# ASIAN PASTA

# ASIAN PASTA

A cook's guide
to the noodles,
wrappers and
pasta creations
of the East

BY LINDA BURUM

ARIS BOOKS

**Addison-Wesley Publishing Company, Inc.**

Reading, Massachusetts   Menlo Park, California   New York
Don Mills, Ontario   Wokingham, England   Amsterdam   Bonn
Sydney   Singapore   Tokyo   Madrid   San Juan

Copyright © 1985 by Linda Burum
Photographs © 1985 by John William Lund

ISBN 0-201-10833-X

(Previously published by Harris Publishing Co.,
ISBN 0-943186-23-4, pbk.)

Aris Books Editorial Office and Test Kitchen
1621 Fifth Street
Berkeley, CA 94710

Cover and book design by Thomas Ingalls + Associates
Composition in Times Roman by On Line Typography

First Addison-Wesley printing, March 1989
ABCDEFGHIJ-VB-89

# CONTENTS

# ACKNOWLEDGMENTS

This book has more contributors than can be mentioned here, including the many restaurant owners, shop keepers, and librarians who answered my hundreds of questions. But for their special contributions I would like to thank: my husband Stephen, for eating all those pasta dishes–even the ones that needed fixing—and for his unfailing support and generous spirit; Antoinette Epstein, for her editorial direction in assembling the historical material as well as for simply cheering me on; Charles Perry, for taking the time to discuss many important historical and linguistic facts pertaining to this work; Maggie Hale, for always answering my questions about Japanese food, customs, and language; Marty Harding and Karyl McGinness, for helping me test and retest the recipes; Jeanie Kim, for the time she spent in the library; David Kim, and Heisun and Paul Chung, for enlightening me on Korean noodle lore; Sue Coe, for introducing me to her grandmother, Mrs. S. Y. Kim, at Korean Gardens Restaurant; Helen Truong, owner of Royal Cuisine Restaurant in Santa Monica, for explaining how to use rice papers and other noodles the correct Vietnamese way, and for checking over the Vietnamese noodle glossary; and Thuan and Trang Lai, for helping me identify the Vietnamese noodle names and for their recipe, *Bun Rieu*.

I would also like to thank the librarians and Asian historians at London University, S.O.A.S.: Professor Mahn-Gunm Yu, Visiting Fellow in Korean Language, Helen Cordell, Charles D'Orban, and Jeremy H. C. S. Davidson. Thanks also to Dr. Angela Little at the University of California, Berkeley.

Finally, thanks to Maggie Klein, my editor, for persevering cheerfully throughout the fine tuning of a very complicated manuscript.

# INTRODUCTION

# Asian Pasta for the American Kitchen

No one knows exactly where noodles and related pastas first originated. Perhaps there is no single birthplace; noodles and flat, unleavened dough wrappers seem to have appeared spontaneously in different cultures, evolving quite naturally from thin, quick-cooking griddle breads that are found almost everywhere. Besides being easy to store and keeping well, noodles cook quickly, saving energy, always a consideration in fuel-scarce cultures. We know they were eaten by at least 100 A.D. in China, when wheat milling techniques were imported from the West, but they may well have been around long before that date. It is commonly thought that Marco Polo brought noodles to Italy, but this is doubtful, for the explorer referred to the Chinese noodles he ate on his journey by an Italian name, suggesting that in some form they were already known to him.

I began my research for this book quite by chance. Every visit to the Orient brought new "pasta" discoveries. While I waited on a train platform in Japan, I ate *udon* noodles in a delicious broth, topped with an egg; the dish was as satisfying as any prepared in good restaurants. After an exhausting day shopping in Tokyo's Ginza area, I came across a tiny hole-in-the-wall that served only *soba;* I then learned that many shops in Japan specialize in just one kind of noodle. In Thailand, I ate noodles in such diverse dishes as breakfast soups and stuffed fried squid or chicken wings. In Malaysia, I became addicted to *laksa* cooked in Indian spices with coconut milk and sometimes mixed with peanuts. In Singapore, I sampled noodles from at least ten regions of China. Throughout Asia, I found noodles nourishing bankers and laborers alike. Certain restaurants take pride in their specialty noodles, while vendors sell noodles and dumplings from makeshift stalls in Asia's crowded market places and in modern supermarkets.

My native Los Angeles, with its vast and varied Asian population, was the perfect place to reinforce my Asian experiences by sampling further a variety of Oriental cuisines. A string of Thai restaurants seems to grace every large thoroughfare. Two large Chinese enclaves, several huge concentrations of Japanese, and a sizeable Koreatown offer a wealth of good, authentic Oriental foods and information for real-life research. The city's rambling streets and boulevards accommodate hundreds of ethnic restaurants and food shops serving an eclectic population. It is not unusual to see French-speaking shoppers in a Vietnamese market looking over seafood and buying fresh coriander (cilantro) and limes, or Mexicans in a Filipino market stocking up on mangoes and *saba* tropical bananas. While researching a food shoppers' guidebook to L.A., I came in contact with many such cross-cultural food exchanges. Adventurous chefs stuffing wonton skins with smoked duck and morel mushrooms and using bean threads in exotic restaurant salads are capitalizing on the best ingredients from both Eastern and Western cuisines.

While checking the ingredients on thousands of market shelves, I realized how many kinds of Asian pastas are locally available—many made here in the United States—and sold nationwide. Several large Japanese noodle factories turn out a full range of fresh and dried products, including *soba, udon, somen,* and *ramen.* (The products sell not only in Japanese and Korean markets, but also in the gourmet and Oriental sections of many supermarkets across the country. More supermarkets than ever before now stock fresh *chao mian* noodles, wonton wrappers, and cellophane noodles.) Several large companies import dried rice papers and rice noodles of all kinds from Thailand to be used in Southeast Asian dishes. From the Philippines come frozen *lumpia* wrappers, which are similar to spring roll wrappers, and a large variety of dried noodle *(pancit)* products. Filipino noodles are also locally made and available fresh. I loved exploring the noodle sections of the large Oriental markets, remembering all the marvelous pastas I tried when traveling and finding many others I wasn't sure what to do with. I brought many kinds home and started to experiment.

To get still more ideas, I ate in as many Asian noodle specialty shops as I could find in Southern California. I was truly surprised at what turned up. In addition to a number of the familiar Chinese noodle houses, I found a Japanese place that makes its own *soba* and *udon* noodles, an Indonesian shop that makes *bahmee* (egg noodles), and several Vietnamese places serving a full complement of traditional noodle dishes and making their own fresh rice wrappers. One restaurant specializes in the Vietnamese beef and noodle soup garnished with fresh herbs and vegetables, *pho,* just as though it were back in Saigon where identical specialty shops are typical and abundant. Some Korean restaurants make their own buckwheat noodles and other "Chinese" restaurants in Koreatown even hand swing their noodles (see page 141). The menu listings of these restaurants allowed me to familiarize myself with the many dishes available in each country. It was an exciting way to educate my palate, tasting many treatments of the same noodle type and getting a sense of how noodles are served and eaten in each part of Asia. I was able to organize what had seemed, when I first traveled in Asia, a mysterious jumble of names and ingredients into a few basic noodle types with variations.

Asian pasta encompasses fresh dough wrappers used for wontons, egg rolls, spring rolls, and *lumpia;* dried and fresh rice papers; and noodles made from a variety of flours and vegetable starches. (The word *pasta,* though Italian, is so well integrated into everyday

American usage that I use it because there is no English term to describe the full range of unleavened, rolled out, or extruded doughs that comprise this food category.) In Asia, pasta, like rice, is central to many meals, in contrast to its role in Italy where it remains the first course. Though an everyday mainstay for one-dish meals, it also appears on banquet tables for birthday and wedding celebrations as a symbol of longevity. Some of the recipes in this book may seem complex, but keep in mind that noodles, meat or seafood, and vegetables combined make a complete meal.

I wanted this book, of course, to be a collection of all my favorite Asian pasta recipes. I knew, however, that cooks would need a guide to sorting out and cooking all the unfamiliar products. So I have designed the book not only as a collection of recipes but also as a primer and handbook, including definitions at the beginning of each chapter and a Special Ingredients and Substitutions section. In selecting the recipes, I've attempted both to illustrate the well-loved, traditional ways noodles and related products are enjoyed in each culture, and to introduce contemporary ideas for their preparation. Versatile eggroll wrappers make whimsical salad bowls when deep-fried around a ladle, and tasty coverings for over-sized ravioli. From pasta-wrapped Thai meatballs to tempting pots of noodle-rich soup, from one-dish meals garnished bountifully with a grand assortment of ingredients to pristine ungarnished noodles eaten with a simple dipping sauce, pastas turn up in every guise.

Every page of this book has been influenced by scores of Asian people whom I met while researching the book. My next door neighbor, Angela Africa, introduced me to a few dishes I hadn't tasted in the Philippines and to many Oriental convenience foods like tamarind concentrate, annatto water, and frozen coconut milk. My former student, David Kim, told me about noodle eating in his Korean homeland, and our neighborhood health-food store owner, Heisun Chung, helped me translate recipes and noodle descriptions I found in *The Encyclopedia of Korean Cooking*. My friend Thuan Lai and her husband made sure I had a complete list of Vietnamese noodles and added a favorite recipe. Through Sue Coe, I spoke to the chef at her grandmother's restaurant who gave me the recipe for Bibim Naeng Myun which, to my knowledge, has not been printed elsewhere in English. These were just a few of many such experiences.

I have done my best to gather all these generous gifts of time and information into a book I hope will endure as a reference as well as a collection of recipes.

LINDA BURUM

Santa Monica
August 1985

# THE SCOPE OF ASIAN PASTA

Trying to choose the right Asian pasta from among the tangle of strange names and unfamiliar packages may leave one mired in confusion. But once a few mysteries are dispelled, cooks will know what to do with each pasta on the market shelf.

Part of the confusion stems from a lack of any official terminology. The same noodle may have a different name in each of many Asian countries; transliterations for names may also vary, making one wonder if *dan mian* and *don mein* are two different noodles or different ways of spelling the same noodle. Each noodle or wrapper may also be given a number of picturesque names. Bean threads, for example, can be called "shining noodles," "cellophane noodles," "silver" or "transparent noodles," and so forth. To clear up this jumble, pages 34 through 35 list each noodle by ingredient, giving the name(s) for it in each country. Thus you can see though bean threads are called *bun tau* in Vietnam and *wun sen* in Thailand, *fen si* in Mandarin and *fun sie* in Cantonese, they are one and the same.

Sometimes package labeling is confusing. Such unappetizing terms as "alimentary paste" or "imitation noodles" are used to describe package contents. This is because, until very recently, the United States Food and Drug Administration required that all products labeled "noodles" contain wheat flour and eggs. This meant that noodles such as *soba* (made with buckwheat flour and water) by the legal definition were not considered true noodles. However, a recent ruling in favor of an Asian-American noodle manufacturer gave them the right to call their nonwheat products "Oriental noodles." Still, many of the old packaging terms persist.

The apparent complexities of Asian pastas can be remarkably simplified by categorizing them according to their major ingredient. Wheat flour noodles are probably the most familiar; the other two major types are the rice flour group and the vegetable starch group, including bean starch, potato starch, and cornstarch noodles. The cooking procedures for noodles within each group are often the same. □

# Wheat and Wheat with Egg Pastas

Within the wheat flour group are egg noodles, nonegg noodles, and wheat pasta wrappers. Descriptions of each country's versions are found in the noodle glossaries at the beginning of every chapter. All the wheat noodles are cooked similarly but the cooking time needed varies widely depending on whether the noodles are fresh or dried, thick or thin.

Nonegg wheat noodles come in many more forms and colors than do egg noodles. Though some may contain a little egg, don't confuse them with those actually labeled "egg noodles" (such as Chinese *dan mian*). Nonegg noodles are more widely distributed than true egg noodles. You'll find them fresh or frozen in air-tight plastic packages with such titles as *ramen* and *chao mian* (or *chow mein*) noodles, *udon* or *pancit miki*.

### General Directions for Cooking Wheat Noodles

Occasionally, fresh wheat pastas are cooked only by deep-frying (as with egg rolls), but, generally, wheat noodles are cooked in boiling water. The cooking time recommended on most packages, if there is such a recommendation, is often much too long, especially for fresh pasta. I suggest simply testing your pasta using the following guidelines.

To cook 1 pound of fresh or dried noodles, bring 4 quarts of water to a rapid boil. Place a colander in the sink under the faucet. If cooking fresh noodles, put them in the colander and fluff them with your fingers to be sure they are separated. Scatter the noodles into the water and return the colander to the sink. When the water returns to a boil, lift and separate the noodles with chopsticks to prevent clumping. Start checking thin fresh noodles after 30 seconds; check thin dried noodles after 2 minutes. Thicker noodles will take up to 2 minutes for fresh or 20 minutes for dried thick noodles such as thick *udon*. (See the Japanese pasta section for further information.) Test the noodles by biting into them at frequent intervals. Remember, overcooking is the cardinal sin in noodle preparation. When the noodles are almost *au point*, rush them to the colander and drain them, then refresh them immediately under gently running water, swirling them in the colander until they are well drained. If the noodles are not going to be used right away, drain them further by turning them onto sturdy paper towels or a cotton tea towel. Place the noodles in a bowl and sprinkle them with 1½ teaspoons Oriental sesame oil, and stir them gently to be sure the oil coats every noodle. If you are not going to use them within an hour or two, cover them tightly or put them in a plastic bag and refrigerate up to two days.

### Cooking Wheat Noodles for Hot Dishes

Noodles precooked for soups or stir-fries should be slightly underdone. They will cook further on reheating. Noodles for dishes with a hot sauce or braised food to be poured over them should also be slightly undercooked.

### Cooking Wheat Noodles for Cold Dishes

Cook the noodles completely, but still *al dente,* following the general directions. Drain the noodles and immediately rinse them first under cool water, then under cold. Swirl the noodles in a colander to drain them well. Drain the noodles on toweling, then oil and store them as described in the general directions.

### The Add-Water Method

Many Japanese cooks like to use the add-water method because they feel it cooks the noodles more evenly throughout, and use the method for Western-style noodles as well. This method is described on page 44.

### Reheating Noodles

The most convenient way to serve noodles of any sort is to have them precooked, just under-done. To reheat the noodles, plunge them into a pot of boiling water for a few seconds or simply pour boiling water over them in a colander while you stir. Drain the noodles and they will be ready for any hot dish. This cook-ahead method is especially handy when you are doing a stir-fry topping and need all your attention for timing the ingredients being fried.

**Amounts to serve.** One pound of fresh noodles will serve four or five as a main dish and eight as a side dish or first course. Count on 3 ounces of dried noodles per main course serving. Substitute 13 ounces of dried noodles for 1 pound of fresh.

### Freezing Fresh Noodles

Whether you buy or make your fresh noodles, it is convenient to have an extra supply in the freezer. I like to freeze all types of fresh noodles in 4-ounce batches and bring out as much as I'll need for a recipe. Simply wrap them in foil, label them, and bag them in plastic; they will keep up to 3 months.

## Rice Pastas

From the familiar, fragile rice vermicelli to the soft, moist, wide, flat rice-noodle sheets, rice pastas, like wheat pastas, come in a panoply of styles, both fresh and dried. The category includes dried rice papers and the thick vermicelli—called *lai fen* in China, *laksa* in Malaysia, and *pancit luglug* in the Philippines. These pastas are most popular in Southeast Asian and southern Chinese cooking. The rice pastas used in each country are described in the noodle glossaries at the beginning of each chapter.

### Cooking with Rice Noodles

Because all rice noodles have been cooked during manufacture, their preparation is simply a matter of heating or rehydrating.

**Fresh rice noodles.** Years ago these noodles could be found only in Chinese *dim sum* parlors, but they are now becoming widely available in Oriental markets. Like bread, they are at their peak when freshly made and not refrigerated. However, they will stay fresh at room temperature for 2 days and will keep up to a week in the refrigerator or 2 months when frozen. For freezing, separate cut fresh rice noodles into half-pound batches and wrap them tightly in plastic wrap, then in foil.

Both cut and sheet noodles come with a light coating of oil. Remove it by pouring boiling water over the pasta before using it in a recipe. If the pasta has been refrigerated, it will be stiff. A light steaming will soften it, but you must not steam it too long or it will disintegrate. Once softened, gently run hot water over the noodles in a colander and they will be ready to use in a recipe. Chilled or frozen noodle sheets that have been folded break easily along fold lines. Therefore, when you are steaming them, turn the noodle square several times; just when it becomes pliable, open it. This is tricky and must be done carefully. Gently rinse the steamed noodle sheet with warm water and it will be ready to use in a recipe.

**Dried rice noodles.** It is a good idea to separate the thin rice vermicelli into the required portions inside a large paper bag. This will keep them from spattering all over the kitchen.

Dried rice noodles are already cooked, so they need only to be rehydrated. Though dried rice noodles may simply be boiled to rehydrate, a preliminary soaking before heating improves the flavor and texture of the noodles. Presoaking and then rinsing also washes away starch that will otherwise cloud soups and sauces.

The noodles should be soaked 15 to 20 minutes until they have softened and untangled. Thin vermicelli will then be ready to be rinsed and used in soups and stir-fried dishes where they will soften further. Thicker noodles must be boiled 4 to 7 minutes after soaking to become tender. They should then be rinsed thoroughly. Rice vermicelli may also be simply boiled 2 to 3 minutes; thick rice noodles may be boiled without soaking, anywhere from 5 to 10 minutes depending on their thickness.

As with wheat noodles, rice noodles should remain *al dente*.

**Amounts to serve.** Serve 6 to 8 ounces fresh, cut rice noodles per person as a main dish or 3 ounces as a first course or side dish, or in soup. For dried rice vermicelli, allow 3 ounces per person as a main course or 1½ to 2 ounces as a first course or side dish.

## Vegetable Starch Pastas

The versatility of Oriental pastas is best demonstrated by vegetable starch noodles. They soak up quantities of flavorful juices and hold them, creating succulent mouthfuls of flavor. This spongelike quality, unknown in Western pastas, is what makes them versatile. The jellylike yam noodle, *shirataki,* readily soaks up a *sukiyaki* sauce; bean thread noodles in stuffings for chicken or squid absorb their juices. When deep-fried, Japanese *harusame* (made of potato and corn starch) or bean threads puff dramatically and add crunch to a chicken salad. Korean *dang myun*, a clear potato-starch noodle, lends its mild flavor to spicy stir-fries.

No matter what their starch base, all vegetable starch noodles are clear and springy when cooked. Unlike wheat pastas, vegetable starch noodles lack gluten to hold them together. As the noodles and pasta sheets are made, they are either steamed or extruded into boiling water. Cooking causes the starch granules to form a cohesive gel network giving them form. Mixing gluten-free starches with water and drying them would otherwise result in a powder. But like cornstarch and water mixtures, they become a solid mass when cooked and cooled. As with rice flour pastas, the cooking during manufacture means the noodles need only be rehydrated.

### Cooking with Vegetable Starch Noodles

If the noodles must be separated or broken into shorter lengths when they are dry, hold them inside a large paper bag as you break them to prevent the brittle noodles from spattering.

To cut soaked noodles into shorter lengths, tie or secure the noodles at one end with a rubber band while they are soaking; they will remain in the same direction and can easily be cut into even lengths with scissors before or after they are drained.

The very thinnest vegetable starch noodles need only soak 10 to 15 minutes before being dropped into hot broths or used in stir-fries.* Thicker noodles require a longer soaking of 15 to 30 minutes and may also need up to 5 minutes cooking. When they turn from partially translucent to perfectly clear they are ready. These noodles may be braised up to 20 minutes without losing their shape and good texture.

If the noodles are being used for stuffing, forcemeat, or in a braised dish, they should be soaked in warm tap water until just pliable. This allows for further absorption of meat or braising juices. They will be watery tasting if allowed to soak too long.

For deep-fried noodles, fry the noodles at 375°. (You can test the temperature of the oil by dropping a noodle into it: the oil is hot enough if the noodle puffs and floats almost instantly.) Cold oil will make noodles tough and leathery. Be sure to push the noodle mass down into the hot oil for a few seconds so all the noodles puff and cook immediately. Reheat fried noodles in a 250° oven just long enough to warm them through.

**Amounts to serve.** Allow 2 ounces per serving for main courses. Other amounts vary according to how the noodles are being used. In soups, ½ to 1 ounce per serving is usually sufficient.

*Soak bean threads manufactured in the People's Republic of China in simmering water for use in cold dishes.

# Notes on Pasta Wrappers

Many dough stuffs used as edible wrappers fall into the pasta category. Occasionally it is hard to decide where pasta leaves off and bread begins, as with some spring roll skins or Filipino *lumpia* wrappers.

**Dumpling wrappers.** Dumpling wrappers include egg roll wrappers, wonton skins, and pot sticker skins (often called *gyoza* skins by Japanese manufacturers), all of which are about 1⅙ inches thick and may be eggless or contain a small amount of egg. Somewhat thinner are the eggless boiled dumpling wrappers; thinner still and the most delicate of all are the *shao-mai* wrappers. Wrappers containing egg are preferred for East-West cooking, especially where a Western flavor, such as in ravioli, is desired. Fresh wrappers are always best, but frozen ones carefully wrapped in foil are satisfactory. If you are going to freeze wrappers, it is a good idea to divide a large package in half or even thirds or fourths so the wrappers can be used in the quantity each recipe calls for and to speed thawing time. Wrappers may be stored about a week in the refrigerator and must be wrapped in several layers of plastic to remain pliable.

When working with wrappers, keep them covered with plastic wrap, a plastic bag, or covered by a damp tea towel so they do not dry out. To get the edges of the wrappers to adhere to one another around the filling, the edges should be grease free. Moisten the edges with water, egg white, or lightly beaten whole egg. Applying the filling with two spoons will help to keep your fingers and wrapper edges grease free, but keep a damp towel handy for occasional finger wiping.

**Fresh rice noodle sheets.** Fresh rice noodle sheets are frequently used as wrappers. If you must chill or freeze them, cut them the size you want and stack the pieces, then wrap them tightly first in plastic wrap and then in foil. A very light steaming will bring them back to life; oversteaming will turn them mushy.

**Dried rice papers.** Dried rice papers *(banh trang)* are sheer, delicate wrappers usually sold in Vietnamese, Thai, and Chinese markets. Their basketweave texture comes from being dried on bamboo mats. They are used moist or deep-fried in Southeast Asian spring rolls or with grilled meats. Complete instructions for their use and handling are on page 75, in the Vietnamese section.

**Spring roll wrappers, *lumpia* wrappers, and *mushi* pork wrappers.** Wrappers for spring rolls, *lumpia,* and *mushi* pork are delicate, almost lacy, slightly air-leavened, and pancakelike. They may be frozen by dividing large amounts into smaller quantities and wrapping them carefully in foil. If they have become too dry, revive them by steaming lightly in an oiled steaming basket for 15 to 60 seconds. If you steam them too long they will disintegrate. When they are stuffed, you must also be careful not to oversteam them.

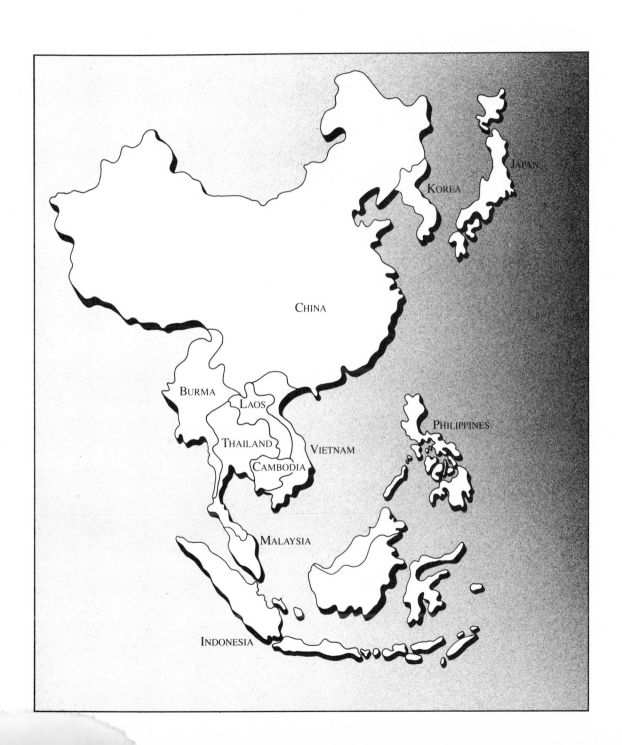

*Annatto seeds*

*Asian chili peppers*

*Star anise*

*Szechwan peppercorn.*

*Galingale*

*Lemon grass*

*Turmeric*

# Special Ingredients and Substitutions

Don't let the names of the exotic sounding ingredients on these pages deter you from trying the recipes. Many of the "exotic" ingredients are easier to get than you might think, and I've recommended substitutions in the cases of those that might send you too far out of your way. Lemon peel can replace lemon grass, ginger and cinnamon will suffice for galingale, and tangerine peel may be dried at home. Quick-to-make recipes are provided for such items as fish balls, pressed tofu, crispy onions and shallots, coconut milk, barbecued pork, and tamarind water.

Many ingredients overlap from country to country. One country's fish sauce, for example, will suffice for all the cuisines herein. But do go out of your way when you can. Stock up on shrimp paste, fermented black beans, *hoisin* sauce, and tamarind pulp when you are near a store that sells them. With items like these on hand, you'll create the more authentic flavors.

Even if you do not live near an Asian market, you may be surprised how many "Asian" ingredients can be found elsewhere. Signature flavorings and ingredients used in Southeast Asian cooking, such as tamarind, fresh coriander (cilantro), annatto seeds, and a variety of chilis, are standard in Mexican and Latin American markets and in stores with inventories geared for American Southwest cooking. Indian grocery stores can be a good source for tamarind pods and paste, bean flours, and sometimes coconut milk. More and more of these ingredients are being stocked in large supermarkets. A Los Angeles produce wholesaler who introduced kiwi fruit and shallots years ago is now shipping fresh lemon grass to many parts of the country. And if you enjoy growing your own herbs and vegetables, mail-order nurseries sell plants or seeds of mint, coriander, and lemon grass.

Many exotic ingredients may be stored almost indefinitely. Some items such as dried mushrooms, though differing slightly from country to country, may be interchanged. Thus you can pare down your shopping list and needed storage space while experimenting with the cuisines of all the Asian countries. □

**Annatto seeds,** also *achuete* (Filipino). Reddish-orange seeds from the annatto tree, used as a coloring agent for sauces. Available in Latin American, Filipino, East Indian, Spanish, and some Chinese markets. Two convenient commercial forms are "annatto water" and "annatto paste," ready to use as coloring. Annatto paste, also known as *achiote* paste, is available in Mexican or Latin American stores. To make your own annatto water, combine 1 tablespoon seeds with ¼ cup boiling water. Allow to soak 30 minutes. Strain while pressing the seeds against the strainer to extract more color. A mixture of paprika and turmeric may be substituted.

**Bamboo shoots, braised.** Braised bamboo shoots are pre-cut and cooked in oil, soy sauce, salt, and sugar.

**Barbecued pork.** See Chinese barbecued pork *(char siu).*

**Bean curd, pressed.** Sold in Chinese markets either plain or seasoned and "baked," ready to cut for stir-fried dishes. Substitute the simple (and better tasting) homemade recipe described for *Ketoprak* (page 130).

**Black beans, salted.** Also known as "fermented black beans" or "Chinese black beans," the beans have been fermented and dried slightly. The beans come in jars and plastic bags. The plastic bags allow you to squeeze to determine freshness; the beans should not be hard. Black beans seasoned with five-spice powder will change the character of a dish calling for unseasoned black beans. Store them in an air-tight container at room temperature.

**Brown bean sauce.** Crushed yellow soy beans, mixed with flour, vinegar, spices, and salt. Sold in jars or cans as whole bean sauce, smooth paste (ground), or bean and paste combination. The latter two are interchangeable. The recipes in this book call for the ground variety. Do not confuse with *hot bean sauce* or *sweet bean sauce,* which are flavored differently.

**Calamari steak.** Pounded and "formed" squid, which resembles abalone. A fairly new product at the seafood market. A good and easy-to-use substitute for squid "cut into rings." Simply cut the steaks into 2-inch-long strips while they are semi-frozen.

**Candlenut** (Indonesian, *kemiri* nut; Malaysian, *buah keras*). A hard, oily tropical nut used in pounded curries of Southeast Asia to unify and absorb flavors. Available roasted in Dutch, Indonesian, and some Indian stores. They are toxic raw. Brazil or unsalted macadamia nuts are a good substitute.

**Chili oil,** or hot chili oil. Made by infusing the flavor of crushed Asian chilis into an oil, then straining. Oil preserves the delicate heat which loses potency in other mediums. Sold in most Asian markets except, perhaps, Japanese. Often used as a table condiment.

**Chili peppers, Asian.** Fiery little red chili peppers, sometimes called bird's eye chilis. Sold in Asian markets, usually in plastic bags. The chilis are much hotter than Western-style chilis. Also come in crushed and powdered forms. Crushed chilis sold in Mexican and American markets are a poor substitute, but if that's all you have, use them and fortify the dish with Tabasco sauce, cayenne, *sambal oeleck,* or *sriracha* sauce to taste.

**Chili peppers, Serrano.** Since it is difficult to get fresh Asian chili peppers in the United States, I have used Serrano chilis wherever fresh chilis are called for. This provides some uniformity, though there are so many variables even among Serranos—including size and age—it is impossible to be accurate regarding how hot a dish will be. I have used them conservatively in the recipes. If you don't care for hot spicy food, remove some or all of the seeds. Fry the seeds in a little oil and, by tiny increments, add them to cooked dishes until you have the hotness you want. For uncooked dishes, mince or crush the seeds lightly and stir them in, a little at a time, until the desired hotness is attained.

**Chinese barbecued pork** *(char siu).* Sold in almost every Chinese delicatessen, and sometimes in other Asian markets. You might even procure some from a local Chinese restaurant. Adds a distinctive flavor to stir-fried dishes. Can easily be made at home and frozen: marinate 2 pounds of boned pork loin for 3 hours in ½ cup *hoisin* sauce, ¼ cup tomato catsup, 2½ tablespoons each packed brown sugar, light soy sauce, and rice wine or dry sherry, ⅛ teaspoon five-spice powder, and 2 medium cloves garlic, crushed. Roast in a preheated 350° oven, hanging from S-shaped hooks (made from poultry lacers) for 40 to 45 minutes, until the pork is cooked through. Place a baking sheet at the bottom of the oven to catch any drippings.

**Chinese chives.** Sold fresh by the bunch, they resemble large blades of grass. Purchase green or yellow, or you can buy Chinese chive flowers. Flavor is reminiscent of garlic.

**Chinese rice wine.** See Rice wine, Chinese.

**Chinese sausage** *(lop cheong).* Rich, rather sweet, small, thin sausages. Widely distributed in both Oriental and Occidental markets and may even be ordered by mail. There are many domestic brands, and an outstanding one from Canada, called "Jimmy's." Steam to soften before slicing. A good item to keep in the freezer for impromptu meals.

**Chinese sesame paste.** See Sesame paste.

**Chinese vinegar, black.** See Rice vinegar, Chinese black.

**Chinese vinegar, red.** See Rice vinegar, Chinese black.

**Citrus leaves.** The leaves of the *Citrus hystrix* or Kaffir lime are used widely in Southeast Asian cooking. Called *makrut* or *Bai Ma Grood* in Thailand and *jeruk purut* in Indonesia. Leaves of any lime or lemon tree may be substituted, as may the zest of half a lime for each leaf. If purchased powdered, substitute ¼ teaspoon powder for one leaf.

**Coconut milk.** Becoming more readily available frozen and canned. Also available dried, and can be made at home in a blender. Recipes in this book specify thin, medium, or thick milk (see instructions, following). Leftover coconut milk may be poured into ice cube trays, frozen, then stored wrapped in foil.

**Thin coconut milk.** Stir canned or thawed frozen coconut milk until the solids are uniformly dispersed. For one cup thin coconut milk, combine ½ cup plus 1 tablespoon coconut milk with ½ cup minus 1 tablespoon water.

**Medium coconut milk.** Combine ¾ cup canned or thawed coconut milk with ¼ cup water.

**Thick coconut milk.** Use canned or thawed coconut milk full strength.

**Coconut cream.** Chill canned or thawed frozen coconut milk in a wide bowl. Skim the creamy part from the top. Use the remaining milk as thin coconut milk. Milk may be refrozen.

**Coconut milk from dried coconut.** Combine 2 cups dried, unsweetened shredded coconut and 2¼ cups very hot water in a blender or food processor. Process until it is a thick pulp. Pour into a fine sieve or several layers of cheesecloth. Press all of the liquid from the coconut. The milk should be chilled at least 2 hours before using. A second extraction using 1½ cups hot milk will yield thin coconut milk. Both may be frozen.

**Coconut milk, fresh.** Pierce the "eyes" with an ice pick and pour out the juice (this is not coconut milk). Place the drained coconut on a large baking pan and heat it in a 350° oven about 15 minutes so the meat will come out more easily. Crack the nut open with a hammer on a hard surface. Pry out the meat in small pieces and coarsely chop it in a food processor or by hand. Measure the meat and return it to the processor or place in a blender. Pour an equal amount of very hot water over the coconut and process until the mixture is a thick pulp. Strain through a fine sieve or several layers of cheesecloth and squeeze out all the liquid, then chill at least 2 hours before using.

**Coriander, fresh; also, cilantro** (*Coriandrum sativum*). Leaves of this herb are often used as a garnish as well as a flavoring agent in spice mixtures. The roots are used in curry mixtures.

**Coriander root.** Fresh root of the coriander plant, often used in Southeast Asian curry mixtures. In my neighborhood, coriander bunches are sold with the roots intact. If this is not true where you shop, you may have to do some hunting and asking. Since the leaves are often used in the same dish, if only for a garnish, it is simple to wash the bunch and trim off the roots.

**Coriander seed.** Sold whole or ground. One of the major flavoring agents in curries; should not be confused with coriander leaves.

**Crispy onions.** Used as a crunchy garnish in Indonesian and Malay dishes. Often available in Indonesian stores. Should be refrigerated after opening; will keep for 6 months. Homemade crispy onions can be made using the recipe for Crispy Shallots (page 136). Cut small onions into eighths lengthwise, then slice them into thin semicircles. Fry as directed in the recipe.

**Curry paste.** Much preferred to curry powder, this oil-based mixture includes chili peppers as well as the standard curry spices. Found in Chinese and Indian stores, but not always available.

**Curry powder.** The deficiencies of American curry powders have long been known. When I do use ready-mixed powder, I have enjoyed 777 brand, Agmark Madras Curry Powder, and a Japanese brand, S & B. All are more interesting than our supermarket varieties.

**Daikon** (Chinese, *lo bahk*). Large white radish, often 1½ feet long and almost 2 inches thick at the base. Unlike the red radish, it has a delicate flavor and absorbs the flavors of soups and sauces when cooked in them.

*Dashi.* Clear stock made from dried bonito flakes and seaweed. Packaged in teabag-like containers. Just simmer in boiling-hot water 5 minutes, or as directed. Much easier than any other stock and very delicious. "Prepared *dashi*," called for in many recipes, is *dashi* prepared as directed on the package.

*Enoki.* See Mushrooms, *enoki.*

**Fettuccelli.** Little noodle ribbons, a narrow version of fettuccini.

**Fish balls.** Found at Chinese butchers and in the freezer case of many Oriental markets. Homemade fish balls, though not the same, may be substituted. See *Bolang Bolang Misua* (page 114).

**Fish cake.** Sold at Chinese butchers or in the freezer case of Chinese markets. Store-bought or homemade fish balls may be substituted.

**Fish sauce** (Thailand, *nam pla;* Vietnam, *nuoc mam;* the Philippines, *patis;* Indonesia, *petis;* Cambodia, *tuk trey;* Burma, *ngan-pya-ye*). Light brown to amber seasoning sauces prepared from salted, fermented fish. Though the idea and odor of the sauce seem less than delectable to many Westerners, the flavor it imparts in cooking has no equal. It seems to bring all the flavoring elements into balance, and the fishy smell disappears in cooking. Although not exactly the same, all fish sauces can be interchanged. While there is no truly ideal substitute for this unique flavoring, you can use a combination of 2 teaspoons each anchovy paste, light soy sauce, and water for each 2 tablespoons fish sauce called for.

**Five-spice powder.** Blend of various spices used in Chinese cooking, usually star anise, cloves, cinnamon, Szechwan peppercorns, and fennel. Store in an air-tight container.

**Galingale or galangal** (Thailand, *kha;* Indonesia, Laos, Malaysia, *lengkuas*). Like ginger, galingale is a rhizome and, like ginger, the dried variety is quite different from the fresh. Comes packaged in dried slices, or ground. If you can't obtain galingale in any form, substitute half as much ginger and add a small pinch of cinnamon.

**Garbanzo flour.** Used to thicken various curries. May be purchased as *channa dal* flour in Indian stores or *besan* in Middle Eastern markets or natural-food stores.

*Gyoza* **skins.** Round Japanese wonton wrappers. Usually more thinly rolled and delicate than Chinese wrappers.

**Ham, smoky.** When smoky ham is called for, use Smithfield, which often comes in slices in large Chinese markets. Westphalian ham, available in German, Polish, and Hungarian delis, is a good substitute. There is also a product called "pork strips," made by Venus Foods, a Chinese-American company. The cured and smoked strips are packaged in vacuum-sealed plastic.

*Hoisin* **sauce.** Popular here when *mushi* pork was all the rage. Now often carried in even the most pedestrian of supermarkets. A sweet and spicy brown paste of ground beans, garlic, sugar, vinegar, and sesame oil.

**Jackfruit.** One of the world's largest fruits. Grown in tropical Southeast Asia. Found in Southeast Asian, Indian, and Latin American markets in cans or jars.

**Jicama.** Round tropical root vegetable with tough light brown skin. Some very large jicama are sold cut, wrapped in plastic. Their slightly sweet flavor and crunchy texture are more like fresh water chestnuts than the soggy canned variety. If you can't get fresh water chestnuts, try jicama, cut into the appropriate shapes. Cooks in only a few seconds.

*Katsuobushi.* Dried bonito fish in thin, almost transparent shavings. Used to make *dashi,* as a condiment in Japanese sauces and cooking, or as a delightful garnish.

*Kecap manis (ketjap).* An Indonesian-style sweet soy sauce found in Indonesian and sometimes Chinese markets. Made with palm sugar, it has a characteristic sweet flavor which makes it unlike other soy sauces. For an easy substitute, combine 1 cup regular soy sauce, ¼ cup each dark molasses and mild honey, 1 small cracked clove garlic, and 1 thin slice ginger or 2 slices dried galingale in a saucepan. Simmer, stirring, 6 minutes; then cool to room temperature. Store with the garlic and ginger in a glass jar. May be kept unrefrigerated.

*Kiaware* **daikon** (hot sprouts). Radish sprouts. Look like bunches of pale clover leaves with a slightly more pneumatic look. Packaged "growing" on strip of plastic sponge and wrapped in plastic. Found in Japanese markets, specialty greengrocers, and some supermarkets. A wonderful addition to salads, and an excellent garnish.

*Konbu.* Dried Japanese kelp used to flavor soups and stocks. Neatly packaged in squares or strips in cellophane wrappers.

*Krupic.* See Shrimp wafers.

**Lemon grass** (citronella). Long woody stalk with fresh scent of lemon. Often found in Asian markets fresh, frozen, or dried in the whole stalk or thinly sliced and dried. Dried lemon grass must be soaked 2 hours in just enough water to cover; add water as the lemon grass expands. Use both grass and water. For soups, it is not necessary to soak dried lemon grass. When using fresh lemon grass, cut away any tough outer layers and the top part of the stalk, using only the inner white stalk to grind into curry mixtures. The whole stalk, cut up, can be used in soups. For one stalk fresh lemon grass, substitute ¼ cup sliced, dried lemon grass, or the zest of one lemon.

**Lentil flour.** Used to thicken some curries. May be made by grinding lentils to a powder in a blender.

*Lop cheong.* See Chinese sausage.

*Makrut* **leaves.** See Citrus leaves.

*Mirin.* A Japanese sweet rice wine used in cooking as a seasoning, never as a drink. Used frequently and a must for anyone cooking Japanese dishes. Found not in liquor stores or in wine departments but with condiments in Japanese markets or the Japanese section of the supermarket. If you don't have *mirin,* add an extra teaspoon sugar for each table-spoon of *mirin* called for. If called for in a dipping sauce, supplement the liquid with an equal part *dashi* or stock as well as adding the sugar.

*Miso,* **red and white.** One of the basic sea-sonings of every Japanese kitchen. A savory paste made from fermented soybeans, grain, salt, water, and a fermentation starter *(Asper-gillus oryzae).* Texture resembles peanut butter. Found in every Japanese market and many well-stocked supermarkets. Of six basic types, the most often used are the red or *hatchomiso,* made with the addition of barley, and the "white" (actually beige) or *shiromiso,* made with rice. Used in soups, sauces, and glazes in Japan. Though it can be kept on the shelf for a month or two, the flavor is best preserved when stored refrigerated in an air-tight container.

*Mitsuba* (trefoil). A delicate, aromatic Japanese parsley sold in bunches in the pro-duce section of Japanese and sometimes other Oriental markets. Resembles Italian broad-leaf parsley with longer stems.

**Mushrooms, Chinese black.** Dried black mushrooms are found in every Chinese and usually other Asian markets. Often markets buy them loose and package them in bags under their own name. Best are the *fah goo* (Cantonese), *hwa-goo* (Mandarin), or "flower" mushrooms, recognizable by the large, irregular light-colored cracks on the surface of the mushroom cap. *Doong goo* (Cantonese), *huang-goo* (Mandarin), or "winter" mushrooms are not as thick and meaty as the *fah goo,* but are perfectly acceptable. All dried mushrooms should be rinsed well to rid them of sand, then soaked in water. After the mushrooms have softened, squeeze out excess water before adding them to stir-fried dishes. Reserve the soaking water for soups and sauces. Though not precisely the same, Japanese *shiitake* mushrooms may be used interchangeably with Chinese black mushrooms.

**Mushrooms, *enoki* (*enokitake*).** Slender stems, 3 to 4 inches long, topped with tiny, pea-sized caps make these elegant little Japanese mushrooms the perfect garnish. Canned *enoki* mushrooms are to be avoided. Grown in the United States, they may be found in Japanese markets, specialty green-grocers, and occasionally in supermarkets. Cut off the woody lower portion of the mushrooms.

**Mushrooms, oyster** ("abalone mushrooms," English; *shimeji,* Japanese; *bao-how-goo,* Chinese). Greyish tan mushrooms with a delicate flavor and strikingly meaty texture. Sold fresh as well as canned. Make a delight-ful addition to salads raw or stir-fried a few seconds. You will find both the small capped, which are less expensive but just as tasty, or the larger capped oyster-sized mushrooms in Japanese and sometimes Chinese markets and specialty greengrocers. Canned oyster mushrooms are not recommended.

**Mushrooms, *shiitake*.** These Japanese mush-rooms, found dried in most Asian markets, are now being cultivated in Oregon and can also be purchased fresh. The best are large, thick, and meaty with caps curled under. Those with flared caps are beyond their prime when fresh, but are perfectly fine dried. Treat dried *shiitake* mushrooms as you would Chinese black mushrooms (above).

**Mushrooms, tree ears and cloud ears.** Sometimes labeled "black fungus" or "wood fungus" on packages, such appellations aptly describe these wrinkled barklike specimens.

The best are the totally black, smaller variety as opposed to the larger black-with-tan-undersides variety. Soak tree ears in warm water until pliable, then cut away the tough inner portion. Cut into strips or dice.

***Nori*.** The sheets of toasted sea vegetable found wrapped around your *sushi*. Sometimes called "toasted laver," an English term which actually refers only to certain species of the sea plant. Come roasted or unroasted. Buy the convenient roasted variety, or roast your own by passing the sheets very briefly over a flame. Roasted *nori* that have absorbed moisture can be revitalized this way too. Used crumbled as a garnish over rice, noodle dishes, and salads, and in *sushi*.

**Oriental sesame oil.** Strong nutty oil made from roasted sesame seeds. Be sure to buy the amber-colored oil rather than the sesame oil sold in natural-foods stores, which is made from unroasted seeds. Used sparingly at the end of any cooking period as a flavoring rather than as a cooking oil. Store in a cool, dark place to prevent rancidity. Available now in some supermarkets.

**Oyster sauce.** By now most cooks who have experimented with Chinese cooking have a bottle of this flavorful brown sauce in their larder. Made from oyster extract, sugar, and vinegar, its sweet-salty taste can give punch to many noodle dishes. Brands vary widely so you must experiment. Contains thickening agents that will thicken other sauces and pan juices slightly.

Nori

Black beans

Dried tangerine peel

Tree ear mushrooms

Shiitake mushrooms

**Palm sugar** (jaggery). A major sweetener in India and throughout Southeast Asia, with a very strong distinctive flavor. Usually made from a certain type of palm, though some varieties are made from sugar cane. Southeast Asian markets and Indian stores are the best source. Substitute brown sugar for a different, but acceptable, alternative.

**Pear—Oriental, Japanese, or Chinese.** Crisp pears even when ripe, with a clean crunchy texture and less sweet flavor than Western pears, and a rounder apple-like shape. Found in Japanese and Korean markets. Sometimes imported from Japan, they are now grown in the U.S. and sold in some supermarkets.

**Pepper paste, Chinese hot.** Do not confuse this garlicky paste with hot bean paste. Though it does contain crushed soy beans, it is primarily made from crushed chili peppers and garlic. Two brands I have had success with are Kim Lan and Lan Chi. The hotness diminishes with age, but you can simply use more as it ages. Be cautious when using a newly opened jar. *Sambal oeleck* may be substituted, but it is slightly hotter and less garlicky, so make adjustments.

**Pork butt.** Pork meat that comes from the shoulder area above the front leg, or "picnic roast." In many Chinese markets, the whole butt is displayed and the butchers will cut off whatever portion you desire. In supermarkets, look for Boston butt, rolled Boston butt, or blade steak—all various cuts from the same area. If you find pork butt unavailable or too fatty, any boneless pork meat may

be substituted.

**Radish, giant white.** See Daikon.

**Rice flour.** Two types of flour are milled from rice: sweet rice flour (called *mochiko* in Japanese stores), and flour made from long-grain rice. The two are not interchangeable. Sweet rice flours are used to make confections, while the regular rice flour is used for noodles and savory pastries. Use regular rice flour unless sweet rice flour is specified.

**Rice vinegar.** Among the many types of white rice vinegars available, the Japanese brands have the most consistently good quality, and I use them wherever rice vinegar is called for. Be sure to check the label of rice vinegar to determine whether it is seasoned or unseasoned. Seasoned vinegars contain sugar and, unless specifically called for, will not work in a dish requiring "rice vinegar."

**Rice vinegar, Chinese black or *chenkong*.** Dark vinegar made from a fermented rice base. Flavors vary widely. In her *Modern Art of Chinese Cooking,* Barbara Tropp suggests Balsamic vinegar as a substitute for, or even preferable to, some Chinese brands. If you do use Balsamic vinegar, decrease any sugar or sweetening agent in the recipe to taste. Chinese red vinegar is similar to black vinegar in flavor but is lighter in color.

**Rice wine, Chinese** (*shao-hsing* wine). This staple Chinese cooking wine is brewed from rice. Like Western wines, it is used in marinades and as a splash of flavor to deglaze pans and add dimension to sauces. A good quality dry sherry can be substituted.

**Rice wine, Japanese.** See *Mirin*.

*Saba*. Tiny tropical bananas, not quite as sweet as our standard bananas. Plantains may be substituted, but in the Banana Lumpia recipe (page 118), regular bananas are preferred.

*Sake*. Japanese rice wine. The same type of *sake* used as a beverage is used extensively in Japanese cooking, where it acts to supress saltiness and helps eliminate fishy tastes. *Sake* is widely available in liquor stores and wine shops, and may be labeled "cooking *sake*" and found with the other condiments in Japanese markets.

*Sambal oeleck*. A hot Indonesian relish made from ground chili peppers. Usually served as a table condiment.

**Seasoned rice vinegar.** See Rice vinegar.

**Serrano chili peppers.** See Chili peppers, Serrano.

**Sesame oil.** See Oriental sesame oil.

**Sesame paste.** Thick brown paste which, unlike Middle Eastern tahini, is made from sesame seeds that have been roasted. Use tahini for a different, but good tasting, substitute; it will require less liquid or oil for thinning. Store in an air-tight container in a cool dark cupboard.

**Sesame seeds.** Available unroasted or roasted, there are white sesame seeds and black sesame seeds, each with a distinctive flavor. Specific seeds required are specified in each recipe. If you are using large quantities of the seeds, buy them in large packages found in Chinese and Korean markets. Small packages found in Japanese stores and in supermarkets are much more expensive.

*Shichimi togarashi*. A spicy Japanese table condiment and garnish made from ground chili peppers, sesame seeds, Japanese pepper, and spices. It is packaged in delightful mini-cans with shaker tops.

*Shiitake*. See Mushrooms, *shiitake*.

**Shrimp, dried.** Tiny, strong smelling shrimp, though not favorably aromatic by themselves, give a delightful lift to Chinese and Southeast Asian dishes. Completely lose their unsavory identity once added to a dish. Often used pounded or ground. They can be purchased in most Oriental groceries and sometimes in Mexican food stores.

**Shrimp paste, moist or dry** (Thailand, *kapi;* Vietnam, *mam ruoc;* Malaysia, *blachan;* Indonesia, *trasi)*. Shrimp pastes are a staple flavoring for Southeast Asian foods, and are available both fresh (in jars) or dried (in logs or individually wrapped in squares). The newer square packaging usually helps keep its strong odor to a minimum. Once cooked, the unpleasant odor disappears into the complexities of soups or sauces, and imparts a special delicious flavor. Once opened, keep fresh paste in the refrigerator and dried paste wrapped air-tight in a cool dark cupboard. Usually a recipe specifies the type of paste required; use 1½ times as much fresh as dried shrimp paste. Anchovy paste is often called for as a substitute and will do, though not having been fermented, it lacks the characteristic Southeast Asian flavor. If using anchovy paste, use slightly more than half as much as you would dried shrimp paste, and a quarter the amount of fresh shrimp paste.

**Shrimp wafers** (*krupek* or *kroepoek*). Sometimes labeled "prawn crackers" or *beignets des crevettes,* the wafers are made from ground shrimp and a starch such as tapioca or rice flour. Often colored pink, green, or yellow; come either boxed or in cellophane bags. Have a delicate, sweet flavor, and must be deep-fried before serving. (Follow the directions for deep-fried bean threads, page 17. Like bean threads, the crackers puff when fried.) They may be fried and then refreshed in the oven before serving at room temperature. I have called for Hawaiian potato chips as a substitute. While they in no way resemble the wafers, potato chips make a delightful crunchy garnish.

*Sirimi*. A new seafood product now being introduced in the markets. It is made from inexpensive fish, such as pollack, then flavored and re-formed to resemble such delicacies as crabmeat, shrimp, and scallops. While unappealingly labeled "imitation" crab, shrimp, or scallops, some *sirimi* products are quite good, especially if served in a spicy sauce. And the price is right.

**Soy sauce, light and black.** Light soy sauce is both lighter in color and different in taste and saltiness from regular or black soy sauce. I have used it where dark soy sauce would mar the color of a dish or where a delicate flavor is desired. If you use regular soy sauce in a dish calling for light, reduce by about one-third, then add more to taste if you wish. Chinese black soy sauce is occasionally called for where a salty flavor with a low volume of liquid is needed. I use Kikkoman brand soy sauce in recipes that do not specify either light or black, and Superior brand black soy sauce where black is specified.

*Sriracha* **sauce.** Bottled fiery chili sauce rather like a *sambal,* made with ground fresh chili peppers, garlic, vinegar, sugar, and salt. Look for sauce labeled "HOT"—I have used the "HOT" sauce in these recipes. *Sambal oeleck* or *sambal badjack* may be substituted, or add a little more garlic and minced fresh chili peppers, or dried crushed chili peppers soaked until they are soft, to the dish.

**Star anise.** Hard, brown star-shaped pods with a slight licorice flavor. Because it is a main component of five-spice powder, you can detect its presence in Chinese barbecue-style foods. Store in an air-tight container in a cool dark cupboard.

**Szechwan peppercorns.** Called "flower pepper" or "fragrant pepper," the hollow brown pods taste a little like black peppercorns. Often crushed and sprinkled onto dishes as a garnish, or lightly roasted in a dry frying pan before being used. Store in a tightly covered jar in a cool dark cupboard.

**Tahini.** Middle Eastern sesame paste made from unroasted sesame seeds. Refrigerate after opening.

**Tamarind paste, pods, concentrate.** The russet colored pulp of tamarind pods adds a sour fruity note to Southeast Asian curries, sauces, and soups. Tamarind pods can be purchased in Latin American or Asian markets. Peel off their thin, brittle coating before using for tamarind water (below). Or buy the convenient compact blocks of pressed tamarind. One tablespoon pressed tamarind is equal to about four large pods. Though even more convenient to use, smooth tamarind concentrate, packed in little plastic jars, is not quite as flavorful as the pulp.

**Tamarind water.** Put 2½ tablespoons of tamarind pulp or 4 or 5 peeled tamarind pods in a bowl and pour ⅓ cup very hot water over it. Allow to stand 30 minutes. Pour the liquid through a coarse strainer, pushing down on the mass to separate the seeds from the pulp. Discard the seeds and use the juice and pulp. Or when using concentrate, for each 2 tablespoons of tamarind water called for, dilute 1½ teaspoons of the concentrate in 1½ tablespoons hot water.

**Tangerine peel.** Dried tangerine peel may be purchased in Chinese grocery stores. It is also quite easy to make your own by scraping the inner white pulp from tangerine peels and allowing the zest to dry in a gas oven with a pilot light for a few days. If you don't have a gas oven, just allow the peels to sit on a rack in a warm dry place. Store the dried peels in a jar with a tight lid.

**Tapioca powder or starch.** A thickening powder much like cornstarch, made from ground dried tapioca (cassava). Packaged in plastic bags and sold in most Oriental markets.

**Thai hot sauce.** See *Sriracha* sauce.

**Tonnarelli.** Square-edged, ¹⁄₁₆-inch-thick fresh egg noodle, similar in thickness to spaghettini.

**Tree ears.** See Mushrooms, tree ears and cloud ears.

**Trefoil.** See *Mitsuba*.

**Turmeric, fresh and dried.** Turmeric is familiar to most cooks in its dried, powdered form, and as the major coloring agent in curry powder. A rhizome (like ginger), the little brown knobby "fingers" are beginning to turn up in Indian stores, specialty greengrocers, and occasionally in fancier supermarkets. Since its usual use is in curry mixtures, turmeric should be pounded or ground with the other flavoring components after it has been peeled with a sharp knife and sliced. Use 2 teaspoons fresh grated turmeric to replace ¾ teaspoon dried ground turmeric.

**Vinegar, Chinese black.** See Rice vinegar, Chinese black.

**Vinegar, rice.** See Rice vinegar.

***Wasabi* powder.** The dried, ground form of the *wasabi* root. A condiment familiar to *sushi* lovers as little green mounds of spicy paste. Its flavor has been compared to horseradish. To reconstitute dried *wasabi*, mix it with just enough water to form a stiff paste. Let the paste sit for 10 minutes before using it.

**Zest, lemon or lime.** The thin colored part of the citrus skin which contains the flavorful oils but none of the bitterness of the skin's white inner pulp.

## Asian Pasta Dictionary

| | CHINESE | JAPANESE | THAI |
|---|---|---|---|
| Generic term for noodle | mian (M),* mein (C)* | men | mee |
| Wheat noodle<br>  dried<br>  fresh<br>  precooked | gan mian<br>sun mian<br>yi mian | somen, hiyamugi<br>udon, ramen<br>ramen, chuka soba | mee |
| Egg and wheat noodle<br>  thin<br>  wide | dan mian (M), don mein (C)<br>kuan dan mian (M),<br>fu don mein (C) | | bà mee |
| Rice vermicelli<br>  thin<br>  thick | mi fen (M), mai fun (C)<br>lai fen (M), lai fun (C) | maifun | sen mee |
| Flat dried rice noodle<br>  (rice sticks) | gan he fen (M),<br>gon ho fun (C) | | jantaboon<br>(chantaboon) |
| Fresh rice noodle | sha he fen (M), sa ho fun (C) | | gwayteeo |
| Bean thread (cellophane<br>noodle, glass noodle,<br>transparent noodle,<br>shining noodle) | fen si (M), fun sie (C) | saifun, harusame | wun sen<br>(woon sen) |
| Buckwheat noodle | qiao mian (M) | soba | |
| | (M) = Mandarin<br>(C) = Cantonese | | |

| VIETNAMESE | FILIPINO | SINGAPOREAN, INDONESIAN, MALAYSIAN | KOREAN | SUBSTITUTIONS |
|---|---|---|---|---|
| | pancit | mee (mi) | gougsou | |
| mì soi | miswa<br>pancit miki<br>pancit canton | mee | mil gougsou | spaghettini |
| | pancit mami | ba mee (Malay)<br>bakmie or mahmee (Indonesian) | | fresh spaghettini or tonnarelli or, for the flat noodles, fettucelli; or 13 ounces dried noodles per 1 pound fresh |
| bún | pancit bihon<br>pancit luglug | beehoon, meehoon (Malay), bihun (Indonesian)<br>laksa | | any fine dried wheat noodle, such as hiyamugi, flat rice noodles, or thin rice vermicelli |
| phở<br>(bánh phở) | | | | |
| bánh uôt (uncut)<br>bánh phở (cut) | | kway teow | | homemade recipe, page 207 |
| bún tau | sotanghon | sohoon or tunghoon (Malay)<br>sotangoon (Indonesian) | dang myun | |
| | | | naeng myun | |
| | | | | |

35

# THE PASTAS OF JAPAN

I t is hard to know just when noodles became a part of Japanese cuisine. We can safely assume that, like much of Japanese culture, noodles and noodle dishes were introduced from China. Waves of immigrants came to Japan from China and Korea from about 300 B.C. to 300 A.D.—just when the Chinese noodle was getting its start. But there was little Chinese cultural infusion until about the 5th century A.D., when Korean scholars brought the Chinese writing system to Japan. From that time to the end of the 8th century, the Japanese adopted much Chinese culture: economic and governmental administrative patterns, religion, arts, and technology. Isolation allowed the Japanese spirit to emerge and reshape its borrowings into something distinctly Japanese. The cuisine of Japan, including noodle dishes, is a prime example. The emphasis the Japanese place on natural flavors is reflected in the way Japanese-style noodles are served—simply, with a little broth or dipping sauce to bring out the noodles' natural qualities. A really great noodle, of course, is essential.

The noodle probably joined Japanese cooking along with *miso,* soy sauce, tofu, and chopsticks during the 6th century A.D. though there is not much discussion of it until the Edo period (1603 to 1868). By then *soba* noodles were part of the diet of peasant farmers who, before that, had eaten buckwheat dumplings. This hearty grain (which is not a true cereal) grew well in the less fertile mountainous soils and produced two crops a year. Not only did buckwheat make economic sense, it was further encouraged by a characteristic government edict that demanded the poor farmers not eat white rice but coarser foods.

At the same time, noodles or noodlelike foods were being eaten in Japanese cities. The diary of a Dutch physician, Englebert Kaempher, describes some of the food he tried on his journey to Edo: "Chinese *laxa* [noodles?] is a thin sort of pap, or paste made of fine wheat flour cut into small, thin long slices and baked. . . .the common sauce for these and other dishes is a little *soje* [soy sauce] as they call it, mixed with *sakki [sake]* or the beer of the country. *Sansjo [sansho]* leaves are laid upon the dish for ornament's sake, and sometimes thin slices of fine ginger and lemon peel."

In modern Japan, noodle eating, especially at lunch time, is a cultural institution. During the bustling Tokyo noon hour, blue-suited business men, shop clerks, and mothers with children sit elbow to elbow on stools, giving their complete attention to their bowls of noodles. In summertime, lunch might be a bowl of fine white noodles over ice with a dipping sauce; in chillier weather, fat *udon* swimming in a bowl of steaming, robust broth would be good for the soul as well as the body. Sucking noodles loudly into one's mouth is considered a proper display of appreciation and not at all offensive.

Lunch is not the only time noodles are eaten: they are a favorite snack food sold at all hours by street vendors. The *soba* man announces his presence by playing a *charumera*. He dishes up steaming bowls of noodles and broth from two large kettles kept warm by charcoal fires in the depths of his house-shaped cart. A tasty bowl of noodles hits the spot before a movie or after a night of *hashigo* (bar hopping), and late at night in Japanese cities groups of people gather around noodle carts, eerily lit by the *soba* man's lantern.

Many tiny three-table *soba-ya* and *udon-ya* noodle houses do a phenomenal take-out business. A photo in Raphael Steinberg's *The Cooking of Japan* depicts a noodle shop delivery boy guiding his bicycle through the mad Tokyo traffic with one hand while balancing a pile of trays, each filled with uncovered bowls of noodle soup. Every hamlet seems to have a noodle shop, usually specializing in a certain kind of noodle.

Despite the associations of noodles with peasant life and fast-food cookery, a level of refinement and subtlety has developed in the creation of various noodle types and their preparation. Certain well-bred *soba-ya* specialize, seeking to please the noodle connoisseur with such regional *soba* as

*Sarashina, Yabu,* or *Sunaba.* Some shops pride themselves on making and cutting the noodles by hand. *Udon* vary widely too, some being fat and chewy while others are thinner (but still chewy). *Udon* gourmets love the hand-cut variety. Hot Japanese-style noodles are best when served in a deep, lidded earthenware *donabe*—something like an individual casserole dish that keeps the soup piping hot until the end of the meal. Traditionally, one drinks the broth from the bowl, and no spoons are provided. In contrast, Chinese-style noodle dishes come to the table in ceramic Chinese-patterned bowls with a ceramic spoon.

As more of Japan's rural population gravitates to the cities, regional variations are not as evident as they once were, although there is still a difference in noodles and broths. Basically, *soba* is considered a northern noodle, while *udon* an Osaka or southern area dish. *Kishimen,* the flat, wide variety of *udon,* is a Nagoya specialty and even has its own *miso*-braced broth typical of the area. Even with the mobility of modern Japanese, it is common to find Osaka-style noodle houses in Tokyo and northern-style noodle shops in southern cities, just as one finds Chicago-style pizza in California.

Throughout Japan it is generally considered *de rigeur* to eat *soba* at New Year's, one of the most widely and exuberantly celebrated of Japan's holidays. *Toshikoshisoba,* "year crossing *soba,*" is thought to bring good luck.

In addition to "buckwheat noodle,"

another translation of the word *soba* is "close to" or "near." A Japanese who has just changed residences may offer *hikkoshi soba*—a bowl of *soba* with the greeting, "three across the street and two on both sides"—to his new neighbor as a token of newly established friendly relations and close harmony.

Stand in front of the noodle aisle in a large Japanese market and you will appreciate the place noodles have in Japanese eating. All kinds of fresh pastas fill a refrigerated case, and shelf upon shelf of dried, artfully packaged noodles are lettered in bold calligraphy. If you investigate all the fresh *udon* (white wheat-flour noodles), you will find everything from precooked noodles, with their packet of soup mix, to the long, fat, and chewy *futonaga udon*, dusted with a snowy cornstarch coating. Sometimes fresh *udon* is labeled *nabeyaki udon* after the dish in which *udon* is used, even though it is the same as simple *nama* (fresh) *udon*.

A good way to start acquainting yourself with Japanese noodles is to buy fresh *soba*—the brownish-grey buckwheat-flour noodles. If you cannot find *soba* fresh, there are always fresh *ramen* (for Chinese-style noodle dishes) or serving-size packages of *miso* soup *ramen* or broth *ramen*. For stir-fried noodles, use the *"yakisoba,"* actually a *ramen* noodle. Don't forget to pick up some fresh *gyoza* skins for dumplings.

If you are not going to eat Japanese noodles soon, it might be better to stock up on the dried varieties to have on hand for spontaneous experimenting. A good store will have a dozen or so dried *udon,* countless *soba* styles and brands, and all types of *somen* (thin white wheat noodles), *hiyamugi* (a slightly thicker wheat noodle), *harusame* or Japanese *saifun* (which are similar to bean threads), and *maifun* (rice stick noodles). □

# THE VARIETIES OF JAPANESE PASTA

Because the cooking requirements for the many unique varieties of Japanese noodles do not fit neatly into the basic cooking instructions beginning on page 14, I have given cooking instructions, with the noodle descriptions here. Words from other languages for similar noodles can be compared on page 34.

## 1. HARUSAME

Japanese version of bean threads or cellophane noodles, made from potato and corn starches and used in salads, soups, and deep-fried. Maloney brand is often served as a specialty noodle in American Vietnamese restaurants. It is flat and about ⅛-inch wide rather than threadlike. *Harusame* is often called Japanese *saifun*. Cook as you would bean threads.

## 2. HIYAMUGI

White wheat noodle similar to *somen* in composition but about twice as thick. Packaged in bunches, bound with a cloth ribbon. A few strands of pink and blue *hiyamugi* are added. Its name means "cold wheat," and it is eaten chilled over ice with garnishes and dipping sauce.

## KISHIMEN

Very much like *udon* but flatter and wider, typically served Nagoya-style in a *miso* broth. Available dried. Sometimes called *himokawa* after the dish it is used in.

## 3. MAIFUN

Japanese name for Chinese-style rice vermicelli noodle. Always found in Japanese markets and often packaged by a Japanese company. Used deep-fried as a garnish and in salads.

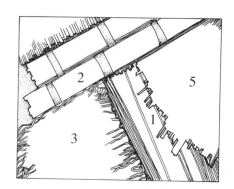

## RAMEN

The Japanese version of the Chinese wheat noodle owes its yellowness to coloring rather than egg. It is sold both fresh and dried. Quite frequently it is labeled according to the way it will be used rather than being called *ramen;* in such cases it will usually be accompanied by a special seasoning or broth packet. For example, *ramen* labeled *yakisoba* is used in stir-fries, while *ramen* labeled *miso ramen* comes with a packet of concentrated *miso* soup. *Ramen* also comes precooked in cups or packages with packets of dehydrated broth.

4. ***Chuka soba.*** Precooked *ramen,* dried in random directions and lumped together in serving sizes. Must be recooked. Use in soups, stir-fries *(chuka-men),* or eaten cold *(hiyashi-chuka).*

## SHIRATAKI

Not truly a noodle, but made of noodlelike strands of *konnyaku,* a Japanese yam. These jellylike threads come in cans or refrigerated plastic tubs and are delicious in *sukiyaki.* It is thought *shirataki* has a beneficial cleansing effect on the intestines.

## 5. SOBA

Well-known buff-colored buckwheat-flour noodle that contains some white wheat flour. Usually eaten hot, in a broth with garnishes, or chilled, with a dipping sauce. Practically all the recipes calling for *udon* may be made with *soba.* Several variations of *soba* are:

***Cha soba.*** Made with powdered green tea as well as buckwheat and white wheat flours. The tea flavor is very subtle when the *soba* is cooked.

***Nama soba.*** Fresh *soba* quite frequently made with a little egg and dusted with potato flour. Often sold frozen.

*Yamaimo soba.* Made with the addition of Japanese mountain yam flour. The texture is chewier and the color lighter than in plain *soba*. Different brands may vary in chewiness. Available dried only.

### 6. SOMEN.

Very fine white wheat flour noodle, the finer the more expensive. *Somen* is almost always eaten cold, though I have seen it garnishing some clear broths. The noodles are packaged with each serving portion bound by a cloth ribbon. Cooks often tie the *somen* together at one end while it cooks to keep the noodles going in one direction. When chilled, they are untied and served attractively swirled on a dish or basket. *Somen's* several variations include:

*Cha somen.* *Somen* with the addition of green tea powder.

*Tomago somen.* Beautiful, bright yellow fine noodle made with egg yolk.

*Ume somen.* Attractive pink *somen,* which includes plum and *shiso* (beefsteak plant) oil in the dough.

### 7. UDON

Wheat and water noodle, square-edged and thick, with a chewy texture. It can be found fresh as *nama udon* in air-tight packages (frequently with a little soup packet), or dried. It is usually served in a broth or as *udon-suki,* a noodle *sukiyaki.* Fresh *udon* freezes well. (For a recipe for homemade *udon,* see page 205.)

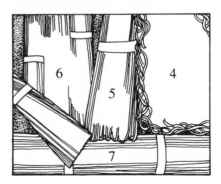

# Cooking Japanese Noodles

The Japanese like to cook their noodles by the *sashimizu* (add-water) method. It is felt that noodles cook more evenly throughout, and some cooks use it for Western noodles too.

Bring 3 to 4 quarts of water to a rolling boil. Never crowd the noodles in the water. Add the noodles to the boiling water gradually so the water remains at a boil. Push long dried noodles down into the pot slowly as they soften. Stir well to keep the noodles from sticking to the bottom of the pot. Let the water come to a full rolling boil again, then add a cup of cold water. When the water boils again, add another cup of cold water (except when cooking *somen*) and bring it to a boil again. The number of times water is added depends on the noodle, its thickness, and whether it is fresh or dried. Consult cooking times that follow.

Test for doneness by biting into a noodle. When the noodles are cooked, drain immediately in a colander and rinse well, tossing them with your fingers to rid them of starch, until they are completely cool.

### Cooking Times for Japanese Noodles

*Hiyamugi.* Using the add-water method, add 2 cups water (1 cup at a time) and steep until *al dente*—about ½ minute after the final boil is reached. Or boil continuously 3½ to 4½ minutes.

**Fresh *soba*.** Using the add-water method, add 1 cup water. Return water to a rapid boil. Test a noodle; if it is not done, let the *soba* simmer a few seconds longer.

**Dried *soba*.** Using the add-water method, add 3 cups water (1 cup at a time) and let the noodles steep 10 minutes after the last boil. Or boil continuously 7 to 9 minutes.

*Somen.* Using the add-water method, add 1 cup water, return to a rapid boil; test immediately. Thicknesses vary, but cooking time is very short after the second boil is reached. Or boil continuously 1½ to 2 minutes.

**Fresh *udon*.** Cooking time will vary with the thickness of the noodle, but 3 cups water (using the add-water method) and a steeping time of 5 minutes will usually be adequate. Without the add-water method, some very fat *udon* must be boiled 25 minutes. Instant fresh *udon*—the kind that come with soup packets—are precooked, so they need a warming period of about 1½ to 2 minutes. After the first ½ minute, gently separate the noodles with chopsticks.

**Dried *udon*.** Times vary greatly depending on the thickness of the noodle. Generally the addition of 4 cups water (added 1 cup at a time), with the water being brought to a full boil between each addition, will suffice. After the last boil is reached, cover the pot, remove it from the heat, and allow the *udon* to steep until *al dente*—about 15 minutes. Or boil continuously 15 to 25 minutes.

# *Somen* Noodles in Steamed Custard

*Odamaki Mushi*

This is a dish that always takes Westerners by surprise. It is not as fluffy as a souffle, or as dense as a quiche or omelette, but is something along those lines with the never-miss flavor combination of smoky ham, chicken, mushrooms, and onions all in a savory noodle custard.

4 dried *shiitake* mushrooms
1 bundle *somen* noodles (about 3¼ ounces)
2½ tablespoons light soy sauce
4 green onions
6 ounces cooked chicken, cut into strips ⅛-inch wide by 2 inches long
5 ounces smoky ham, cut into fine slivers
5 eggs, lightly beaten
3¾ cups prepared *dashi*
2 teaspoons *mirin*
¼ teaspoon salt
6 lemon wedges

Soak the mushrooms in warm water to soften them. Cook the noodles in 3 to 4 quarts rapidly boiling water for 1½ minutes; drain in a wire strainer and rinse well with cold water. Spread the noodles out on a towel to dry a few minutes, then cut them into 4-inch lengths and toss them in a bowl with 1 tablespoon of the soy sauce. Cut the green onions into 1-inch lengths, then halve each piece lengthwise. Drain the mushrooms and cut off the tough stems and discard them. Cut the caps into thin strips.

In a large bowl, combine the mushrooms, chicken, ham, eggs, *dashi, mirin,* 1½ tablespoons soy sauce, and salt; mix them well, then gently stir in the noodles and onions. Ladle the mixture into six 1¼-cup-capacity Pyrex or heatproof bowls and cover them very tightly with foil. Place the bowls on a steaming rack or cake rack in a large pot, and add boiling water to a depth of 1½ inches. Cover the pot and steam the custards about 25 minutes or until a knife inserted just off center comes out clean. Remove the custards from the water and allow to cool almost to room temperature before serving them garnished with the lemon wedges.

Serves 6 as a first course or part of a multicourse meal.

# Japanese Stir-Fried Noodles
## *Yakisoba*

Every outdoor celebration, carnival, or festival in Japan is well supplied with food booths that sell everything from cotton candy to corn on the cob to barbecued squid. And there is always *yakisoba,* a spicy Japanese version of Chinese stir-fried noodles, flamboyantly grilled on huge castiron griddles under canvas awnings. *Yakisoba* isn't made with *soba* noodles at all, but with Chinese-style wheat noodles or fresh *ramen.* Sometimes a dried *ramen,* labeled *chuka soba,* is used; it might be fun to try the wiggly looking *chuka soba* when you have no fresh noodles on hand. My favorites for *yakisoba* are fresh Chinese egg noodles or actual *soba* noodles.

1¼ pounds fresh Chinese wheat or egg noodles or fresh *ramen,* or 1 pound dried Chinese noodles or *chuka soba*
1 pound, 6 ounces lean pork, cut into strips ⅛-inch wide and 2 inches long
About 6 tablespoons vegetable oil
2 cups finely slivered yellow onions
1 large carrot, cut into strips ⅛-inch wide and 2 inches long
4 cups coarsely shredded white or Nappa cabbage
6 to 7 tablespoons soy sauce
2 teaspoons sugar
1½ teaspoons minced fresh ginger
¼ teaspoon salt
4 teaspoons *sake,* or dry sherry
4 green onions, thinly sliced
5 sheets toasted and flaked *nori*
Hot red pickled ginger *(beni shoga),* slivered (optional)

Cook the noodles in boiling water until *al dente*. Drain and rinse in a colander and spread them on a tea towel to dry slightly.

In a large skillet or wok, saute the pork in 2 tablespoons of oil over high heat, stirring until the pork is no longer pink. Add the onions and carrot, and stir-fry until the onions begin to turn translucent and the carrot begins to soften. Add the cabbage and stir-fry about a minute more.

In a separate bowl, combine 6 tablespoons soy sauce, sugar, ginger, salt, and *sake.* Mix well and pour over the cabbage mixture. Toss well and remove from the pan.

Heat the rest of the oil, then add the noodles. Toss the noodles with two wooden or plastic spoons as you would a salad, until the noodles begin to brown. Add the meat and vegetable mixture and toss until well combined. Taste and add more soy sauce if necessary.

Mound the noodles onto a serving platter or individual plates and garnish with green onions, *nori,* and pickled ginger strips.

Serves 4 or 5 as a main course or 8 as a first course or accompaniment.

# Sauteed Chicken
# Dumplings with Dipping Sauce

*Torigyoza Yaki*

The standard *gyoza,* the Japanese version of Chinese potstickers, are made with minced pork. This is my chicken version to be served with a traditional sauce or a refreshing orange sauce.

1 large dried *shiitake* mushroom
1⅓ cups shredded Nappa cabbage leaves
¼ pound ground pork
½ pound chicken, ground or minced
¼ cup minced green onions
1 clove garlic, pressed
1 tablespoon minced fresh ginger
1½ tablespoons soy sauce
⅛ teaspoon salt
1 tablespoon Oriental sesame oil
One-half 10-ounce package round wonton
    or *gyoza* skins (35 to 40)
6 tablespoons vegetable oil
¾ cup chicken broth
*Gyoza* Dipping Sauce (following)
                or
Walnut Dipping Sauce (page 57) with 2
    teaspoons grated orange rind stirred
    into it

Soak the mushroom in warm water. Blanch the cabbage about 1 minute; drain and pat dry. Squeeze the water from the mushroom, remove the tough stem, and mince the cap.

In a medium bowl, combine the mushroom, cabbage, pork, chicken, onions, garlic, ginger, soy sauce, salt, and sesame oil. Mix together well.

Unwrap the skins, put them on a plate, and cover them with plastic or a slightly damp towel. Have another damp towel handy. Spread about four wrappers on a work surface. Fill each with 1 heaping teaspoon of filling. Moisten the wrapper edges with water and fold the wrapper in half. Starting at one end, pinch the edges closed. As you seal the edges, make three evenly spaced tucks along only one side of the wrapper so the dumpling curves. Place the *gyoza* on a plate and keep them covered with plastic wrap as you work. Uncooked *gyoza* may be frozen on the plate and, when hard, wrapped in foil and kept frozen.

There are two ways to cook the *gyoza:* the classic pot-sticker method, and my method for novices, which I use. For the pot-sticker method, heat 2 tablespoons vegetable oil in a large skillet. Arrange 12 *gyoza* in the pan and cook until lightly browned on the underside. Add ¼ cup of the broth and enough hot water to barely cover the *gyoza.* Cover the pan and simmer until all the water disappears. Loosen the *gyoza* with a spatula. Place a large plate over the skillet and invert the dumplings onto the plate, or simply remove the *gyoza* with a pancake turner. Repeat with the remaining *gyoza.*

# *Soba* and Chicken with Walnuts

Or, in 2 tablespoons vegetable oil, saute one-third of the *gyoza* on both sides. When they are sauteed, arrange them so they do not touch and pour in ¼ cup broth and enough water to barely cover. Cover the pan and simmer the *gyoza* 3 minutes. Uncover the pan and simmer until most of the liquid is evaporated. Remove the *gyoza* from the pan with a spatula. Repeat with the remaining *gyoza*. Serve with the following Gyoza Dipping Sauce or Walnut Dipping Sauce with orange rind.

Makes 35 to 40.

**Gyoza Dipping Sauce**

Combine ¼ cup soy sauce, ¼ cup rice or seasoned rice vinegar, 1 teaspoon Oriental sesame oil, and a dash of hot chili oil or *shichimi togarashi*. Serve the sauce in individual dishes.

This dish is traditionally served warm, but because it is just as delightful cold, I always double the recipe and serve it twice, adding a few blanched broccoli florets or snow peas for embellishment the second time.

3 raw chicken breast halves, boned and skinned
1 tablespoon *sake* or dry sherry
1¼ teaspoons cornstarch
½ inch fresh ginger
1 pound fresh or 12 ounces dried *soba* or Chinese wheat noodles
Cooking oil
½ cup chopped green onions
1½ cups prepared *dashi*
4½ tablespoons soy sauce
4 teaspoons sugar
½ teaspoon salt
4 teaspoons rice vinegar
⅓ cup finely chopped walnuts
*Katsuobushi* (dried bonito flakes) optional
Toasted *nori* (optional)

Cut the chicken into strips ⅛-inch wide and 2 inches long. In a mixing bowl, stir the *sake* with the cornstarch until smooth. Cut the ginger to fit a garlic press and squeeze about 1 teaspoon ginger juice into the wine mixture. Add the chicken pieces, mix thoroughly, and allow to marinate about 10 minutes.

*Asian Pasta*

Cook the *soba* in 3 to 4 quarts boiling water until *al dente,* following the directions on page 44. Drain in a colander and rinse with warm water; set aside. In the same pan, heat about 2 teaspoons cooking oil; add the chicken and its marinade and the chopped green onions. Saute 2 minutes and add to the drained noodles in a large mixing bowl. Add *dashi,* soy sauce, sugar, salt, 1 tablespoon oil, and the rice vinegar to the pot. Simmer 5 minutes; remove from heat and allow to stand 5 minutes. Add noodles and chicken mixture and toss. Return pot to very low heat and heat mixture through, stirring occasionally. When heated through, divide among serving bowls. Sprinkle with chopped walnuts. Garnish with *katsuobushi* and crumbled *nori,* if desired, just before eating.

Serves 4 as a main course.

## Curry *Udon*

2 tablespoons vegetable oil
1½ cups finely chopped yellow onions
12 ounces lean beef or pork cut into strips ⅛-inch wide and 2 inches long
1 carrot cut into strips ⅛-inch wide and 2 inches long
3½ cups East-West Soup Stock (page 51)
or
3½ cups chicken stock mixed with 1½ teaspoons soy sauce and 2 teaspoons sugar
2 teaspoons Japanese or American curry powder
½ teaspoon *wasabi* powder
6 tablespoons tapioca starch or cornstarch
1½ pounds fresh *udon* or 1 pound dried *udon*
3 green onions, minced, or several sprigs of *mitsuba,* or *kiaware* daikon sprouts (hot sprouts)

In a large skillet or saucepan, heat the oil and saute the onions, meat, and carrot together until the onions are soft and translucent and the meat is slightly browned. Pour the East-West broth or stock mixture and curry powder into the meat and vegetable mixture, stir, and simmer 3 minutes. Mix the *wasabi* powder, starch, and 4 tablespoons of water together until smooth and stir the mixture into the curry. Cook, stirring until the mixture boils and thickens. Cover the sauce and set it aside while you prepare the *udon.*

Cook the *udon* in 4 quarts of boiling water as directed on page 44. Drain the *udon* well. Serve the noodles on individual plates. Reheat the sauce, pour it over the noodles, and garnish with green onions, *mitsuba,* or *kiaware* daikon sprouts.

Serves 4 as a main course.

# Japanese-Style Soup Noodles

W hile looking through a book I bought in Japan called *Eating Cheap in Japan,* I counted 16 illustrations of Japanese soup-noodle dishes. The authors include an equally long list of Chinese-style soup-noodle dishes, explaining where travelers in Japan can find such delicacies. Their collection only scratches the surface. With these and scores of other possibilities, how could I decide on what would be a representative selection? I narrowed my choices for this book to a few well-loved favorites, providing cooks with a choice of broth recipes that yield the same volume and may be interchanged. To the basic recipes, either 1½ pounds of fresh or 1 pound dried cooked *soba* or *udon* noodles or even linguine or Chinese *mian* may be added.

To garnish the noodles and expand your repertoire, follow the recipes and choose among suggestions for variations that follow each recipe.

# Basic Noodle Broth
### *Kake Jiru*

K *ake jiru* means soup for pouring on (the noodles). I wish all broths were as delicious and easy to make as these; you need simply boil water, and add a bag of instant *dashi* and a few condiments.

### #1

5 cups prepared *dashi*
2 teaspoons sugar
⅓ cup *mirin* or sweet sherry
About ¼ cup soy sauce

---

Combine all the ingredients in a saucepan. Taste and add more soy sauce if needed. Cover and simmer 10 minutes. Adjust soy sauce if necessary.

### #2

5 cups prepared *dashi*
4½ teaspoons sugar
3 tablespoons *sake* or dry sherry
About 3 tablespoons soy sauce

---

Follow directions for recipe #1.

**#3– East-West Soup Stock**

3 cups fat-free chicken broth
2 cups water
One 2-inch square piece *konbu*
About ¼ cup soy sauce
1 tablespoon sugar
2 tablespoons *sake* or dry sherry

Simmer the broth, water, and *konbu* together for 10 minutes. Remove the *konbu*, stir in remaining ingredients, and simmer 5 minutes more.

# Classic Chicken and Noodle Pot

*Tori Nanban*

2 dried *shiitake* mushrooms
1 recipe Basic Noodle Broth (page 50)
3½ ounces *enoki* mushrooms (optional), ends of stems trimmed
2 green onions, trimmed and cut lengthwise
1½ chicken breasts, cooked, boned, and cut into strips
8 spinach leaves cut into ½-inch ribbons
1½ pounds fresh *udon* or 1 pound dried *udon*, cooked and drained (see page 44)
*Shichimi togarashi* (optional)

Soak the dried mushrooms in water to cover until they are soft. Squeeze the water from the mushrooms and remove the tough stems and discard. Cut the caps into thin strips. Divide the broth equally into two pans. Heat the broth in one pan to boiling. Add the dried mushrooms, *enoki*, and green onions and simmer 1 minute. Remove the *enoki*, then the green onions, with a slotted spoon. Hold separately until assembly. Heat the broth again, add the chicken meat, and cook just until the meat is heated through. Add the spinach leaves and turn off the heat. Heat the second pot of broth and add the noodles to heat through.

Divide the noodles among four bowls. Top with the broth, chicken, *shiitake* mushrooms, spinach, and onions. Garnish the bowls artistically with *enoki* and serve the *shichimi* as a table condiment.

If you have *donabe* bowls, cook everything except the *udon* and the *enoki* right in the bowls, adding the noodles last just to heat through. Then garnish with the *enoki*.

Serves 4 as a main course.

## Chicken, Seafood, and Noodle Pot
### Nabeyaki Udon or Soba

Follow the recipe for Classic Chicken and Noodle Pot (page 51) omitting the spinach and *enoki* mushrooms. To each serving add a whole large cooked shrimp (shelled and deveined) and two slices of Japanese fish cake *(kamaboko)*. Warm them along with the chicken.

# Pork and Leeks with Noodles
### Buta Udon

1 recipe Basic Noodle Broth (page 50)
1 medium leek, quartered lengthwise, then cut into 3-inch lengths
8 to 10 ounces very lean pork meat, sliced wafer thin ½ inch by 2 inches
1½ pounds fresh *udon* or *soba,* or 1 pound dried *udon* or *soba,* cooked and drained (page 44)
2 green onions, minced
*Shichimi togarashi*

Heat the broth to boiling, add the leek, and cook 10 minutes or until almost tender. Add the pork and cook, stirring to keep the meat slices separate, about 5 minutes or until the pork is no longer pink. Remove the pork and leeks with a slotted spoon. Add the noodles to the broth and heat them through. Divide the noodles among four bowls, top with the pork slices and leeks, then add the broth. Sprinkle with green onions and serve the *shichimi* as a table condiment.

Serves 4 as a main course.

# Moon Viewing Noodles

This poetic name comes from the image of a poached egg floating in the middle of a bowl of noodles.

> 1 recipe Basic Noodle Broth (page 50)
> 4 fresh eggs
> 1½ pounds fresh *udon* or 1 pound dried *udon*, cooked and drained (page 44)
> Finely shredded *nori*
> 2 green onions, minced

In a wide saucepan, poach the eggs in 2 cups of simmering broth just until the whites begin to become opaque. Cover the pan with the lid askew while heating the noodles in the remaining broth in another saucepan. Distribute the noodles in broth among four bowls and sprinkle them with shredded *nori* and green onion. Float an egg on each serving of broth and noodles, being careful not to break the yolks. Distribute any remaining broth around the eggs.

Serves 4.

**Garnishing Suggestions for *Udon* or *Soba* Soup-Noodles**

• Four pieces deep-fried bean cake *(aburage)*, rinsed with boiling water, drained, and cut into thin strips.

• 1 pound ground pork or beef, sauteed, broken up, and seasoned with a little soy sauce.

• One recipe fried, pressed tofu as described in *Ketoprak* (page 130).

• For each serving, 2 tablespoons sauteed, minced yellow onion mixed with an egg and scrambled.

• Strips of salmon fillet, lightly cooked in the soup broth before the noodles are heated.

# Chilled Noodles

One of the better ways to stave off the discomforts of a baking Tokyo August afternoon is to sit down to a serving of chilled noodles with chilled dipping sauce. One Tokyo restaurant, specializing in cold *somen (hiyashi somen),* is equipped with a circulating ice-cold brook. Guests help themselves to chilled noodles from the brook and, at the table, eat them with a dipping sauce. A less exotic way to eat chilled noodles is in a bowl with a few ice cubes to keep the noodles chilled throughout the meal. *Hiyamugi* is served this way. I am particularly fond of the musky flavored buckwheat *soba* noodles on their slatted bamboo tray *(zaru),* sprinkled with crunchy, toasted *nori* flakes.

To accompany any of the following cold noodle recipes, I include a collection of dipping sauces and variations using ginger or *wasabi* for a piquant flavor lift. However simple these dishes are, they never fail to refresh.

# Iced Fine Wheat Noodles with Gingered Dipping Sauce

*Hiyashi Somen*

1 pound dried *somen* noodles
12 ice cubes
3 green onions, thinly sliced
2 tablespoons finely grated fresh ginger
Any dipping sauce (page 57)

---

Cook the *somen* in 3 to 4 quarts water according to the information on page 44. Drain the noodles and rinse well under cold water. Chill the noodles completely.

Divide the noodles among four bowls and top each with three ice cubes and a tiny sprinkling of green onions. (Reserve most of the green onions.) Each serving should be accompanied by its own bowl of dipping sauce, and a small dish with a mound of ginger and a mound of green onions for mixing into the sauce.

Serves 4 as a light meal or snack.

# Tri-Color Noodles with Mushrooms, Omelette Strips, and Walnut Sauce

This dish is a colorful tangle of three different colored and flavored noodles, with simmered *shiitake* mushrooms and omelette strips. Serve it chilled with Walnut Dipping Sauce.

> 6 ounces dried or 10 ounces fresh *soba*, cooked (page 44)
> 6 ounces *hiyamugi* noodles or thin dried spaghetti, cooked (page 44)
> 6 ounces dried *tomago somen* or *uba somen*, cooked (page 44)*
> Vegetable oil
> 8 medium dried *shiitake* mushrooms
> 3 tablespoons prepared *dashi*
> 3 teaspoons light soy sauce
> 2½ teaspoons sugar
> 2 eggs, lightly beaten
> 1 teaspoon *sake* or dry sherry
> 4 green onions, minced
> ½ medium cucumber, peeled, seeded, and cut into strips ⅛-inch wide
> Walnut Dipping Sauce (page 57)

Cook the noodles, drain them, and mix them with 1 tablespoon vegetable oil. Refrigerate in a covered container until well chilled. Soak the mushrooms in warm water until they are soft, about 15 minutes. Cut off stems and discard; squeeze the water from the caps and cut into slivers. In a small saucepan, combine the mushrooms with 2½ tablespoons of the *dashi,* 2 teaspoons of the soy sauce, and 2 teaspoons of the sugar. Simmer a few minutes until all the liquid is absorbed. Set aside.

Make the egg strips by blending the egg with ½ tablespoon *dashi*, 1 teaspoon soy sauce, ½ teaspoon sugar, the *sake,* and 1 tablespoon vegetable oil. Heat a 6- to 8-inch skillet, brush with oil, and pour in about 2 tablespoons of the egg mixture. Swirl the pan so the bottom is evenly covered with egg; cook until firm. Flip the omelette and cook about 30 seconds, then transfer it to a plate. Repeat about three times with the remaining egg mixture and more vegetable oil. Stack the omelettes, roll them into a cylinder, and cut them into ¼-inch-wide ribbons.

In a large bowl, gently mix the noodles, mushrooms, and egg strips with your fingers, reserving some of the mushrooms and egg strips for garnish. Divide the noodles among four or more bowls and garnish with the green onions and cucumbers, and the remaining mushrooms and egg strips. Serve with Walnut Dipping Sauce.

Serves 4 or 5 as a main course or 6 or 7 as a first course.

*You may substitute any colored or uncolored thin wheat noodles.

# Basket *Soba*
## *Zaru Soba*

1 pound dried *soba* noodles or 1¾ pounds
    fresh or fresh-frozen *soba*
2 sheets dried *nori*
Dipping sauce with *wasabi* variation
    (page 57)
2 green onions, thinly sliced

---

Cook the *soba* in 3 to 4 quarts boiling water either by simply boiling it or using the add-water method described on page 44. Drain the noodles in a colander and rinse them well; chill completely.

Toast the *nori* under the broiler or in an ungreased heavy skillet. When it is cool, crumble it or cut it into thin strips with scissors. Divide the *soba* among four bowls or baskets *(zaru)*. Garnish with the *nori* and green onion, and serve with dipping sauce and *wasabi* or horseradish.

Serves 4 as a main course.

# Tea *Soba*
## *Cha Soba*

The subtleties of Japanese cuisine are illustrated in this dish in which the noodle cooking water, with its delicate flavor and slight thickness, is used as a broth for the final course.

1 recipe Basket *Soba* using *cha soba* in
    place of regular *soba*
Cooking water from the noodles
Traditional Dipping Sauce (page 57)

---

Save the cooking water from the noodles. After the Basket *Soba* have been served and eaten, mix 1 cup of the noodle cooking water per person *(soba-yu)* with the remaining dipping sauce to make a broth and serve.

# Japanese Noodle Dipping Sauces

## Walnut Dipping Sauce

2½ cups prepared *dashi*
7½ tablespoons soy sauce
½ cup *katsuobushi* (flaked bonito)*
5 tablespoons *sake* or dry sherry
½ cup sugar
½ cup rice vinegar
⅔ cup walnut pieces

Combine all ingredients except walnuts and simmer 3 minutes. Grind or chop the walnuts very fine and stir them into the sauce. Serve cooled or chilled.

## Traditional Dipping Sauce

*Tsuke Jiru*

1⅓ cups prepared *dashi*
3 tablespoons *mirin*
1 teaspoon sugar
¼ cup *katsuobushi* (flaked bonito)*
¼ cup soy sauce

Simmer all the ingredients 2 minutes; strain. Serve chilled.

*¼ cup toasted *nori* may be substituted, or omit the *katsuobushi* altogether.

*Ginger variation*
Stir 1½ teaspoons grated or very finely minced fresh ginger into the cooled sauce.

*Wasabi variation*
Mix 2 tablespoons *wasabi* powder with just enough water to make a thick paste. Serve Traditional Dipping Sauce with little mounds of the paste on the side; the desired amount may be stirred into the sauce by each diner. Or serve *wasabi* in the same way with any of the following dipping sauces. Freshly grated horseradish may replace the *wasabi* powder.

## Rice Vinegar Dipping Sauce

1 cup rice vinegar
¾ cup soy sauce
⅔ cup prepared *dashi*
3 tablespoons and 2 teaspoons sugar
2 teaspoons Oriental sesame oil

Combine all ingredients except the sesame oil in a small saucepan and simmer 5 minutes. Stir in the oil and chill.

*Variations*
Stir in 1 teaspoon grated fresh ginger, or ¼ cup peeled, seeded, matchstick-cut cucumber, or 2 teaspoons crushed, roasted black or white sesame seeds just before serving.

# Cold *Soba* and Chicken in White *Miso* Sauce

The traditional way to serve cold *soba* is with a dipping sauce. But the rich sauce in this recipe—using white *miso*—is so delicious I use it to toss with chicken and *soba* as well as simply a traditional noodle dipping sauce *(tsuke jiru)*.

> White *Miso* Dipping Sauce (following)
> Two whole chicken breasts, boned, skinned, and halved
> ¾ cup braised bamboo shoots, or slivered, plain bamboo shoots
> A few *enoki* mushrooms, trimmed (optional)
> 1½ pounds fresh or frozen *soba,* or 1 pound dried *soba*
> Sliced green onion or *mitsuba* sprigs

Make one recipe of White *Miso* Dipping Sauce. Cut each breast in half, then cut each half chicken breast diagonally into fine strips. Heat ½ cup of the sauce to simmering in a small saucepan and add the chicken and bamboo shoots; simmer, stirring occasionally, until the chicken pieces are firm and opaque. Remove the chicken and bamboo shoots with a slotted spoon. If you are using mushrooms, add 3 more tablespoons of the sauce to the pan and simmer the mushrooms just until they wilt slightly. Remove mushrooms and set aside and return any remaining sauce to the original container of sauce. Chill the sauce, chicken, bamboo shoots, and mushrooms.

Cook the *soba* in 4 quarts of rapidly boiling water as directed on page 44. Rinse the noodles well with cold water; drain them well and chill them.

Divide the noodles among four wide, shallow soup dishes for a main course or among smaller bowls for hors d'oeuvres. Heap the noodles into mounds. Top each mound with the chicken, bamboo shoots, and mushrooms. Divide the sauce among the servings, pouring it around the base of each noodle mound. Garnish each serving with sliced green onion or *mitsuba* sprigs.

Serves 4 as a main course or 6 as a first course.

*Variation: Plain* Soba *with White* Miso *Dipping Sauce*
Follow the recipe for Cold *Soba* and Chicken in White *Miso* Sauce, omitting the chicken and bamboo shoots. If you like, serve the sauce separately in small bowls and the *soba* in larger bowls or on a traditional noodle serving basket-tray *(zaru)*.

**White *Miso* Dipping Sauce**
> 4 tablespoons white *miso*
> 4 tablespoons toasted white sesame seeds, pulverized in a *suribachi* or mortar
> 2 tablespoons sugar

2½ tablespoons *mirin* or *sake*
5½ tablespoons soy sauce
2⅔ cups prepared *dashi*

In a small saucepan, heat the *miso* until it softens and bubbles. Stir in the sesame seeds and sugar and heat through. Add the *mirin* and blend until smooth. Blend in the soy sauce and then the *dashi* a little at a time until the sauce is smooth. Continue to cook and stir until the mixture boils; cool to room temperature.

# Deep-Fried Noodle Brush Garnish

These deep-fried fine noodle brushes can garnish almost anything, from *sashimi* to sirloin steak or even a noodle salad.

1 sheet toasted *nori*
About 1½ ounces *somen* noodles (½ of a bundle)
1 egg white, lightly whisked
Vegetable oil for frying

With a sharp knife or scissors, cut the *nori* into ⅜-inch by 1¼-inch rectangles. Brush a strip of the *nori* with egg white and use it to bind 10 to 12 noodles together. If your noodles are 10 inches long, you can bind the bundles in the center, cutting them in half with a very sharp knife after the *nori* has dried (about 5 minutes). If your noodles are only 8 inches long, you will have to break off 1 to 3 inches depending on how long you want the brushes to be, and then wrap each noodle bundle at one end with the *nori*. Wrap the other bundles (10 to 12 bundles may be made with 1½ ounces of noodles), and allow the *nori* to dry.

In a heavy pot or deep fryer, heat 5 inches of oil to 350°. Holding each bundle with tongs at the *nori* end, fry each bundle, swishing it gently in the hot oil until the noodles fan out, about 30 seconds. Drain on a rack or absorbent paper.

Makes 10 or 12 bundles.

8-inch noodles

10-inch noodles

# THE PASTAS OF VIETNAM, LAOS, AND CAMBODIA

E ven before the mountainous borderlands of the Southeast Asian subcontinent were visited by Chinese and Indian traders, their intricate culture was well developed. The cultural characteristics of Indochina, as the area came to be known in the French colonial period, have staunchly survived the comings and goings of the military and mercantile factions of more powerful countries. Interaction between the Chinese and Southeast Asian peoples repeatedly stimulated cultural cross-fertilization from the earliest times. Later, Indian trading posts and settlements added other dimensions to the cultures, including to the established culinary arts—inspiring, for example, such developments as coconut milk/lemon grass sauces seasoned with Indian spices on Chinese noodles. Later came the overlay of French culture and its particular effect on the cuisine of Vietnam.

I first was introduced to Vietnamese food when I was living in Paris in the early seventies. A friend advised me that "it was good, and not expensive—close to Chinese but different." My budget was small, I liked "Chinese," and was in Paris, after all, to experience life. I allowed my friend to order, having no idea about anything on the menu. My first bite of *Pâté Impérial à la Viet-*

*namienne* was perfection, with its tissue-thin rice pasta covering and delicate filling of ground meats and vegetables. Our order of *Soupe des Nouilles Garnies à la Hanoienne,* "a cross between a soup and a salad," as my friend said, was a broth of mysterious flavors afloat with chewy rice noodles. This was my first experience of noodles made from rice flour. The unusual (to me) combination was habit-forming and I returned frequently during my Paris stay.

The place was always crowded with an unlikely mix of people. The atmosphere and food seemed to cut through cultural barriers, and cause the French customers to abandon their chauvinism about food. Each week my menu-French broadened its scope as *galette de riz, pousses de bambou,* and *germes de soja* joined my vocabulary. The dish that transformed my concept of pasta was *Fondue Variée.* Its title, hinting nothing of pasta, promised only an assortment of meats, seafood, and vegetables to be cooked at the table. But along with those were bowls of delicate rice vermicelli and tissue-thin moistened rice papers, served with a dipping sauce. The cooked foods were to be wrapped in the rice pasta along with the noodles and some fresh herbs; one could then dip this already complex mouthful into the light and intricate sauce. Like all good things, my stay in Paris and my earliest association with Vietnamese food came to an end.

My next real experience with the food of Vietnam was in Tulsa, Oklahoma. I thought Tulsa an unlikely spot to acquaint oneself with Vietnamese food, but the Ri-Le Restaurant proved to be a Vietnamese oasis during my several-month stay there. Although Ri-Le billed itself as a Vietnamese family restaurant and was in an out-of-the-way location, Oaklahomans somehow found their way there. The building had once been a doughnut shop and still bore a red and white striped exterior and 1950s-shaped sign, re-lettered by hand to read Ri-Le. The owner, Ri-Le, and his wife worked together cooking and serving, and somewhere in the background was a grandmother or great auntie who occasionally shuffled out from the kitchen with more plates of food. The children were always playing in the dining room where cassettes of popular Vietnamese songs played on the stereo.

At Ri-Le I discovered *bun nem nuong*—charcoal-browned barbecued pork balls on a bowl of rice noodles served with a dipping sauce and platters of herbs, cucumbers, and lettuce. One could eat all these things separately with chopsticks, or wrap the balls, noodles, herbs, and cucumber in lettuce and dip the package in the sauce. Diners always fell to the task with gusto. Sometimes the special of the day would be *goi cuon,* shrimp and pork with noodles and herbs rolled in moist rice paper (page 75). I realized the extent to which Oriental pasta is used when our stuffed barbecued chicken came to the table filled with savory ground meats, their juices absorbed by cellophane noodles. Ri-Le gave me his recipe for *banh-xeo*—a kind of pancake stuffed with meat and onions—which I still possess, hand-written on the back on an envelope.

With the recent large influx of Vietnamese into the United States and the consequent availability of Vietnamese foodstuffs, it would be easy to limit this chapter to Vietnamese dishes. I did, however, want at least to acknowledge that Cambodia (Kampuchea) and Laos also make use of noodles. Two particularly useful sources for the study of Lao and Cambodian cuisines are the narrative of Pearl Buck's *Oriental Cookbook,* and *Traditional Recipes of Laos,* the work of Phia Sing brought to life by Alan Davidson. Davidson, a British food scholar, tells us Phia Sing's dishes are "almost purely Lao, not having much French or other influence."

What is "purely" Lao? Phia Sing's recipes seem a delicate balance of native and Chinese cuisines with occasional glimmers of the Indian-influenced Khmer ancestry of Laos. One recipe tells the cook to stir-fry pork and garlic in pork fat in a wok, but the recipe takes a Southeast Asian turn when it says to add fish sauce, great quantities of bruised garlic, and coconut milk. Although one recipe for duck uses curry powder and coconut milk, as might be found in a southern Indian-style recipe, in general, Indian spices are absent. Instead, there is a heavy reliance on fresh chilis, garlic, shallots, and coriander leaves pounded to a pulp as they would be throughout Southeast Asia. The abundant use of fresh herbs, lettuces, and raw vegetables is a hallmark, as is the wrapping of pureed foods (like fish or seasoned eggplant mixture) in lettuce.

The most noticeable Chinese influence in *Traditional Recipes of Laos* is the sizable number of recipes using Chinese rice vermicelli *(khao poon)* or bean threads *(khao poon Chin)*. The noodles are sold in Lao markets in bunches, arranged around a circular bamboo tray, each bunch overlapping the next and weighing about half a kilo. The most well-known Lao dish to take its name from *khao poon* is a robustly spiced coconut milk and noodle soup garnished with sliced banana flowers (similar to those found in Malaysia). Often referred to as the "national breakfast soup," it is sold even in rural areas by traveling vendors who set up rickety stands in any available spot.

Cambodia has the same profusion of unusual curry flavors Laos has but with a stronger Indian influence. Pounded curry mixtures season strongly spiced stews, with characteristic Southeast Asian touches of fish paste and lemon grass. As in Laos, there are plentiful leafy vegetables, and foods wrapped in lettuce are typical. Cambodian dishes frequently include rice noodles. □

# THE VARIETIES OF VIETNAMESE PASTA

## 1. BÁNH CANH

Clear short noodles, about the thickness of spaghetti, made from rice, wheat, corn, and other starches. Used in soups, stir-fries, and in place of rice vermicelli. Sold fresh in Vietnamese markets. The noodles soften when heated in boiling water for just a few seconds. They have an interesting chewy texture.

## BÁNH CUỐN

Fresh rice papers sometimes served in restaurants and occasionally available in Vietnamese delicatessens, bakeries, and snack shops. Served plain with dipping sauce or wrapped around barbecued meats. A reasonable facsimile may be made at home from the recipe on page 208.

## BÁNH HỎI

Extra thin and delicate rice vermicelli.

## 2. BÁNH PHỞ

Flat rice noodles that come both fresh and dried. Usually used in soups, notably the northern breakfast soup *pho*. Consult the section on cooking dry rice pastas for cooking information.

## BÁNH TRÁNG

Thin translucent rice papers made from rice flour, salt, and water, then dried on bamboo mats which give the papers their characteristic crosshatch pattern. The papers come in two shapes: round (6-, 8-, and 13-inch diameter) and quarter circle or triangular shape. Must be stored in air-tight packages or they will absorb moisture and curl. Consult the section on pasta wrappers for information on their use.

## BÁNH UỚT

Uncut rice noodle sheets. The sheets can be cut up and used in soups and stir-fried dishes. Consult the section on cooking fresh rice noodles for more detailed instructions on their use.

### 3. BÚN

Rice vermicelli used in myriad dishes from soups to an ingredient in rice paper-filled rolls (along with meats, lettuce, fresh herbs, and grilled meat) or as an accompaniment to grilled meats and seafood.

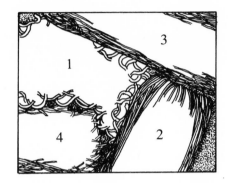

### 4. BÚN TAU

Bean threads commonly used for stuffings and steamed loaves.

### HÙ TIÊÚ DAI

Chewy noodles, often made from tapioca starch. Similar to bean threads but flat instead of round. In the United States, Vietnamese cooks use Maloney brand Japanese *saifun*, made from potato and corn starches. Cook as you would bean threads.

### MÌ SOI

Thin stringlike Chinese egg noodles.

# Vietnamese Barbecued Pork Salad

If served in true Vietnamese fashion, this salad would not be dressed but rather accompanied by a dipping sauce. While this works well for intimate dining, it is not successful for buffets. Guests find it easier to serve themselves to a fully dressed salad; for additional spiciness, a side dish of extra sauce may be offered.

*Meat and marinade*
    8 ounces pork butt or loin, partially frozen
    2 medium cloves garlic, cut up
    1 fresh green or red Serrano chili pepper,
        seeds removed
    2 shallots (about 3 tablespoons), chopped
    1¾ teaspoons sugar
    1 tablespoon and 1 teaspoon fish sauce
        (*nuoc mam*)
    2 teaspoons fresh lime juice
    ¼ teaspoon grated lime zest

*Salad ingredients*
    1 large, thick carrot
    ⅓ cup plus ¼ cup raw or roasted unsalted
        peanuts
    10 ounces thick rice vermicelli or thin
        rice vermicelli
    1⅔ cups fresh bean sprouts
    1 teaspoon vegetable oil
    Salad bowl or red leaf lettuce leaves
    Nuoc Cham Dressing (recipe follows)
    ½ hot house cucumber, peeled, seeded,
        and thinly sliced
    1 bunch fresh coriander

1 bunch fresh mint
3 green onions, finely sliced

Slice the meat wafer thin into ½-inch by 2-inch pieces. Combine the garlic, chili pepper, shallots, and sugar in a food processor or mortar and process or grind to a paste (you will not get as smooth a paste with the processor). Add fish sauce, lime juice, and lime zest and stir together or process to a puree. Combine the meat and the spice mixture in a glass or ceramic bowl and mix them together well; let marinate 30 minutes.

Preheat the oven to 450°. Slice the carrot very thin on a sharp diagonal, then into fine matchsticks; or use the fine julienne blade of a food processor. Set them aside.

If using raw peanuts, roast them on a baking sheet 10 to 15 minutes, stirring at least three times, until lightly browned. Transfer to a plate to cool. Line the baking sheet with foil. Spread the meat slices on the foil with edges touching, and bake about 7 minutes on each side until the meat is just firm. (Use a pancake turner to turn several meat slices at a time.) Or you can cook the meat over charcoal. Cool the meat to room temperature.

Bring 3 quarts of water to a boil. Add the noodles and stir until they are separated. Continue to boil the noodles, 8 minutes for the thick rice vermicelli or 3 minutes for the thin, or until they are tender. Add the carrots and bean sprouts to the boiling noodles for 15 seconds, then drain. Rinse the mixture with cool, then cold, water. Add the oil and mix well with your fingers. The vermicelli mixture may be chilled. Do not chill the thick rice noodles, however, or they will become stiff. The noodles can stay at room temperature at least 4 hours.

Chop ¼ cup of the peanuts almost to a meal. Chop the remaining ⅓ cup peanuts coarsely.

Line a large platter with the lettuce leaves, outer edges at the circumference of the platter. Mix about ⅓ cup of the dressing with the finely ground peanuts and stir into the chilled noodle mixture. Add enough additional dressing to thoroughly coat the salad. Reserve the rest of the dressing to serve at the table. Mix in the meat and about 2 tablespoons each chopped fresh coriander and mint leaves.

Mound the salad in the center of the lettuce-lined platter. Arrange the cucumber slices around the noodles, sprinkle the noodles with the coarsely chopped peanuts, and scatter green onions and additional sprigs of mint and coriander over the salad. Serve cold or at room temperature with additional dressing on the side.

Serves 4 as the main part of a meal or 8 as a side dish.

## Nuoc Cham Dressing

> 2 large cloves garlic, minced
> 2 fresh green or red Serrano chili peppers*
> 2½ tablespoons sugar
> ⅓ cup water
> ¼ cup fish sauce (*nuoc mam*)
> 5 tablespoons fresh lime juice

Combine the garlic, chilis, and sugar in a food processor or mortar and process or grind to a paste. (You will not get as smooth a paste with the processor.) Add the remaining ingredients and process to a puree or stir together.

*For a less spicy salad, remove the seeds from one of the chilis before processing or crushing it.

# Barbecued Beef in Fresh Rice Wrappers

Marinated beef cooked over charcoal is the traditional filling for this appetizer, but the baked version is delicious too. The fresh rice paper wrappers, called *banh cuon,* available everywhere in Vietnam, are very difficult to find in this country. In Los Angeles, I buy them from a "truck-kitchen" parked in Chinatown. Such professionally made wrappers are so thin they are translucent. And though the homemade variety aren't that thin, they are quite good, and as easy to make as French crêpes. Some Vietnamese markets even have a *banh cuon* mix— just add water and cook. The problem for most American cooks is the directions, which are in Vietnamese. Fresh rice noodle sheets *(banh uot)* may be substituted for the rice papers in this dish, but are not as delicate.

2 thick stalks fresh lemon grass or 2 tablespoons dried, chopped lemon grass
1 pound boneless top or bottom beef round, 1-inch thick and partially frozen
3 tablespoons minced shallots
1¾ teaspoons minced garlic
1 small, fresh green or red Serrano chili pepper, seeds removed*
2½ teaspoons sugar
1 tablespoon fish sauce *(nuoc mam)*
1 tablespoon Oriental sesame oil
1 tablespoon sesame seeds
1 recipe *Banh Cuon* (page 208)  or

1½ pounds commercial fresh rice noodle sheets or recipe on page 207
Fresh mint leaves
Fresh coriander sprigs
Dipping Sauce (recipe follows)

---

If using dried lemon grass, pre-soak it 1½ hours in hot water. Or peel the tough outer layers from fresh lemon grass and slice the tender inner portion thinly. Slice the meat wafer-thin to obtain slices 1 inch by 2 to 2½ inches. Place the meat in a glass or ceramic bowl. Combine the lemon grass, shallots, garlic, and chili pepper in a food processor or mortar, and process or grind to a paste (you will not get as smooth a paste with the processor). Add the sugar and process or mix again about 30 seconds. Add the fish sauce and oil, and process to a puree or mix them into the paste in the mortar. Mix in the sesame seeds. Mix the seasoning paste and the meat slices together well; let marinate about 30 minutes. Meanwhile, start the barbecue fire or preheat the oven to 450°.

Barbecue the meat briefly on both sides, just until firm to the touch. Or line a baking sheet with foil and place the meat slices on it with edges touching; bake about 10 minutes or just until firm to the touch.

Cool the meat to room temperature. Cut the fresh rice papers in half. If you are using commercial rice noodle sheets, you may need to steam them about 2 minutes to make them pliable. (Be careful—more steaming will make them mushy.) Cut the rice noodle sheet into 2-inch by 3-inch rectangles. Wrap the meat in the fresh rice paper or rice noodle pieces along with a mint leaf and coriander sprig, tucking in the lose edges of fresh wrappers (but not the noodle sheets) as you roll. Serve the rolls with the following dipping sauce as a first course or appetizer.

Serves 8 to 10 as an appetizer.

*Leave the seeds in if you like very spicy food.

### Dipping Sauce

 1 large clove garlic, chopped
 1 fresh Serrano chili pepper, seeds re- moved and chopped
 10 seeds from the chili
 2 teaspoons sugar
 4 teaspoons fish sauce (nuoc mam)
 2 teaspoons white rice vinegar or fresh lime juice
 ¼ cup water

Combine the garlic and chili pepper with the sugar in a mortar; grind to a paste. Add the remaining ingredients and mix well.

# Pâté of Crab, Pork, and Mushrooms
## Cha Trung Hap

The name *cha trung hap* (steamed egg) aptly describes this Vietnamese-style meatloaf. I had eaten it in a family-style restaurant but couldn't get the recipe until I found one in a French pamphlet on Vietnamese food. This is my version of that recipe. I find it is easier, and just as effective, to bake the pâté in a large pan of boiling water (a *bain-marie*), instead of using the steaming method.

 2 ounces fine bean threads (bun tau)
 6 ounces coarsely chopped domestic mushrooms (about 2 cups)
 ½ cup fresh or thawed, frozen tiny tender peas
 1 medium yellow onion, finely chopped (about 1 cup)
 2 cloves garlic, minced
 ½ teaspoon baking powder
 1½ tablespoons all-purpose flour
 1 tablespoon fish sauce (nuoc mam)
 ⅛ teaspoon freshly ground pepper
 4 ounces ground pork
 3 ounces crabmeat, crumbled (about ¾ cup)
 3 whole eggs and 2 egg yolks
 Vegetable oil
 *Nuoc Cham* Dressing (page 67)

# Vietnamese Spring Rolls
*Cha Gio*

Soak the bean threads in warm water to cover just until soft—about 5 minutes. Preheat the oven to 350°. Drain the bean threads thoroughly, spread them on paper toweling, and cut them into 1½-inch lengths.

In a large bowl, combine the mushrooms, peas, onion, garlic, baking powder, flour, fish sauce, pepper, pork, crab, and drained bean threads. Beat the three eggs lightly and add them to the mixture. Mix together well.

Lightly oil an 8-inch round glass or ceramic baking dish or cake pan. Spread the noodle mixture in the dish and cover very tightly with aluminum foil. Set the dish in a larger pan and fill the larger pan with boiling water reaching almost to the top of the pâté dish. Bake 1 hour at 350°, remove the cover, and bake 20 to 30 minutes more until the pâté is firm.

Beat the egg yolks slightly. Remove the foil from the pâté and drizzle the yolk over the surface, spreading it evenly with the back of a spoon. The heat of the pâté will cook the egg topping. Cool the pâté to room temperature and cut into wedges to serve. Serve with *Nuoc Cham* sauce (page 67) for dipping. Try serving pâté as an entree with rice and salad.

Makes 6 servings.

About 28 6-inch round rice papers (*banh trang*) or the triangular papers, or about 7 13-inch-diameter round papers, quartered
1 tablespoon sugar
5 cups warm water
Selected filling (recipes following)
1 egg white
Vegetable oil
Vietnamese Vegetable Platter (page 85)
*Nuoc Cham* Dipping Sauce (page 84)
*Hoisin* Peanut Dipping Sauce (page 84)

---

If you are using the large rice papers, cut them into quarters with scissors. Dissolve the sugar in the warm water. Working with three or four rice papers at a time, dip each into the water or use a pastry brush to moisten each rice paper with the solution. Place on a flat surface and allow them to soften about 3 minutes. As you work, rotate dipping and filling so there will be no waiting.

With your hands, form about 1½ tablespoons of the filling into a 2-inch-long log. Center the log horizontally about 1½ inches from the circumference of the round paper and fold the short edge over the log of filling (see Diagram A). Fold in the sides of the papers, like a blintz or burrito, and roll them up, moistening the edges with egg white to ensure a seal. (If you are using wedge-shaped or cut papers, follow Diagram B.) Place the finished rolls on a tray and cover with plastic wrap to prevent drying out.

In a deep 3- to 4-quart pan or wok, heat 1½ inches of oil to 325° or until a bread cube, dropped in the oil, browns quickly and rises to the surface. Add six or seven rolls and fry, stirring occasionally, until the rolls are golden and crisp, about 4 to 6 minutes. Lift out with tongs and drain on paper toweling. Keep warm in the oven on low heat until all the rolls are fried. *Cha gio* may be refrigerated and re-fried just to crisp and heat through.

Serve the rolls, sliced into thirds, arranged on a lettuce-lined plate, accompanied by the Vietnamese Vegetable Platter and individual dishes of dipping sauces. Diners should roll each piece of *cha gio* in a lettuce leaf along with a little coriander, mint, and selected vegetables, and dip the whole package into the sauce.

Allow 3 to 4 rolls per person as an appetizer. Makes about 28 rolls.

A

B

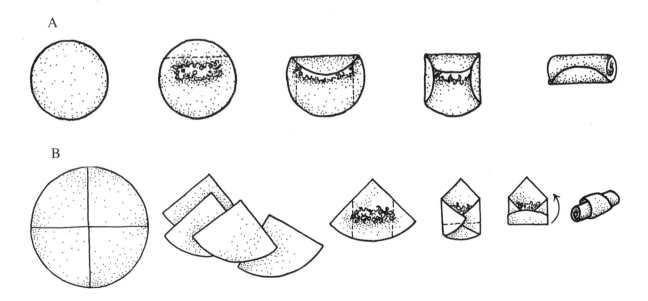

# Fresh Spring Rolls

*Goi Cuon* and *Bi Cuon*

**Pork and crab filling for** *cha gio*

6 medium tree ears
2 ounces fine bean threads *(bun tau)*
12 ounces ground pork
6 ounces chopped crab meat
¾ cup bean sprouts, beans removed, and
    cut into 1-inch lengths
2 medium cloves garlic, minced
⅓ cup minced red onion
3 tablespoons minced shallots or green
    onions (white part)
2 teaspoons sugar
¼ teaspoon freshly ground black pepper
1 teaspoon fish sauce *(nuoc mam)* or
    ¾ teaspoon salt

Soak the tree ears and bean threads, in separate bowls, in warm water to soften about 20 minutes. Drain the bean threads and cut them into 1½-inch lengths. Drain the tree ears, remove and discard the tough stems, and chop the tree ears finely. Combine the remaining ingredients in a large bowl, add the bean threads and tree ears, and mix thoroughly with your fingers.

*Variation*
**Chicken and shrimp filling for** *cha gio*
Follow the directions above, substituting 10 ounces minced, skinless, boneless chicken meat for the pork and 6 ounces shrimp, ground or finely minced, for the crab meat. Add ¼ pound ground pork fat or ¼ pound chicken skin and fat ground together.

Rice paper rolls—*goi cuon* and *bi cuon*—are filled burrito-style with shrimp or pork or both, aromatic leaves, and rice vermicelli. Cooks can put a personal stamp on these traditional bundles with their own selection of aromatics and dipping sauce. "Very refreshing," according to my Vietnamese friend and advisor, Mrs. Thuan Lai.

## Goi Cuon

2 cups chicken broth mixed with ¾ cup
    water
1 teaspoon fish sauce *(nuoc mam)*, or
    ¼ teaspoon salt
⅛ teaspoon freshly ground pepper
⅛ teaspoon sugar
1 pound pork butt or boneless pork loin,
    partially frozen then cut into ⅜-inch by
    1½-inch strips
4 ounces rice vermicelli *(bun)*
About 24 rice papers, 6 or 8½ inches in
    diameter *(banh trang)*
1 bunch bronze leaf or salad bowl lettuce,
    thick stem-ends removed
12 large shrimp, shelled, deveined,
    cooked, and cut in half lengthwise
3 large celery stalks, cut into strips ⅛-
    inch wide by 2 inches long
1 red onion, cut into very thin strips
1 bunch of any of the following fresh
    aromatic herbs: Chinese chives, corian-
    der, celery leaves, sweet basil, purple
    basil, fresh dill, mint

1 carrot, cut into strips ⅛-inch wide by
   2 inches long (optional)
*Hoisin* Peanut Dipping Sauce (page 84)
Other dipping sauce of your choice (optional) (page 84)

---

In a large saucepan, combine the broth mixture, fish sauce, pepper, and sugar. Bring the liquid to a boil, drop in the pork strips, and simmer, stirring occasionally, just until the pork is no longer pink. With a slotted spoon, transfer the pork to a plate; return any juices to the saucepan. Return the broth to a boil and add the vermicelli. Cook the noodles until they are tender, 2½ to 3 minutes; drain well. Spread them on a plate to cool. Toss the noodles occasionally to prevent them from sticking together.

Have a large bowl of water ready to moisten the rice papers. Dip two or three papers into the water for an instant or brush both sides lightly with a moistened pastry brush. Lay them flat on a work surface, and when they are pliable fold one-third of the rice paper over. Lay the pliable part of a lettuce leaf over the folded rice paper with about ½ inch of the frilly part of the leaf extending over the fold line. Place on the lettuce several strips of pork, ½ shrimp, 1 strip celery, 1 strip onion, assorted aromatic herbs, a few noodles, and a sprinkling of carrot if you are using it. Fold the bottom portion of the rice paper up over part of the filling, then fold one side of the rice paper over the filling and keep rolling the paper into a cylinder. Moisten the edge of the final flap of rice paper so it will stay shut. Place the rolls on a plate covered with plastic wrap so they will stay moist as you fill the remaining wrappers. Serve with one or more dipping sauces.

Makes 8 to 10 appetizer servings of 3 rolls per serving.

### *Bi Cuon*

Follow the directions for *Goi Cuon,* omitting the shrimp and increasing the pork to 1½ pounds. Serve with *Nuoc Cham* or *Hoisin* Peanut Dipping Sauce (page 84).

 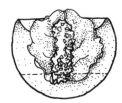 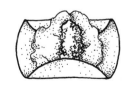

# Rice Paper-Wrapped Foods

Highly seasoned Vietnamese grilled meats are often eaten wrapped in lettuce and moistened rice paper. Sometimes rice vermicelli are included in the bundle to soak up the juices. The flavors of barbecued meat balls, barbecued beef strips, or simmered pork and shrimp are given an added dimension in these "sandwiches."

## Barbecued Meatballs in Moist Rice Wrappers
### Nem Nuong

1 pound pork shoulder
2 teaspoons minced garlic
1 shallot, minced
⅛ teaspoon freshly ground pepper
½ teaspoon salt
1 teaspoon sugar
1 tablespoon all-purpose flour
Lettuce leaves to line the serving platter
Moistened Rice Papers (following)
Vietnamese Vegetable Platter (page 85)
Aromatic leaves (page 85)
*Nuoc Cham* (page 84) or *Hoisin* Peanut
    Dipping Sauce (page 84)

Cut the pork into 1-inch chunks and grind it coarsely in a food processor or meat grinder. Combine the meat with the garlic, shallot, pepper, salt, and sugar. Allow the mixture to marinate a few hours at room temperature or overnight in the refrigerator. Return the meat mixture to the food processor, stir in the flour, and process to a fine paste. (This may also be done in a mortar.)

Form the meat paste into ¾-inch balls, skewer them on flat metal or water-soaked bamboo skewers, and barbecue over medium heat or broil until they are firm and browned, turning the skewers from time to time.

Serve the meatballs on a lettuce-lined platter and accompany them with a plate of Moistened Rice Papers, a Vietnamese Vegetable Platter, Aromatic Leaves, and, if you like, a bowl of cooked rice vermicelli and your choice of dipping sauces. Diners should place a piece of lettuce over a sheet of rice paper, add the meat and selected vegetables, herbs, and vermicelli, then roll up the bundle and dip into the sauce.

Serves 6 as an appetizer or 4 as a main course.

### Grilled Shrimp Balls in Moist Rice Wrappers

Use the Grilled Shrimp Patties (page 76) mixture instead of the meatballs. Form the patties into small ovals for easy wrapping and eating out of hand, skewer, and grill them, turning from time to time. Serve as you would the meatballs. This is particularly good with Mint Dipping Sauce (page 84).

# Using Dried Rice Papers

Dried rice paper wrappers may be rehydrated either by dipping them momentarily in a large bowl of water, brushing them with a moist pastry brush, or spraying them lightly with water from an atomizer. If the wrappers are to be deep-fried, a little sugar added to the water gives a golden color to the fried paper.

Dampen only a few papers at a time, then let them rest on a work surface until just pliable. Do not let them lie in a puddle or they will disintegrate. Use the wrappers as they become pliable. If you alternate between moistening and wrapping, you will save time.

### Serving Moistened Rice Papers

Serving a platter of moistened rice papers at the table can be tricky. If the papers are too moist, they stick together; if too dry, they are leathery. Attention to their degree of wetness is all-important. Using an atomizer works best in this case. The paper will become pliable and almost soggy at first. Allow the papers to dry until they can be folded in half without sticking together but are still pliable. This will take about 20 minutes. Stack the still-damp papers on a plate and cover them with plastic wrap, then a very lightly dampened towel, until you are ready to serve them.

# Rice Vermicelli Dishes
## *Bun*

The menu of the Dong Phuong Cafe in Los Angeles lists at least a dozen *bun* dishes in which the central ingredient is rice vermicelli. Some of these are soups, but most are the typical bowl of plain cooked pasta topped with well-seasoned grilled meat or seafood. With this plain dish comes a fresh, undressed salad plate and a zesty dipping sauce.

Unlike the Chinese renditions, the dishes are not sauced, stir-fried, or seasoned during the cooking. The Vietnamese prefer to blend their flavors at the table. The diner designs each bite according to the whim of the moment. Grilled Shrimp Patties with Mint on Rice Noodles typifies this serving style, and the one recipe may become several by substituting Pork Meatballs (page 74), Barbecued Beef (page 68), or Barbecued Pork (page 66) for the shrimp patties. All are authentic. The second dish, Stir-Fried Beef and Onions with Rice Noodles, is a national favorite.

# Grilled Shrimp Patties on Rice Noodles with Mint Sauce

1 pound raw shrimp, shelled and deveined
1 teaspoon salt
1½ ounces pork fat
2 shallots, minced
2 medium cloves garlic, minced
1 teaspoon rock sugar pounded to a powder, or 1 teaspoon granulated sugar
⅛ teaspoon freshly ground pepper
1 tablespoon fish sauce *(nuoc mam)*
1 egg white
1 tablespoon cornstarch
10 ounces thin rice vermicelli
Mint sprigs
Vietnamese Vegetable Platter (page 85)
Mint Dipping Sauce (page 84)

---

Sprinkle the shrimp with salt, mix very well, and allow them to stand 30 minutes. Wash away the salt thoroughly and drain the shrimp on paper toweling. In a food processor or mortar, grind the shrimp, pork fat, shallots, and garlic to a paste. In a bowl, blend the shrimp mixture with the sugar, pepper, fish sauce, egg white, and cornstarch. Chill the mixture about 30 minutes. With oiled hands, make eight 1½-inch patties.

Soak and cook the rice vermicelli as directed on page 16 while you cook the patties. Either grill the patties over a medium-hot charcoal fire on an oiled grill until they are firm to the touch and browned in spots, or deep-fry the patties in 2 inches of 375° vegetable oil for 2 to 3 minutes and drain them well on paper toweling. Keep the patties in a warm oven while you cook the noodles.

Drain and rinse the noodles and divide them among four or five bowls. Top with the shrimp patties, garnish with mint sprigs, and serve with the Vegetable Platter and Mint Dipping Sauce. To eat the dish, diners dip morsels of the patty along with noodles and salad into the sauce.

Serves 4 or 5 as a main course.

# Stir-Fried Beef and Onions with Rice Noodles
### *Bun Bo*

12 ounces thin rice vermicelli *(bun)*
4½ tablespoons vegetable oil
3½ cups chopped yellow onion
1½ pounds lean beef steak such as sirloin or rump steak, ½-inch thick and partially frozen, then cut into strips
3 teaspoons fish sauce *(nuoc mam)*
¼ or more teaspoons freshly ground pepper
½ cup roasted, unsalted peanuts, chopped
Vietnamese Vegetable Platter (page 85)
*Nuoc Cham* Dipping Sauce (page 84)

In 4 quarts of boiling water, cook the vermicelli about 3 minutes. Drain and rinse the noodles well, turn them onto a platter, cover with foil, and keep warm (not hot) in the oven on the lowest setting.

Heat 3 tablespoons oil in a large skillet or wok. Add the onions and stir-fry until they are soft and nicely browned. Transfer the onions to a plate. Heat a little more oil and stir-fry half of the meat until it is well browned. Add it to the onions and cook the remaining meat. Return the meat and onions to the pan. Stir in the fish sauce and pepper and continue to cook on high heat about 40 seconds. Mound the meat and onions onto a warm platter and sprinkle with peanuts.

Serve the vermicelli, Vegetable Platter, and stir-fry separately, accompanied by the *Nuoc Cham* Dipping Sauce. Diners may serve themselves portions, wrapping some of the stir-fry, vermicelli, and vegetables in a lettuce leaf before dipping it in the sauce; or they may simply eat the stir-fry, noodles, and salad separately.

Makes 5 or 6 servings as a main course.

# Crab Dumpling Soup with
# Rice Vermicelli

*Bun Rieu*

This recipe was adapted from a well-known Vietnamese dish by my friend Thuan Lai. I first ate the dish in a restaurant and when I asked the Lais, to my surprise, they knew all about it. Thuan Lai's husband explained, "At home we used little river crabs to make this dish. *Cua roc* are the best, but these are tricky to catch so some people use the *cua ram* crabs instead. The crabs are small and are pounded, shells and all, to a pulp. This is what is used for the dumplings in the soup—so you see it has a stronger crab flavor than this version. But this is good too."

3 ounces ground pork
6 ounces crabmeat
1 teaspoon moist shrimp paste, or 2 teaspoons fish sauce *(nuoc mam)*
¼ teaspoon salt
2 teaspoons vegetable oil
10 green onions, very coarsely chopped
1 Serrano chili pepper, seeded and minced
2 medium-large very firm tomatoes, cut into wedges
5½ cups chicken broth
1⅔ cups water
Additional fish sauce
¼ teaspoon sugar
3 tablespoons white rice vinegar
3 eggs, lightly beaten
Freshly ground black pepper

7 ounces rice vermicelli, cooked *al dente* (page 16)
2 cups fresh bean sprouts
Fresh coriander sprigs
Fresh lime or lemon wedges
Hot chilis packed in vinegar, or fresh jalapeño chilis, seeded and cut into slivers

In a food processor or mortar, combine the pork and one-third of the crabmeat; process to a smooth paste. Mix in the shrimp paste, salt, and the remaining crab by hand.

In a soup pot at least 10 inches wide, heat the oil and saute all but ⅓ cup of the onions over high heat until the edges begin to brown. Add the chili pepper and tomato wedges, and saute them about 1 minute until the tomatoes begin to soften but still hold their shape. Add the broth, water, 4 teaspoons fish sauce, sugar, and vinegar.

Beat the crab mixture into the eggs with a fork. Bring the soup to boiling and, with a soup spoon, form tablespoon-sized dumplings of the crab/egg mixture. With another spoon, slide them into the boiling soup. Cover and simmer 4 minutes or until the dumplings float and are firm. Season the soup with freshly ground black pepper and more fish sauce to taste.

Divide the noodles among six bowls and top with a few bean sprouts, the soup, and the dumplings. Garnish with coriander sprigs and the remaining green onions. Serve with lime or lemon wedges, hot chilis, additional bean sprouts, and coriander sprigs at the table.

Serves 6.

# Laotian Minced Fish and Rice Vermicelli in Cabbage Rolls

The Laotians grill the fresh-water fish of their land-locked country over charcoal embers, then pound and mix them with fresh herbs and rice vermicelli as a sort of pâté. Mildly flavored white fish, rock fish or snapper can substitute for the catfish called for in this recipe. If you are not cooking the fish over charcoal, broil it very close to the flame.

3½ ounces thin rice vermicelli
One 2¾-pound whole catfish, or 2 pounds catfish fillets or other mild white-fleshed fish steaks
2 tablespoons chopped fresh mint
8 green onions, minced
10 fresh basil leaves, minced
6 sprigs fresh dill, fennel, or celery leaves, chopped

1 thin (⅛-inch) slice fresh galingale or half as much fresh ginger, minced
Salt
1 head Nappa or white cabbage
1 head salad bowl lettuce
6 to 8 green onions, thinly sliced
1 cucumber, peeled, seeded, and cut into strips ⅛-inch wide and 2 inches long
1 bunch coriander
1 bunch mint or a mixture of mint and fresh basil sprigs
Dipping Sauce (following)

Cook and drain the rice vermicelli (page 16), and set aside. Skewer the fish lengthwise with two long skewers or sandwich it in a hinged barbecue grill and grill it over hot embers, turning once; or grill it on a rack close to the flame of a broiler, turning once. Cool the fish until you can handle it and remove the bones, head, and tail. Pound the fish to a paste in a mortar or process it in a food processor. Blend in the chopped mint, onions, basil, dill sprigs, and galingale. Salt the mixture to taste. Cut the vermicelli into ½-inch lengths and combine it with the fish mixture. Refrigerate until the vegetable platter and dipping sauce are prepared. Serve the fish mixture at a cool room temperature.

Remove about 10 leaves from the Nappa cabbage and cut away the tough white center.

Or, if you are using white cabbage, plunge it into a large pot of boiling water, remove it from the heat, and let it stand 5 minutes. Remove 10 to 12 outer leaves from the cabbage, repeating the plunging process to soften the leaves if necessary. Remove any inflexible parts from the lettuce leaves. Arrange several lettuce leaves on a large plate as a bed for the fish mixture. Arrange the remaining leaves on another platter with the cabbage leaves, sliced green onions, cucumber, coriander, and mint.

To serve the dish, bring the fish mixture, salad platter, and individual bowls of dipping sauce to the table. Each person selects a leaf, scatters salad ingredients over it, centers some of the fish mixture on it, rolls it up, and dips the bundle.

Serves 8 as an appetizer.

### Dipping Sauce

    1 small head garlic, unpeeled
    2 small, fresh red Serrano chili peppers,
        seeded
    2½ tablespoons fish sauce (use *nuoc
        mam*)
    6 tablespoons water
    3½ teaspoons sugar
    1 tablespoon minced coriander

Peel off the papery layers of the garlic bud leaving one thin layer. Impale the garlic on a metal skewer and roast it over a flame until it is slightly charred. Roast the chilis similarly. Peel the garlic, remove the charred parts from the chilis, and pound them together to a paste in a mortar. Combine the remaining ingredients in a bowl, stirring well to dissolve the sugar. Stir in the garlic/chili paste.

# Lao Salad of Green Papaya, Chicken, and Rice Vermicelli

This dish was originally made with duck. I love this version made with the dark meat of chicken.

    7 medium chicken thighs
    2½ cups chicken stock
    1 cup water
    1 tablespoon fish sauce
    Five ¼-inch slices fresh galingale, or 10
        slices dried, or substitute
    5 green onions
    3 fresh coriander sprigs with roots
    8 ounces rice vermicelli
    1 small very green papaya
    6 Nappa cabbage leaves, sliced crosswise
        into thin ribbons

One 10-ounce can braised bamboo shoots
3 tablespoons chopped fresh coriander
3 green onions, thinly sliced
2 to 4 fresh red chili peppers, thinly slivered lengthwise
Sugar
Fish sauce (use *nuoc mam*)
Salt

---

Remove as much fat as you can from the chicken, but leave the skin intact. In a soup pot, combine the stock, water, fish sauce, and galingale. Slice off the onion roots, slice the onions in half lengthwise, and tie them together with string or thread. Add the onions and coriander sprigs to the soup pot. Simmer the chicken in the stock about 45 minutes, or until the chicken is fork tender. Meanwhile, cook the noodles in 4 quarts of boiling water about 2½ to 3 minutes, until *al dente*. Rinse well in a colander with cold water and drain well.

Remove the chicken and set aside. Strain the stock and return it to the pan. Skim as much fat as possible from the stock and simmer it, uncovered, until it is reduced to 1½ cups. Cool the stock. Cut the chicken meat from the bones and shred it. Remove the skin of the papaya with a vegetable peeler. Cut it in half and seed the papaya, then cut it into strips ⅛-inch wide by 2 inches long or coarsely shred it.

Mix the papaya, cabbage, and bamboo shoots and spread them on a platter. Top with the vermicelli, leaving a circle of the papaya mixture showing. Top the noodles with the shredded chicken and sprinkle the chopped coriander and onions over it. Sprinkle a cup or more of the stock over the salad to moisten. Serve the salad accompanied by small dishes of chilis, sugar, fish sauce, salt, and the remaining stock. Diners flavor their own salads with these condiments.

Serves 6 as part of a meal.

### Variation—Lao Duck Salad

Follow the above recipe using a whole duckling, about 4 pounds. Remove the wings and back and reserve them for another use. Quarter the breast and legs. Cut away as much fat as possible. Proceed as with chicken in the recipe above. You may want to add up to another cup of water to almost cover the meat. Extend the cooking time to 1 hour, or until the duck is fork tender. If you have time, chill the stock to remove the fat—duck has considerably more fat than chicken.

# Cambodian Rice Noodle
# and Sour Beef

The meat for this dish is lightly cooked in a tangy tamarind-braced soup-stew. It is served over fresh herbs, the effect being miles apart from a Western-style beef soup.

6½ cups water
1 beef knuckle or other soup bone
1 stalk fresh or 2 tablespoons dried lemon grass
1 small head garlic
1 large shallot
Six ¼-inch-thick slices fresh or dried galingale or four ¼-inch-thick slices fresh ginger
Two 1-inch-long "fingers" fresh turmeric or 1 teaspoon dried turmeric
6 tamarind pods, peeled, or 1 rounded tablespoon tamarind paste
1½ teaspoons sugar
1¼ teaspoons shrimp paste or anchovy paste
3 teaspoons soy sauce
8 ounces daikon (giant white radish), halved lengthwise and sliced ⅜-inch thick
4 round, golfball-sized white Southeast Asian eggplants, quartered*
1 pound tender beef steak, such as sirloin or top round, sliced into 2-by-¾-by-⅛-inch pieces
4 ounces fine rice vermicelli
2 medium tomatoes, cut into wedges
Fish sauce
Salt
Vietnamese Vegetable Platter, modified (page 85)
Tiny fresh red chili peppers, thinly sliced, or dried chili flakes

---

In a large soup pot, combine the water and soup bone and boil 10 minutes, skimming off any scum that rises to the top. Remove the tough upper leaves and outer leaves of the lemon grass and slice the stalk in half lengthwise and then crosswise. Add it to the soup pot. Add the turmeric and galingale if you are using them dried. Simmer the soup for 45 minutes.

Peel off the papery layers of the garlic head leaving one thin layer. Impale the garlic on a metal skewer and roast it over a flame until it is slightly charred. Roast the shallot similarly. Peel the garlic, shallot, and galingale and turmeric if you are using them fresh. Grind them together to a paste in a mortar. Add this mixture to the soup along with the tamarind, sugar, shrimp paste, and soy sauce. Give the pot a brisk stir. Add the daikon and eggplants and cook 5 minutes. Add the beef and simmer soup 12 to 15 minutes, until the meat is cooked. Boil the rice vermicelli (page 16). Drain and rinse it well with cool water in a colander. Set it aside on a plate. When the meat is almost cooked, stir in the tomatoes and cook them about 1 minute.

With a slotted or Chinese wire mesh spoon, remove the vegetables and meat from the soup. If using tamarind pods, remove and crush with a little of the broth to liberate the soft pulp; return the pulp to the soup. Strain the broth, mashing the flavoring agents lightly against the strainer. Return the broth, vegetables, and meat to the pot and season the soup to taste with fish sauce and salt.

Modify the Vegetable Platter (page 85) by cutting the lettuce into ½-inch-wide ribbons and using only lettuce, aromatic leaves, and possibly bean sprouts. Serve the sliced chili peppers or chili flakes in small condiment bowls. Place a tureen of soup, a plate of noodles, and the Vegetable Platter in the center of the table, giving each diner his own soup bowl. Eaters help themselves first to noodles, then to a little salad, then top it with a ladleful of soup. They garnish the soup with their choice of aromatic leaves and chili peppers.

Serves 6.

*Two zucchini, thickly sliced, may be substituted.

# Vietnamese Dipping Sauces

### *Nuoc Cham* **Dipping Sauce**

¼ cup fish sauce *(nuoc mam)*
2 tablespoons distilled white vinegar
3 tablespoons fresh lime juice
¼ cup water
2 tablespoons sugar
1 clove garlic, pressed
⅛ teaspoon cayenne pepper

Mix all the ingredients together until the sugar is dissolved. Makes about ¾ cup—enough for 6 to 8 individual dipping bowls.

### *Hoisin* **Peanut Dipping Sauce**

4 medium cloves garlic
¾ cup peanuts, roasted and unsalted
2 tablespoons hot bean paste*
½ cup *hoisin* sauce
1 tablespoon sugar
1½ tablespoons distilled white vinegar
⅔ cup chicken broth

Mince the garlic in a food processor or by hand. Grind the peanuts to a coarse meal. Combine and mix in the remaining ingredients.

*If you don't have hot bean paste, add *sambal oeleck* or minced fresh Serrano chili peppers to taste.

### **Mint Dipping Sauce**

2 cloves garlic, peeled and diced
½ fresh Serrano chili pepper, cut up
⅓ cup fresh mint leaves, lightly packed
2 tablespoons distilled white vinegar
3½ tablespoons fresh lemon juice
2 tablespoons light corn syrup
1 tablespoon sugar
5 teaspoons fish sauce *(nuoc mam)*
2 tablespoons water

In a food processor or by hand mince the garlic, chili pepper, and mint together. Add the remaining ingredients and mix well until the sugar is dissolved.

# Vietnamese Vegetable Platter

A bountiful vegetable platter is the table centerpiece at almost every Vietnamese meal. The lettuce and herbs are an integral part of many dishes, rather than being a dish or course unto themselves. The platter almost always includes mint, and quite frequently several varieties of mint that are not found here. But Vietnamese in the United States make do nicely with only one or two mints and an assortment of aromatic leaves.

Arrange the herbs and vegetables attractively over the lettuce. Any vegetable platter should include:
• Soft-leaf lettuce, either bronze leaf, salad bowl, or butter lettuce (2 to 3 leaves per person)
• ½ cucumber, peeled, cut in half lengthwise, seeded, and sliced
• 6 or 8 sprigs each fresh coriander and mint (any variety or varieties) per person
• 1 carrot, cut into thin circles or flowers, or shredded
• Bean sprouts

If you have access to any of the following, add them to the platter:
• Green (unripe) mango, shredded
• Green (unripe) papaya, shredded
• Green onions, cut into 2-inch lengths and then into thin strips
• Chinese white radish (or Japanese daikon), shredded
• Red radish, thinly sliced

**Aromatic Leaves**
A smaller platter of fresh aromatic leaves may be served in addition to the vegetable platter. Or any of these may supplement the mint and coriander on the vegetable platter:
• Celery leaves
• Carrot leaves
• Sweet basil
• Lemon basil
• Purple basil
• Dill weed
• Yellow onion cut into thin strips
• Red or Maui onion cut into thin strips

# THE PASTAS OF THAILAND AND BURMA

If the intoxicating cooking aromas from a Thai noodle shop lure you off the sultry Bangkok streets—especially such a shop as Wang Hsiou Nan at Sukhumvit Soi 8—you can expect to experience a wide range of Thai noodle dishes and the gamut of culinary elements that bring distinction to this habit-forming cuisine. Some dishes are direct transplants from China, such as *gwaytio lard nah*—a combination of pork, broccoli, and oyster sauce tossed with fresh wide rice noodles. Others, like the *laksa*-style red curry noodle (either *bahmee,* an egg noodle, or thick rice vermicelli in a coconut milk base, spiced with a searingly hot curry) are typical Indian-influenced dishes of the Malaysian peninsula. If you prefer a more mellow flavor combination, you will find a salad of *wun sen* (bean threads), with shrimp, crisp vegetables, and a tartly sweet and slightly hot dressing, to be more delicate. If you have chosen something bland, you can perk it up to suit your taste with the range of Thai condiments that decorates every noodle-house table: bowls of fiery *priky-noo* chilis preserved in vinegar, sugar, and *nam pla* (fish sauce).

When in season, tan-colored *hoi-lay* clams, usually sauteed with curry spices, fresh basil, and chili peppers, are served in their own broth on a thick nest of noodles. Almost anything you eat is likely to be garnished with fresh coriander or a sprinkling of chopped mint leaves and very often a touch of green onions.

Heady aromas, brilliant colors, and contrasting textures and flavors that could be unsettling, if poorly prepared, harmonize beautifully in the hands of Thai cooks, who have mastered the Chinese concept of balancing bitter, salty, sweet, and sour flavors as suggested in the 3rd century B.C. Chinese poem, "Summons of the Soul."

At what point pastas became integrated into Thai food remains a mystery. Even now, formal Thai meals pay only fleeting attention to noodles. Since a large segment of the Thai population came at one time or another from China, noodles could go back many centuries, beginning about 100 A.D. with the migrations of Chinese into Thailand from the Yunan Valley in Southern China. These early Chinese immigrants blended culturally and racially with the indigenous peoples, creating a thriving civilization which greeted the heavier migrations of the 13th century and later.

But I suspect the noodle, which was at first a northern specialty, waited for the later and more ethnically distinct Chinese migrations. By the 14th century, the Chinese were very visible in Thai society and were well established as merchants, artisans, and cooks, and in such trades as pig breeding (the pork undoubtedly being used in Chinese food). Though at times they intermarried with the Thai, they remained to a large extent culturally distinct. According to a 14th century journal of a French traveler, "there were three to four thousand Chinese living in the capital of Ayutthaya in their own quarters or in port settlements all around the Gulf of Siam."

Regardless of when they arrived in Thailand, noodle dishes have not remained thoroughly Chinese. Ancient Indian and later Khmer influences, evident in other aspects of Thai culture, are manifest in Thai food ways. Thai curries are a good example of the cultural borrowings that have gone on in Thai kitchens for centuries. Into a base of shallots, garlic, lemon grass, and fish paste—which some experts feel was the original Thai curry mixture—a sprinkling of Indian curry spices is skillfully incorporated. The whole mixture is fried in oily coconut cream and mixed with meats or vegetables that have been simmered in coconut milk. Fresh chilis (the ingredient that supplanted black pepper when Portuguese traders brought them to the area from the New World in the early 16th century) are usually added before fresh herbs are finally blended in toward the end of the cooking time, preserving their clarity of flavors. The curry is finally garnished with more fresh herbs lending further dimension. A curry may occasionally be served with Chinese noodles or have an ingredient such as tofu mixed into it, all the varied elements being flawlessly combined.

The Burmese and Thai civilizations have borrowed and stolen heavily from each other during the course of their war-torn histories. Burma, the small, isolated "Royal and Golden Country," shares traces of a Mon-Khmer ancestry and Indian cultural influences with its Thai neighbor. Even so, the two cuisines differ significantly, India having exercised a stronger cultural and culinary influence through the trading port of Rangoon. Both countries are known for their pungent curries. While many of the same ingredients and flavorings are used, Burmese curry sauces are made in the Indian way by gently cooking freshly powdered spices in hot oil before adding vegetables, meats, and any liquids. At the same time, Burmese cooks have a decidedly Southeast Asian way with lemon grass and fish sauce.

"The Burmese idea of a meal is to eat rice in as appetizing a way as possible," explains Mi Mi Khaing in her book, *Cook and Entertain the Burmese Way*. Still, her slim volume devotes considerable space to the explanation and use of noodles. While Chinese cooking has not been a strong influence in Burmese cooking, all the basic Chinese noodle styles are readily available and eaten frequently. In Burma, rice vermicelli are made fresh daily from slightly fermented rice flour. Burmese housewives may buy these from their local *moh* seller (*moh* is the word used for flour and everything made with wheat or rice flour). Other noodle styles, both dried and fresh, such as bean threads, rice noodles, plain wheat noodles, wheat and egg noodles, and very fine dried wheat vermicelli (*muswa,* an obvious derivation from the Chinese *miswa),* are all on hand.

Noodles are always used as a base for one-dish meals and, as one might guess in this land of curries, curries are what go on top of the noodles. Often served at celebrations and large family gatherings, *mohinga* is based on noodles and curried fresh-water fish. *Oh-no kaukswe,* the festive Burmese Curry Chicken and Noodle Feast, is a richly flavored coconut-milk curry served with a banquet of assorted garnishes. Both outstanding curries give the familiar Chinese egg noodle a new personality. □

# THE VARIETIES OF THAI AND BURMESE PASTA

Few Thai and Burmese noodles differ from the standard Chinese noodles. The cooking directions for all may be found in the cooking section of the chapter entitled "The Scope of Asian Pasta."

## BÀ MEE (Thailand)
## KYET-OO KAUKSWE (Burma)

Chinese-style egg noodles that come stringlike or flat. Used much as the Chinese would use them in soups or stir-fries in Thailand, and as a base for curry in Burma.

## GWAYTIO (Thailand)
## KYASANGYI (Burma)

Fresh wide rice noodles, which may come in wide sheets *(sha he fen* in Chinese markets*)* or cut into ⅜-inch ribbons. Two-inch-square dried rice sheet flake noodles (3), packaged in cellophane bags in Thai and Vietnamese stores, can replace *gwaytio* in soup but are less successful in stir-fries, nor will they work as wrappers for fillings. Soak them 20 minutes, then boil about 4 minutes. *Gwaytio*

is not only the name of a noodle, it is also the name of the popular Thai breakfast soup containing it. Wide dried rice noodles are called *hsan kwkswe* in Burma.

## 1. JANTABOON NOODLES (Thailand)

Flat, thin, dried rice noodles, often used in *pad Thai*. Unlike the thinner rice vermicelli, which need only be soaked before heating, these must be soaked then boiled 3 to 4 minutes. (See Cooking Rice Noodles, page 16.)

## KAUKSWE (Burma)

Thin dried wheat noodles, cooked and eaten with a curry topping. (Cook as for any wheat noodle.)

## MONDI or MOHINGA-MON (Burma)

Small fresh rice noodles used in *mohinga*.

**MONDI-CHAUK** (Burma)

Medium-size round dried rice noodles found in Filipino markets as *pancit luglug*.

**MUSWA** (Burma)

Ultra-thin wheat noodles sold in the United States as *miswa* in Filipino markets.

2. **SEN MEE** (Thailand)
**HSAN KYASAN** (Burma)

Rice vermicelli. Used deep-fried in Thai *mee krob*. In *mee Siam* they are tinted bright pink, stir-fried, and served with coconut-milk sauce, any number of garnishes, and sometimes tofu. *Sen mee* may usually replace thicker flat or round rice noodles *(jantaboon)* called for in some Thai and Burmese recipes.

**WUN SEN** (Thailand)
**PEKYASAN** (Burma)

Bean thread or "gelatin string" noodles, used in Thai salads under bits of warm stir-cooked meat or seafood and served on a bed of cool greens, garnished with onions, cucumbers, and aromatic leaves, and finished with a slightly tart dressing. Used in Burmese soups and a curry dish called *panthe kaukswe* sold in the food stalls of Rangoon.

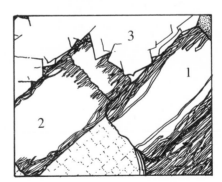

# Thai Crispy Noodles
*Mee Krob*

Almost every lover of Thai food has tried *mee krob*, a dish synonymous with Thai restaurant cooking in America. And a chapter on Thai noodle recipes would be incomplete without it. In Thailand, it is not an everyday dish, but reserved for festivities.

I have altered the usually sticky-sweet dish to this less sweet version which better suits my tastes and the tastes of my guests. If the recipe seems complex, it is because I am giving two sets of instructions: for the traditional, lacy fried-egg garnish and for the simpler stir-fried egg garnish.

*For the sauce mixture*
> 2 tablespoons fresh lime juice
> 3 tablespoons fish sauce *(nam pla)*
> 3 tablespoons distilled white vinegar
> 1 tablespoon soy sauce
> 2 tablespoons tomato paste
> 2 tablespoons sugar
> 3 tablespoons palm or light brown sugar
> ¾ teaspoons grated lemon zest
> 1½ teaspoons grated orange zest

*For the noodles and topping*
> Vegetable oil for frying
> 6 ounces very fine rice vermicelli *(sen mee)*
> 5 eggs, lightly beaten
> 1 medium yellow onion, finely chopped
> 3 cloves garlic, minced
> 2 small fresh or dried hot chili peppers, finely minced

½ pound lean boneless pork, cut into ½- by 2- by 8-inch pieces
1 whole chicken breast, skinned, boned, and cut into strips
½ pound small, raw shrimp, shelled
3 cups bean sprouts, beans removed

For garnishes: finely sliced green onions, lime wedges, or coriander leaves, or any combination

Stir together the lime juice, fish sauce, vinegar, soy sauce, tomato paste, sugars, lemon zest, and orange zest and set aside.

In a wok or large, wide, heavy pan, heat 2 to 2½ inches of oil to 375°, or until a single rice noodle puffs instantly when placed in the oil. Drop in about an ounce of the noodles. As they puff, push them into the oil; turn the noodle mass over when the crackling stops. Cook the noodles until all are puffed and no longer crackling—about 15 seconds; drain briefly on paper toweling. Skim any lost noodle bits from the oil before frying the next batch of noodles. Hold the noodles in a 200° oven while you prepare the remaining ingredients.

When the noodles are cooked, slowly drizzle half of the eggs in a lacelike pattern over the hot oil (or wait to cook eggs as directed below); when golden, transfer to absorbent toweling; repeat with the remaining

# Hugh Carpenter's Thai Shrimp Dumplings with Lime and Chili Sauce

eggs. Set aside. Heat 2 tablespoons of oil in a wok or large skillet. Add the onion, garlic, and chili peppers and stir-fry until the onion is almost translucent. Add the pork and stir-fry about 2 more minutes until the pork is almost browned. Add the chicken and shrimp; stir-fry until they are about half-way opaque. Add the bean sprouts and continue stir-frying until the shrimp are nearly pink. If you have not deep-fried the lacy egg, remove the meat mixture to a plate. Add about ½ tablespoon oil to the pan and cook the eggs to the hard-scramble stage. Remove the eggs to a small plate and return the meat mixture to the pan. Add the sauce mixture and cook, stirring constantly until the sauce turns glossy. Let cool about 3 minutes. Fold in the noodles and eggs about one-fourth at a time, using two large cooking forks to completely coat each noodle. Heap the noodles on a platter and garnish with your choice of garnishes.

Serves 6 to 8 as part of a meal.

P opular Los Angeles cooking teacher Hugh Carpenter, a Thai and Chinese food authority, contributes this recipe for Thai Shrimp Dumplings with its dipping sauce full of fresh, sparkling flavors.

8 ounces shelled, deveined raw shrimp
1 raw egg white
8 ounces ground pork
2 green onions, minced
2 large shallots, minced—about 3½ tablespoons
1 tablespoon finely minced fresh lemon grass
2 cloves garlic, minced
1 tablespoon fish sauce (*nam pla*)
1 tablespoon Thai hot sauce (*sriracha sauce, hot*)
6 water chestnuts, minced
½ teaspoon galingale powder
½ teaspoon salt
1 package round wonton skins
3 tablespoons peanut oil
1 tablespoon toasted white sesame seeds
Lime and Chili Sauce (following)

In a food processor, chop the shrimp to a fine mince, gradually adding the egg white. Do not puree the shrimp. Add all the remaining ingredients except sauce and process just to mix. Or mince the shrimp by hand adding the egg white as you chop, then mix in the remaining ingredients except the sauce by hand.

Unwrap the wrappers, put them on a plate, and cover them with plastic or a slightly damp towel. Have a damp towel handy to wipe your fingers. Spread four wrappers on a work surface. Using two spoons, fill each wrapper with 2 teaspoons of the filling. Moisten the wrapper edges with water and fold the wrapper in half. Starting at one end, pinch the edges closed; as you seal the edges, make three evenly spaced tucks along one side. Place the finished dumplings, pleated-side-up, on a piece of cornstarch-dusted wax paper. This can be done an hour ahead of cooking.

Heat a large heavy skillet and add the oil. Fry the dumplings until they are golden on the bottom. Add ½ cup water. Cover and cook the dumplings until their skins are translucent, about 4 minutes. Remove the cover and cook until all the water disappears and the dumplings turn dark brown on the bottom. Invert the dumplings onto a large plate, sprinkle with the sesame seeds, and serve immediately with individual bowls of Lime and Chili Sauce.

Makes about 30 dumplings.

### Lime and Chili Sauce

2 tablespoons fresh lime juice
2 tablespoons Thai hot sauce (*sriracha* sauce, hot)
2 tablespoons minced fresh coriander
1 tablespoon minced fresh mint
1 tablespoon minced fresh basil

Blend all the ingredients together and whisk well.

# Spicy Beef, Squid, and Noodle Salad

10 ounces top round or flank steak, ½- to ¾-inch thick
6 ounces dressed, small squid, cut into rings
Dressing (following)
4 ounces bean threads (*wun sen*)
1 head Bibb lettuce
About ¼ head Romaine or iceberg lettuce, torn
½ medium red onion, slivered
1⅓ cups bean sprouts
¾ peeled cucumber, halved lengthwise, seeded, and thickly sliced
½ cup chicken broth
Tomato wedges
Lime wedges
Coriander sprigs
Mint or fresh basil sprigs

Preheat the broiler and grill the steak to medium-rare. In a large pot of boiling water, blanch the squid about 1½ minutes, until it turns completely white. Drain and rinse with cold water. Slice the steak as thinly as possible on the diagonal into strips ¼-inch thick and 2 inches long. Combine the squid, beef, and dressing and allow to marinate 1 hour at room temperature or 3 hours refrigerated.

Soak the noodles in warm water until they are soft, about 10 minutes. Drain and immediately rinse with cold water. You may want to cut them into shorter lengths. Put them aside. Line a platter with half the Bibb lettuce leaves. Tear the remaining leaves and mix them with the Romaine or iceberg lettuce. Layer the torn lettuce, red onion, bean sprouts, and cucumber over the Bib lettuce lining. Heat the chicken broth in a skillet, add the bean threads, and cook, stirring, until they are translucent—1½ to 2 minutes. With a slotted spoon, transfer the marinated squid and beef to the noodles in the pan along with 3 tablespoons of the dressing. Stir them into the noodles. Heap the noodle mixture in the center of the vegetables and sprinkle the remaining dressing over all. Alternate wedges of tomato and lime around the edge of the mound and garnish the platter with the coriander and mint or basil sprigs.

Serves 4 to 6 as part of a meal.

**Dressing**

⅔ cup fresh lime juice
⅓ cup fish sauce *(nam pla)*
4 teaspoons minced ginger
2 large cloves garlic, pressed
1½ teaspoons Thai hot sauce *(sriracha chili sauce)* or ⅜ to ½ teaspoon dried, crushed Asian chili peppers
5 teaspoons sugar
1½ tablespoons minced fresh Thai, purple, or sweet basil, mint, or coriander

---

Mix all the ingredients well. Press down on the minced ginger in the sauce with the back of a spoon to release a little of its juices.

# Ladies in a Sarong
*Noodle-Wrapped Meatballs*

I first came across Ladies in a Sarong at the Siamese Princess Restaurant in Los Angeles. Even the name of these whimsical noodle-wrapped meatballs conjures up the delights of a Thai garden party, with laughter floating through the warm air, abundant gossip, plenty of icy Thai beer, and delicious things to nibble on.

For this recipe, it is best to use a flat, ⅛-inch-thick Chinese egg noodle, which becomes very tender when fried; but ¹⁄₁₆-inch fresh noodles will do, or you can even use fresh spaghetti.

>    8 ounces ground pork
>    12 ounces ground beef
>    ¼ cup minced shallots
>    3 tablespoons minced green onions
>    4 teaspoons minced garlic
>    2 tablespoons chopped fresh coriander
>    2 coriander roots, minced
>    4½ teaspoons fish sauce *(nam pla)*
>    ½ teaspoon sugar
>    ¼ teaspoon freshly ground pepper
>    ¼ teaspoon salt
>    1 egg, lightly beaten
>    12 ounces fresh Chinese egg noodles,
>       ⅛-inch wide
>    Vegetable oil for frying
>    Plum Dipping Sauce (following)

Mix the pork, beef, shallots, onions, garlic, coriander leaves and roots, fish sauce, sugar, pepper, and salt. Roll the mixture into small balls about ¾ inch in diameter. Dip each meatball in egg, then wrap it in a noodle as though wrapping a ball of yarn. Leave a little of the meatball showing. If the noodle breaks while you are wrapping, press it into the meatball and continue wrapping. Wrapped meatballs may be refrigerated several hours before frying.

Heat oil at least 2 inches deep in a deep fryer or kettle to 350°. (If the oil is too hot, the noodles will brown before the meat is cooked.) Test cook one meatball and keep regulating the heat to keep the temperature as consistent as possible. The meatballs will be done when the noodles are golden and the meatballs are firm. Drain on paper toweling and keep warm in a 200° oven until all the meatballs are cooked. Serve with Plum Dipping Sauce.

Serves 10 to 12 as an appetizer.

**Plum Dipping Sauce**

>    ½ cup Chinese plum sauce
>    1 tablespoon fish sauce *(nam pla)*
>    2 tablespoons fresh lime juice
>    1 teaspoon grated lime zest
>    2 teaspoons light soy sauce

Whisk all ingredients together thoroughly.

# Thai Breakfast Soup
*Kwayteeo*

In Thai Breakfast Soup, chewy squares or ribbons of fresh rice noodle come immersed in a light savory broth, and the eater garnishes his portion with a choice of aromatic leaves, perhaps a few slices of vinegared hot chili pepper, some *nam pla,* vinegar, or sugar.

If you can't find fresh rice noodle, substitute a product called "dry rice sheet flake," available in Thai and Vietnamese markets; or you can even substitute *sen mee*—dried rice sticks or rice vermicelli.

14 ounces homemade or commercial regular-strength beef broth
14 ounces homemade or commercial regular-strength chicken broth
2½ cups water
12 ounces lean pork, cut into strips 2 inches by ½ inch by ⅛ inch
2 tablespoons fish sauce *(nam pla)*
2 slices dried galingale, soaked
1 stalk lemon grass, or 2 tablespoons dried chopped lemon grass, soaked
5 green onions
1 large clove garlic, sliced
2 dried Asian chili peppers, split
About ½ teaspoon salt
2 tablespoons rice vinegar
1½ teaspoons sugar
12 ounces fresh uncut or cut rice noodle, or 6 ounces dried rice sheet flake or dried rice noodle
3 tablespoons chopped fresh coriander
3 tablespoons chopped celery leaves
1½ tablespoons vinegar-packed chili peppers

Condiments: sugar, vinegar, fish sauce, flaked dried Asian chili peppers (or thinly sliced fresh chili peppers, toasted), and unsalted peanuts, finely chopped

In a soup pot, combine the beef and chicken broths, water, pork, fish sauce, galingale, lemon grass, two of the green onions cut into 1-inch lengths, garlic, chili peppers, and salt; simmer until the meat is no longer pink, about 15 minutes. Remove the meat with a slotted spoon and continue to simmer the broth about 20 minutes more. Strain the broth. Return the broth to the pot and add the rice vinegar, sugar, and more salt if you like.

If the noodle is uncut, cut it into 2-inch squares. Immerse the noodles in boiling water a few seconds and drain them. Or soak dried noodles 20 minutes and cook them in boiling water 4 to 5 minutes (2 to 3 minutes if you are using rice vermicelli); drain the noodles well.* Divide the noodles among four soup bowls. Top each portion with pork, coriander, celery leaves, vinegared chili peppers, and thinly sliced green onion. Then ladle on the simmering broth. Each person may add additional condiments to his soup.

Makes 4 servings.

*Dried noodles may be cooked ahead, rinsed, and cooled, then reheated by dipping briefly in boiling water just before they are served in the soup.

# Stuffed Rice Sheet Noodles
## with Thai Basil Sauce

About 3 tablespoons tree ears
½ cup bean sprouts
4 ounces crab meat
8 ounces ground pork
2 teaspoons minced garlic
⅓ cup chopped domestic mushrooms
2 tablespoons minced white of green
   onion
2 teaspoons fish sauce *(nam pla)*
⅛ teaspoon freshly ground pepper
1/16 teaspoon cayenne pepper
¾ teaspoon salt
2 eggs, lightly beaten
1½ pounds uncut fresh rice noodle or egg
   roll skins*
Vegetable oil
5 teaspoons dried shrimp, pounded
   to a powder (optional)
Thai Basil Sauce (following)

Soak the tree ears in water to cover until they are soft, about 20 minutes. Blanch the bean sprouts in boiling water about 1½ minutes; drain, rinse with cold water, and chop them coarsely. Cut away and discard the tough stems from the tree ears and mince them.

Combine the tree ears, bean sprouts, crab meat, pork, garlic, mushrooms, onion, fish sauce, pepper, cayenne, salt, and ⅓ cup of the beaten egg. Cut the noodle sheet into 4½-by 4-inch rectangles. Place about 2 tablespoons of the filling on each and roll lengthwise. Seal the seam edges with some of the remaining beaten egg.

Place the rolls in a lightly oiled steamer basket. Sprinkle them with the dried shrimp and steam over low heat for 10 to 15 minutes, or until the filling feels firm to the touch. Place the rolls on a plate and cut each into three pieces. Serve with individual bowls of Thai Basil Dipping Sauce.

Makes about 24 pieces, or 6 to 8 appetizer servings.

*Use the heavier egg roll skins rather than the more delicate spring roll skins.

### Thai Basil Sauce

2 large cloves garlic
½ fresh Serrano chili pepper, cut up
2 teaspoons sugar
3½ tablespoons distilled white vinegar
3 tablespoons corn syrup
4 teaspoons fish sauce *(nam pla)*
⅓ cup lightly packed fresh Thai or purple
   or sweet basil leaves

In a mortar or processor, mash the garlic, chili pepper, and sugar to a paste. In a small pan, combine the vinegar, corn syrup, and fish sauce. Bring to a boil and stir to blend well. Cool the syrup to room temperature, then add the paste. Stir in the basil leaves and process until the leaves are well minced or mince the leaves and stir them in.

# My *Pad Thai*

*Pad Thai* is found on nearly every Thai restaurant menu, and prepared differently by each chef. This is my version, prepared, just for fun, with a deep-fried basil garnish.

3½ tablespoons distilled white vinegar
2 tablespoons water
2½ tablespoons fish sauce *(nam pla)*
3 tablespoons tomato paste
2½ tablespoons sugar
½ tablespoon dried shrimp, pounded to
  a powder (optional)
9 ounces flat rice sticks, ⅛-inch wide
  (*jantaboon* noodles*)*
Vegetable oil
⅓ cup fresh Thai or purple or sweet basil
  leaves
2 red Serrano chili peppers, seeded and
  very finely minced
4 cloves garlic, minced
1½ large, boned chicken breast halves,
  cut crosswise into ⅜-inch-thick strips
    or
1 pound lean pork, cut into thin slices ⅜
  inch by 2 inches
8 ounces small, cooked shelled shrimp
2 eggs, lightly beaten
2 cups fresh bean sprouts, beans removed
¼ cup roasted, unsalted peanuts, coarsely
  ground
Cherry tomatoes, halved
Lime wedges
Mint sprigs or sliced green onions

Combine the vinegar, water, fish sauce, tomato paste, sugar, and dried shrimp in a small bowl; mix until well blended and reserve. In a large pot, soak the noodles in enough water to cover. In a small skillet or pot, heat vegetable oil ¾ to 1 inch deep to 350°, or until a dried rice noodle puffs instantly when dropped into the oil. Deep-fry the basil leaves a few at a time, turning them once or twice until they are crisp, or 40 seconds to a minute; drain on paper toweling.

Bring the noodles to a boil and cook them 2 minutes, or until they are almost tender. Drain and rinse them well, then spread them on paper toweling to dry slightly. Heat a wok or large skillet and add about 2½ tablespoons vegetable oil. Fry the Serrano peppers about 30 seconds, then add the garlic and stir-fry until it is soft. Add the chicken or pork and stir-fry until the chicken is almost opaque throughout or the pork is browned. Stir in the shrimp and the sauce and mix completely. Make a well in the center of the mixture and pour in the eggs. When they are almost set, scramble them evenly. Add half the noodles, thoroughly incorporating them into the mixture; stir in the remaining noodles and half the bean sprouts. Cook just until the bean sprouts are nearly wilted.

Heap the meat and noodles onto a platter. Cover one half of them with ground peanuts and the other half with uncooked bean sprouts. Ring the noodles with lime wedges, cherry tomatoes, and mint sprigs and garnish the top with the fried basil.

Serves 6 as part of a meal or 4 as a main course.

# Warm Salad with Thai Crab Sausage

½ recipe Thai Sausage (following) or 4
   or 5 Chinese sausages (lop cheong)
Dressing (following)
4 ounces bean threads (wun sen)
4 leaves Romaine lettuce and 2 leaves
   Bibb lettuce
4 cups torn Romaine and Bibb lettuces
½ small red onion, cut into thin strips
1 cup jicama, cut into strips ⅛-inch wide
   and 2 inches long
1 medium cucumber, peeled and cut into
   thick slices
2 green onions, thinly sliced
1 tablespoon vegetable oil
1 tablespoon minced garlic
1½ tablespoons finely minced ginger
½ cup chicken broth
Garnishes: 3 tablespoons roasted unsalted
   peanuts, coarsely ground; lime wedges;
   tomato wedges; coriander sprigs
   (optional)

If using homemade sausage, broil and cool the sausage. Cut it on the diagonal into ⅜-inch slices; set aside. If using the Chinese sausage, cut it on the diagonal into ¼-inch slices; set aside. Prepare the dressing and have it ready. Soak the bean threads in warm water to cover until they are soft, about 7 minutes. On a large platter, arrange the Romaine lettuce leaves like the spokes of a wheel and top with the Bibb lettuce leaves, stem ends in. Top with the torn lettuce, red onion, jicama, cucumber, and green onions.

In a large skillet, heat the oil and saute the sausage until it is slightly browned. Add the garlic and ginger and saute just until the garlic is soft; reduce the heat. Drain the bean threads. Add the chicken broth and bean threads to the sausage mixture and cook, stirring, about 1½ minutes, until all the moisture is absorbed and the noodles are translucent. Stir in one-third of the dressing. Sprinkle the remaining dressing over the lettuce. Heap the sausage and noodle mixture in the center of the lettuce arrangement and distribute the garnishes over them.

Serves 6 as part of a meal.

**Dressing**
½ cup fresh lime juice
1 tablespoon distilled white vinegar
3 tablespoons fish sauce (nam pla)

2 tablespoons sugar
1 or 2 Serrano chili peppers, minced to
a fine pulp, or ½ teaspoon dried,
crushed Asian chili peppers

Combine all the ingredients in a small bowl and stir until the sugar is dissolved.

### Thai Crab Sausage

2 dried Asian chili peppers
1 stalk lemon grass, or ¼ cup sliced
lemon grass, or the zest of one lime
5 medium shallots or the white part of
5 green onions, chopped
5 cloves garlic
Three ¼-inch slices fresh galingale or
¾ teaspoon powdered galingale
12 peppercorns
2 stalks coriander, with leaves and roots
if possible
¾ teaspoon salt
3 tablespoons fresh or reconstituted thick
coconut milk
1 egg, lightly beaten
2 teaspoons minced ginger
2 teaspoons minced coriander leaves
3 teaspoons fish sauce *(nam pla)*
1 teaspoon sugar
12 ounces minced pork
6 tablespoons roasted, unsalted peanuts,
coarsely ground
6 ounces minced crabmeat
Sausage casings or caul fat (optional)

Soak the chilis in very little warm water until they are soft, about 30 minutes. Peel off the tough outer part of the lemon grass and mince the inner white part only. When the chilis are soft, drain them, and in a mortar or food processor combine them with the lemon grass, shallots, garlic, galingale, peppercorns, coriander stalks, and salt; grind to a paste. Stir in the coconut milk, blending it in well.

In a bowl, combine the egg, ginger, minced coriander leaves, fish sauce, sugar, pork, ground peanuts, crab, and paste mixture. Stir to combine well.

If you are using the sausage casings, rinse them under running water. Soak them in warm water for 30 minutes, then, holding them open with two fingers, rinse them inside and out with fresh water. With a funnel (or stuffing nozzle for electric mixers or food processors), pack the sausage into the casing being careful not to make air bubbles. Twist or tie the sausage as you stuff it at 6- to 7-inch intervals. Tie off the sausage end with thread or light string. Or form the sausages by hand into ¾-inch-diameter sausages. Wrap the hand-formed sausage in caul fat if you like.

Curl the formed sausages into flat coils on a broiling rack. Broil the sausages about 6 inches from a medium flame and cook, turning once, until they are firm. Cool completely before slicing the sausages for the salad.

# Seafood Hot Pot

The authentic way to serve this Thai-style *cioppino* is in a "Mongolian hot pot"— the kind with a chimney and heat source in the center. If you don't have one, a tureen, or simply individual soup plates, will serve this hot-tart soup nicely.

8 cups chicken broth
2 cups water
1 slice peeled ginger, bruised
1 stalk fresh lemon grass, or ¼ cup sliced
    dried lemon grass, or the zest of one
    lime
4 dried *makrut* leaves, or 3 fresh citrus
    leaves
6 to 7 dried red Asian chili peppers, split
3 ounces rice vermicelli *(sen mee)*
6 fresh, unshelled mussels, well scrubbed
10 to 12 small live clams, scrubbed
4 to 6 crab claws, or 8 ounces firm white
    fish, cut into 1-inch cubes
1 pound large shrimp, shelled and de-
    veined, with tails on
4 medium cleaned squid, cut into rings
½ cup fresh lime juice
1 tablespoon distilled white vinegar
2 tablespoons fish sauce *(nam pla)*
3 green onions, cut into 1-inch lengths
⅓ bunch fresh coriander sprigs
Lime wedges
Two seeded Serrano chili peppers, slivered

In a large soup pot, combine the broth and water. In a moistened square of cheese-cloth, loosely tie the ginger, lemon grass, *makrut,* and chili peppers. Add the *"bouquet garni"* to the soup pot. Simmer the soup for 45 minutes, then discard the seasonings, squeezing the bag into the soup to release all the flavor. While the soup is simmering, soak the rice vermicelli in water 15 minutes, then drain.

When the broth is cooked, add the mussels and clams. Cover the pot and simmer a few minutes until they open. Add the crab claws or fish, shrimp, and squid, and simmer until the shrimp turn pink, about 3 minutes. Lift out the seafood with a slotted spoon or Chinese wire mesh spoon. Add the lime juice, vinegar, fish sauce, green onions, and ver-micelli, and cook about 1½ minutes, until the noodles are *al dente*. Return the seafood to the pot. Put the soup in the serving vessel or bowls and garnish it with the coriander sprigs. Serve with lime wedges and slivered peppers.

Serves 4 to 6 as a main course.

# Thai Sticks

This appetizer is a favorite at the Royal Cliff Restaurant in Santa Monica, near Los Angeles. A noodle and chicken forcemeat surrounding a large half-shrimp is dipped in a coconut milk batter and deep-fried. Though this sounds elaborate, it is quite easy to make. The appetizers can be assembled ahead of time and cooked or reheated just before serving.

2 ounces bean threads *(wun sen)*
6 large raw shrimp in the shell
Bamboo skewers, soaked in water 20
    minutes
8 ounces ground chicken
6 ounces ground pork
¼ teaspoon salt
¼ teaspoon Asian chili pepper flakes,
    or ⅛ teaspoon freshly ground black
    pepper
1 egg, lightly beaten
4 teaspoons fish sauce *(nam pla)*
3 water chestnuts, minced
3 cloves garlic, minced
1 tablespoon minced fresh coriander
    (optional)
2 green onions, minced
Coconut batter or simple coating

*For the coconut batter*
   ½ cup all-purpose flour
   ⅔ cup cornstarch
   ½ teaspoon salt

1½ cups medium coconut milk
4 teaspoons white vinegar
½ teaspoon baking soda
Water

*For simple coating*
   1 egg white
   Flour for coating

Vegetable oil for frying
Thai Basil Sauce (page 98), Plain
    Dipping Sauce, or Cucumber Sauce
    (page 104)

Soak the bean threads in warm water to cover only until they are soft, about 7 minutes; drain, cut into 2-inch lengths, and pat dry. Shell the shrimp leaving the tails intact. Cut the shrimp in half lengthwise leaving a segment of the tail attached to each half. Put a

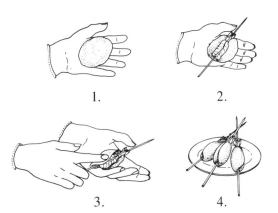

1.          2.

3.          4.

skewer lengthwise through the center of each shrimp half. Fill a saucepan with water to a depth of 6 inches. Bring the water to a boil, and poach the shrimp by holding them in the boiling water by the skewers until they are pink, about 1 minute. Cool the shrimp.

In a bowl, combine the chicken, pork, salt, chili pepper flakes, egg, fish sauce, water chestnuts, garlic, coriander, onions, and bean threads. Mix together well. Place about 3 tablespoons of the mixture on the palm of your hand, form it into a 2½-inch round, and top it with a shrimp half. With dampened hands, roll the "filling" to enclose the shrimp. When all the shrimp are covered, distribute any remaining forcemeat among the shrimp rolls by pressing bits of it onto the rolls. Chill the rolls until they become slightly firmer, about 20 to 30 minutes.

Make the coconut batter or use a simple coating. For the batter, blend the flour, cornstarch, and salt in a bowl. Mix in the coconut milk and vinegar a little at a time until the mixture is smooth. Sprinkle the soda over the batter and blend it in. If needed, thin the batter with a little water. It should coat the shrimp rolls thinly. For the simple coating, beat the egg white until foamy. Roll the shrimp rolls in it and dust with a little flour.

Fill a large deep kettle with oil to a depth just exceeding the length of the shrimp rolls.

Heat the oil to 365°. With the skewers, dip each stick in the batter or simple coating to lightly coat it and deep fry until golden and firm, about 6 to 8 minutes. Drain well on paper toweling and keep warm in a 200° oven. Serve on the skewers with Thai Basil Sauce, Plain Dipping Sauce, or Cucumber Sauce.

Makes 12 rolls—6 servings.

### Plain Dipping Sauce

1 cup distilled white vinegar
1 cup water
1 cup sugar
2 to 3 teaspoons *sambal oeleck*
1 tablespoon pressed garlic
1 teaspoon salt

Combine all the ingredients in a heavy saucepan. Bring to a boil and boil until the mixture becomes a light syrup, about 15 minutes. Cool before serving.

### Cucumber Sauce

Prepare the Plain Dipping Sauce. Peel and seed a medium-sized cucumber. Cut in half lengthwise, then slice it into thick slices. Mix the cucumber into the Plain Dipping Sauce and allow it to stand at least an hour before serving.

# Burmese Fish Soup and Noodles
## *Mohinga*

Often called "the national dish of Burma," this fish-noodle curry soup is eaten everywhere, from roadside stands to huge family gatherings and birthday celebrations. Usually the dish is made with freshwater fish, catfish in particular. But it is just as delicious made with a mild sea fish.

2 tablespoons garbanzo or yellow pea flour,\* or 4 tablespoons yellow split peas
About 2 pounds whole dressed fish with the head on, such as catfish, carp, or whiting; or 1½ pounds fish steaks with skin and bones
2½ cups water, or 2 cups water mixed with ½ cup bottled clam juice\*\*
3 stalks fresh lemon grass, or 6 tablespoons dried lemon grass, soaked
4 large yellow onions
2 small dried Asian chili peppers, split
2½ tablespoons fish sauce (use *nam pla, nuoc mam,* or *patis*)
4 cloves garlic, chopped
7 slices ginger, ¼-inch thick
½ teaspoon dried shrimp paste (use *terasi* or *blachan,* or substitute anchovy paste)
1 teaspoon ground turmeric
3 fresh Serrano or dried Asian chili peppers
¼ cup vegetable oil
2¼ cups medium coconut milk
¼ medium Nappa cabbage, cut crosswise into thin strips
2 hard-cooked eggs, sliced
12 ounces rice vermicelli *(hsan kyasan),* cooked (page 16)
Lime or lemon wedges
Salt
As many of the following garnishes as you like: chopped green onions, chopped fresh coriander, fried garlic (page 107), fried dried crushed chili peppers (page 107)

---

If you are using the split peas, grind them to a flour in a blender. Roast the flour in a dry heated skillet until it is lightly toasted; transfer it to a bowl and reserve.

Place the fish in a large pot with the water or clam-juice mixture. Split the lemon grass stalks lengthwise; mince half of one lemon grass stalk and reserve. To the fish, add the split lemon grass or 4 tablespoons of the soaked lemon grass, 2 of the onions, finely chopped, the split chili peppers, and the fish sauce. Cover the pot and simmer until the fish flakes easily with a fork. Carefully remove the fish from the broth at once. Place it on a plate and set aside. Reserve the broth with the seasonings in it.

In a food processor or mortar, combine the garlic, ginger, dried shrimp paste, tur-

# Burmese Chicken Curry and Noodle Feast

meric, the remaining minced lemon grass, and fresh or dried chili peppers and process or pound them to a paste. Slice the two remaining onions lengthwise into slivers. In a large skillet, heat the oil and add the onions. Saute them until they are soft and golden. Add the paste and saute over medium heat until there is a "cooked" aroma, about 1 minute. Remove the meat from the fish, flake it with a fork, and add it to the sauteed mixture. Discard the fish head, skin, and bones.

Strain the fish broth into a large saucepan. Mix in 2 tablespoons garbanzo or pea flour a little at a time. Bring the broth to a boil, stirring slowly. Stir in the coconut milk and simmer the mixture 5 minutes. Add the cabbage and simmer until it is tender. Pour the coconut sauce into the fish mixture, mixing them together. Squeeze in 1½ tablespoons lime or lemon juice and season to taste with a little salt. Stir in the eggs.

To serve the dish, divide the rice noodles among the serving bowls and ladle fish sauce over the noodles. Each diner may season his dish with additional lemon or lime juice and garnish his dish as he likes.

Serves 6 as a main course.

*You may substitute 1½ tablespoons cornstarch.
**Use the water mixed with clam juice if you are using the fish steaks.

The best part of serving this feast is watching guests enthusiastically garnish their noodle- and curry-laden plates with crisp fried garlic, fried chili, and the other condiments to make a festive plate.

½ cup vegetable oil
½ teaspoon ground turmeric
3 large onions, chopped
4 cloves garlic, minced
2 tablespoons ginger, finely minced or pressed (through a garlic press)
1 teaspoon cayenne pepper
2 teaspoons ground cumin
1 teaspoon ground coriander
4 teaspoons curry powder
4 whole chicken breasts and 3 whole chicken legs
1 cinnamon stick
1 bay leaf
8 cups chicken broth
½ cup yellow pea flour or dried yellow split peas*
⅓ cup lentil flour or lentils*
2½ cups thick coconut milk
About 1 tablespoon fish sauce (use *nam pla, nuoc mam,* or *patis*)
Salt to taste
2 pounds fresh Chinese egg noodles (page 14), or fresh or dried spaghettini, cooked
Condiments (following)

Heat the oil in an 8- to 12-quart pan or Dutch oven. Stir in the turmeric and cook it for 1 minute. Add the onions and cook, stirring occasionally, until the onions are limp but not browned, 20 to 30 minutes. Add the garlic, ginger, cayenne pepper, cumin, coriander, and curry powder. Cook and stir the mixture about 1 minute. Add the chicken pieces and stir to coat them with the onions and spices. Add the cinnamon, bay leaf, and chicken broth, cover, and simmer 25 minutes.

Mix the flours with 1⅓ cups water, or grind the peas and lentils to a flour in a blender or mortar and mix ¾ cup of the resulting flour with 1⅓ cups water. Stir the mixture into the soup. Add the coconut milk, cover, and simmer an additional 30 minutes. Remove the pan from the heat and carefully lift out the chicken pieces. Remove the meat from the bones and return it to the sauce. Add fish sauce and salt to taste.

Serve the noodles on a platter and the curry and condiments separately. Diners serve themselves first to noodles, then the curry, then to whichever condiments they like. They should season their food to taste with squeezes of fresh lime or lemon juice.

Serves 8 to 10 as a main course.

*½ cup cornstarch may be substituted for the pea and lentil flour.

**Condiments**

• Peel and slice 12 garlic cloves crosswise. Fry them in about 4 tablespoons vegetable oil until they are golden and will stay crisp when cooled.
• 3 hard-cooked eggs, quartered.
• 2 red onions, slivered lengthwise.
• 6 green onions, thinly sliced.
• 2 limes or lemons, cut into wedges.
• 1 bunch fresh coriander sprigs, trimmed.
• 2 tablespoons crushed, dried Asian chili peppers sauteed in 1 tablespoon vegetable oil.

Serve each condiment in a separate dish.

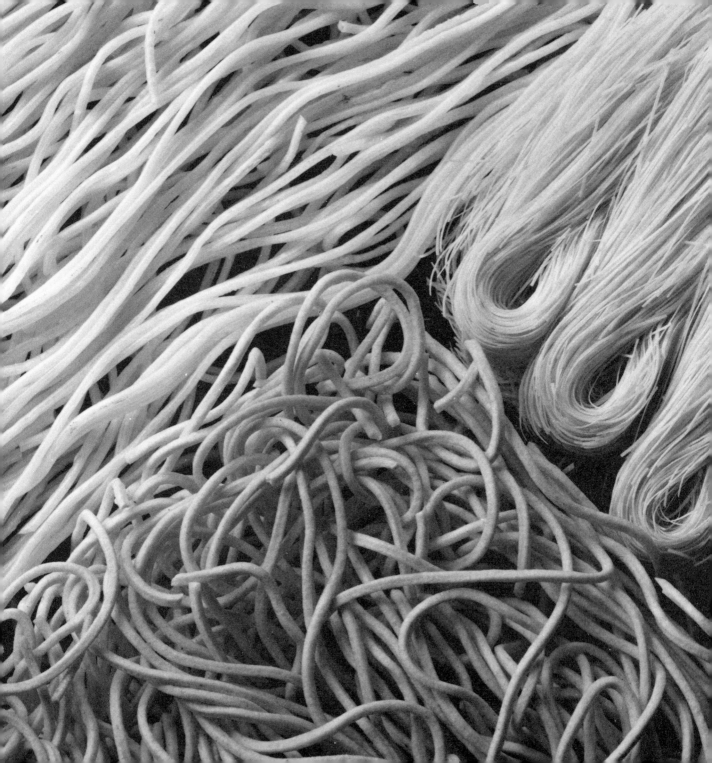

# THE PASTAS OF THE PHILIPPINES

In the bustling Chinatowns of Filipino cities, and even in provincial areas, chatting customers pass the time on lazy, heat-filled afternoons in *panciterias*—noodle shops. At these economical and quick shops, a few pesos will bring a choice of a plate heaped with fried noodles, shrimp, and chicken, or steamed *siomai* (meat-filled Chinese-style dumplings), or a bowl of *pancit molo,* a kind of Filipino wonton soup.

The word *panciteria* itself suggests the merging of two cultures. *Pancit,* Filipino for noodle, evolved from the Chinese term *fenxi,* meaning bean thread; *eria* is, of course, the Spanish suffix for *store*. Home cooks have adapted the *pancits* of the islands' Chinatowns to local ingredients and tastes, giving the noodle a uniquely Filipino character.

Although the Chinese were in contact with the Philippine Islands centuries before the Spanish ever reached their shores, cultural interchange remained minimal. According to the chronicles of Arab traders, the Chinese had been trading briskly at least as early as the Tang Dynasty (618 to 906 A.D.). But trading was all that took place. The Chinese preferred not to mingle with the islanders, and, in the 10th century, Philippine chieftains restricted the traders to living on their junks.

In the 13th century, Chinese trade superintendent for the Philippines, Ju Kua, documented the arrival of Chinese cookware. But such things as woks, cleavers, and cooking shovels were not widespread throughout the islands until the 16th century. Even today they are often used for *guisado* (sauteeing) and not for stir-fry. The culinary history of the Philippines differs from that of most of Southeast Asia and Indonesia because of its strong Hispanic influence, and the early restriction of Chinese influences.

By the time the Spanish established Manila as the colonial capital in 1571, the harbor was already a bustling port for Indian, Chinese, and Malay traders. *Parians* (Chinese sections) were thriving, and, while they are not documented, it is quite likely that convenient and economical eateries, such as noodle shops, had begun to spring up. The Spanish initiated cultural exchange between the Chinese and Filipinos and encouraged Chinese immigration.

With acculturation under way, intermarriage among Chinese, Spanish, and Filipinos fostered the evolution of a monied mestizo middle class, and an even freer flow of cultural influences was a natural by-product. Thus Chinese imports such as tofu, soy sauce, eggplant, bitter melon, and soy and mung beans were added to the Filipino diet, even though indigenous regional food customs still dominated. Noodles had no precedent in the native cooking traditon, and their Chinese preparation soon changed to accommodate native ingredients and Spanish cooking methods. As Nick Joaquin, Filipino national artist, explains, "In the Philippines, pancit is Spanish, Christian and creole, although Chinese in origin." In practice, the *guisado* method transformed the Chinese *pancit* into *pancit luglug, pancit Malabon, pancit palabok,* and so on.

As a result of such diverse origins, today's *pancit* cookery is delightfully unpredictable. A *pancit miki,* for example, will be an entirely different dish in the hands of different cooks. Even the same restaurant may vary it significantly, depending on what is available at the local *sari-sari* (general store). Some *pancits* are loaded with meats and seafoods, while others may be garnished with only a bit of bacon and a few peas.

My local newspaper carried a recipe for "Elsa's *Sotanghon Manok"* (bean threads and chicken). It calls for a chicken, beef bones, *chorizo de Bilbao* (Spanish sausage), tree ears, peas, fish sauce, 10 cloves of garlic, and green onions. Other renditions of the same dish, however, might call for Chinese sausage, Filipino sausage, ham, or bacon; I suggest the use of pepperoni if you cannot find *chorizo*. The chicken could be replaced by pork, and cooks might throw in a few shrimp if handy. Most Filipino cooks would stick with the 10 cloves of garlic, the onion, fish sauce, and of course the bean threads, but might substitute fresh or Chinese mushrooms for the tree ears and zucchini for the peas.

The names of noodle dishes usually include the name of the noodle. For example, you know you will get rice vermicelli in a dish with the word *bihon*. Beyond that, what comprises the dish is up to the chef. This *laissez faire* attitude toward recipes makes assembling ingredients mostly a matter of practicality and creativity.

Like the Chinese, Filipinos regard noodles as a symbol of longevity and prosperity. Because of this association, pastas are welcome at weddings, birthdays, and baptisms, besides being a popular choice for a light meal.□

# THE VARIETIES OF FILIPINO PASTA

## LUMPIA WRAPPERS

Thin crêpe-like pasta wrappers, sold frozen in Filipino and Chinese grocery stores. Their texture is very different from eggroll wrappers. Spring roll wrappers or *mu shu* pork wrappers may be substituted. If you can't get them, homemade wrappers are as easy to make as French crêpes; a recipe is included on page 208.

## 1. MISWA

Wheat noodles, possibly the thinnest noodles on earth and finer than hair. They need almost no cooking. Just sprinkle them into a boiling soup and wait a few seconds, then test for doneness. Simmer a few more seconds if the noodle is not done. Sometimes spelled *misua*.

## PANCIT BIHON

Usually thin rice vermicelli, although thick rice vermicelli, *pancit luglug*, is a type of *bihon* too. *Bihon* is usually sauteed with meats and vegetables or used in soups. Refer to cooking instructions for rice vermicelli in the General Cooking Instructions section.

## 2. PANCIT CANTON

Chinese-style wheat noodles, partially pre-cooked and dried in large disks. Much like the Japanese *chuka soba,* which may be substituted, only round. Used in soups and stir-fries or with a sauce. Cook in a large amount of boiling water about 4 minutes.

## 3. PANCIT LUGLUG

In Tagalog (a Filipino dialect) *luglug* is the sound of a long-handled bamboo basket containing noodles being dipped in and out of boiling water. Most Filipino cooks here rely on dried noodles and simply boil them, though they may reheat them using the dipping method. This thick, spaghetti-size rice vermicelli is also used as *laksa* in Malaysian recipes. *Lai fun,* a shorter Chinese rice noodle, may be substituted.

## PANCIT MAMI

Chinese egg noodle, usually ⅛-inch wide and flat. Served as Chinese soup noodles with various toppings. Their preparation diverges from the Chinese by the addition of garlic and *patis* (fish sauce) in the broth. See General Instructions for Wheat Noodles for cooking information.

## PANCIT MIKI

Chinese-style wheat noodles that resemble cooked spaghetti. They contain less egg than *mami* and are much coarser than Chinese wheat noodles from Chinese groceries. Spaghetti may be substituted. *Miki* are usually sold fresh in the produce or refrigerator section of Filipino markets. Cook as you would fresh Chinese wheat noodles described in the General Instructions section.

## PANCIT SOTANGHON

Bean threads. They are usually sauteed, then simmered—a treatment referred to as *guisado* in Filipino cooking terms. Complete instructions for cooking are in the General Cooking Instructions section.

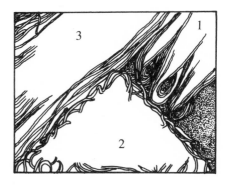

# Shrimp and Cellophane
# Noodle-Stuffed Oriental Eggplant
### *Rellenong Talong*

Shrimp, pork, fresh tomato, and bean-thread noodles, cooked Filipino-style, fill tender 6- to 8-inch-long Oriental eggplant halves in this dish.

2 ounces bean threads (*sotanghon*)
6 large or 7 medium Oriental eggplants
6 ounces raw, shelled shrimp
1 tablespoon vegetable oil
1 large or 2 small cloves garlic, minced
1 cup chopped yellow onion
6 ounces ground pork
4 teaspoons fish sauce (*patis*)
2 eggs, lightly beaten
⅛ teaspoon sugar
⅛ teaspoon freshly ground pepper
¼ teaspoon salt
1 medium tomato, peeled, seeded, and diced
Oriental sesame oil

Soak the bean threads in warm water about 10 minutes until they are soft. Cut the eggplants in half lengthwise. Line the broiler pan with foil, place the eggplants cut-side down on the foil, and broil them 6 to 8 minutes, or until the inside is just soft enough to remove and the shell will still hold its shape. Remove the eggplants from the broiler and scoop out the meat, leaving a ⅜-inch-thick shell. Chop the eggplant meat and reserve it.

Grind the shrimp in a food processor or mince them very fine, almost to a paste. Heat the oven to 400°. Heat the oil in a medium-sized skillet and saute the garlic and onion until they are soft but not browned. In a large bowl, combine the onion mixture, the shrimp, pork, fish sauce, eggs, sugar, pepper, and salt. Drain the bean threads and cut them into 1½-inch lengths with scissors; add them to the filling ingredients in the bowl and mix together thoroughly. Fold in the diced tomato and eggplant meat until well combined.

Distribute the filling among the eggplant halves, smoothing the mounds. Arrange the stuffed eggplants in a large baking dish and brush the filling lightly with sesame oil. Bake at 400° for 25 to 30 minutes until the filling is firm and the pork is no longer pink.

Makes 12 or 14 pieces, or enough for 4 main-dish servings or 6 to 12 or 14 servings as part of a meal.

# Fine Vermicelli and Fish Balls in Soup

## Bola Bolang Misua

Filipino *misua* resembles the finest angel's hair. The thinnest pasta I have ever seen, it needs only a few seconds to cook. Here, *misua,* fresh spinach, and little fish dumpling-like balls combine perfectly in a garlicky broth.

*Ingredients for the fish balls*

> 1 small clove garlic
> 2 green onions, white part only
> ½ small yellow onion
> 1 pound lean fish fillets such as seabass, perch, rock cod, or red snapper, cut into 1-inch-square chunks
> 2 egg yolks
> 2 tablespoons all-purpose flour
> 2 teaspoons fish sauce *(patis)*
> ½ teaspoon salt
> ⅛ teaspoon freshly ground pepper

*Ingredients for the soup*

> 2 teaspoons vegetable oil
> 1 tablespoon minced garlic
> ¼ cup minced yellow onion
> 5 cups water
> 3 cups chicken broth
> About 20 large spinach leaves, washed and stemmed
> About 15 turns of the pepper mill
> 4½ teaspoons fish sauce *(patis)*
> ¼ teaspoon salt or more
> 2 ounces Filipino fine wheat vermicelli *(misua)**

For the fish balls, mince the garlic in a food processor. Add the green onions and mince, then add the onion using the pulser button. Do not puree the ingredients. Transfer the onion mixture to a holding bowl and add the fish to the work bowl of the processor; process it to mince very fine. Add the onion mixture, egg yolks, flour, fish sauce, salt, and pepper and process just until well mixed but not a fine paste. Chill well. Alternatively, mince the appropriate ingredients by hand and mix together well; chill the mixture.

For the soup, coat the bottom of a large soup pot with vegetable oil and heat it. Saute the garlic and onion until they are soft. Add the water and chicken broth and simmer together while you are forming the fish mixture into ¾-inch balls. Bring the soup to a boil and drop in the fish balls a few at a time; simmer 10 minutes or until the fish balls are firm. Remove the balls with a slotted spoon or Chinese mesh spoon. Cover the soup pot and turn off the heat.

Stack the spinach leaves into two or three even stacks and roll the stacks like cigars. Slice the rolls crosswise making ¼-inch ribbons. Add the pepper, fish sauce, and salt to the pot and bring the soup to simmering. Drop in the spinach leaves and cook them just until they wilt, about 2 minutes. Add the fish balls and sprinkle the *misua* over the

# A Variety of *Lumpia*

surface of the soup. Adjust the salt. Remove the pot from the heat, cover, and let stand 1 minute before serving. Test the *misua* to be sure it is tender. If it is not, allow the soup to sit, covered, a little while longer. Serve immediately.

If you wish to prepare the soup in advance, do everything except cooking the spinach and *misua*. The broth and fish balls can be reheated and the soup finished just before serving.

Serves 4 as a main course or 8 as a first course.

*You may substitute any very fine wheat pasta, such as angel hair or *fideo*.

*L*umpia, a light crêpe-like wrapper enclosing a sweet or savory filling, is the Filipino version of egg roll. It is eaten any time of day, but is especially popular at *merienda,* the late afternoon custom of snacking and visiting adopted from the Filipinos' Spanish heritage. The wrappers are delicate and slightly eggy, and the fillings decidedly Southeast Asian. *Lumpia* are served either "fresh" (with the filling wrapped first in a lettuce leaf and then in the *lumpia* wrapper and eaten without further cooking) or deep-fried. The variety of *lumpia* fillings has no end; Filipino cooks might combine whatever they have available. Seafood and pork mixtures, vegetables such as sweet potato, garbanzo beans, and hearts of palm, and even sweet fruits such as small, fat cooking bananas *(sabas)* and jackfruit—all turn up in these pasta wrappers.

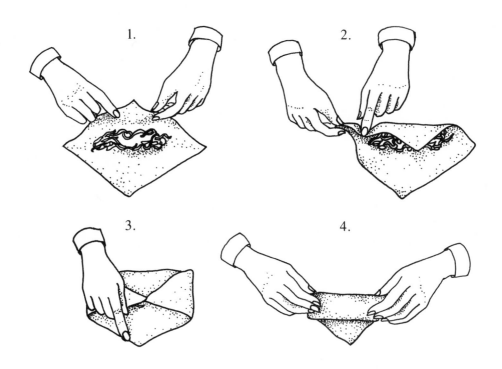

1.

2.

3.

4.

# Crab and Bean Thread
# *Lumpia* with Two Sauces

2 ounces bean threads *(sotanghon)*
5 medium dried Chinese mushrooms
6 ounces crabmeat
¼ pound ground pork
1 medium clove garlic, minced
½ cup finely chopped green onions,
　 white part only
1 teaspoon fish sauce *(patis)*
¼ teaspoon salt
10 grinds of the pepper mill
12 to 14 *lumpia* wrappers
12 to 14 Chinese chives (optional)
Vegetable oil for frying
Peanut Sauce (page 120) and Pineapple
　 Sauce (page 120)

----

Soak the bean threads and mushrooms in separate bowls of warm water until softened, about 15 minutes. In a large bowl, combine the crabmeat, pork, garlic, green onions, fish sauce, salt, and pepper.

Drain the mushrooms, squeeze them dry, remove the tough stems, and cut the caps into very thin strips. (You should have about ⅓ cup mushroom strips.) Drain the bean threads well and cut them into 2-inch lengths with scissors. Add the mushrooms and bean threads to the mixture in the bowl and stir to blend thoroughly.

Place about ¹/₁₂ of the filling on the *lumpia* wrapper as shown in the diagram. Before enclosing the filling, place a single Chinese chive along the length of the filling, trimming it to fit the finished *lumpia*. Finish wrapping the *lumpia*. In a large deep skillet, pour oil to a depth of ¾ inch. Heat the oil to 375°, or until a dry bean thread puffs instantly when dropped into the oil. Fry four or five *lumpia* at a time without crowding—crowding encourages sogginess. Turn the *lumpia* occasionally as they fry, regulating the heat to avoid overbrowning; fry about 7 minutes or until golden on all sides.

Lift the *lumpia* from the oil with tongs, a slotted spoon, or Chinese mesh spoon, and drain them on paper toweling. Place in a barely warm oven until all the *lumpia* are fried. Serve with Peanut Sauce (page 120) and Pineapple Sauce (page 120) for dipping.

Makes 12 to 14 *lumpia*.

# Banana or Jackfruit *Lumpia*

In the Philippines, small cooking bananas called *sabas* are used to stuff these crunchy sweets. The golden *lumpia* are lifted from the hot oil and sprinkled with a snowy drift of powdered sugar, creating a sort of tropical strudel. Sometimes the filling is a combination of banana and jackfruit, sometimes banana with a little freshly grated coconut, and sometimes only banana. With the following recipe you can create any of them.

> Six regular bananas or *saba* bananas
> and
> One 12-ounce jar preserved jackfruit,
>    well drained
> About ⅔ cup granulated sugar
> Vegetable oil for frying
> Powdered sugar
> 12 *lumpia* wrappers

Cut each banana into thirds lengthwise and, if you are using regular bananas, trim them to a length of 4½ inches if necessary. Sprinkle each strip with a little sugar (about ¼ teaspoon per strip). Put a strip of banana and two slices of jackfruit on the *lumpia* wrapper and roll as directed on page 117. Fry the *lumpia* following the instructions for Crab and Bean Thread *Lumpia* (page 117). The cooking time will probably be reduced to 4 minutes.

Drain the *lumpia* on paper toweling and let them cool about 5 minutes before sprinkling with powdered sugar (using a strainer or sifter). If you are going to hold the *lumpia* in the oven, sprinkle with sugar just before serving.

Makes 10 to 12 *lumpia*.

*Variations*

For plain banana *lumpia,* use two strips of banana and omit the jackfruit.

For banana-coconut *lumpia,* use two strips of banana sprinkled with 1½ tablespoons grated fresh or frozen coconut.

# Sweet Potato *Lumpia*

For Westerners, this might seem quite an unusual way to use sweet potato, but it always gets raves when I serve it.

> 2 tablespoons vegetable oil
> 2 medium cloves garlic, minced
> 1 medium yellow onion, finely chopped
> ¼ cup minced smoky ham
> 8 ounces cooked pork, either roasted
>    or boiled, cut into ¼-inch cubes
> 1 cup cut green beans sliced diagonally
>    into 1-inch lengths

6 ounces raw shelled shrimp, cut into
   thirds
2⅔ cups shredded cabbage
½ cup cooked garbanzo beans, split
3 cups peeled, cubed yam or sweet potato,
   steamed until barely tender
1 stalk celery, minced
Salt
12 to 14 bronze leaf or salad bowl lettuce
   leaves, washed
14 to 16 *lumpia* wrappers
Plain *Lumpia* Sauce (page 120) or Pine-
   apple-*Lumpia* Sauce (page 120)

---

Heat the oil in a large skillet and saute the garlic and onion until soft and translucent. Add the ham, pork, and green beans, and stir-fry until the beans soften. Add the shrimp and stir-fry until the shrimp begin to turn pink. Add the cabbage and stir it in well. Add the garbanzo beans and sweet potatoes, cover the pan, and cook the mixture about 2 minutes, until the cabbage softens. Remove the pan from the heat, remove the cover, and let the mixture stand about 10 minutes. Pour off any pan juices, pressing down to extract them, and reserve them for the dipping sauce. Make the dipping sauce and stir ⅓ cup of it into the filling. Add salt to taste.

To assemble the *lumpia,* spread a wrapper, leaving the edges clean, with about 2 teaspoons

dipping sauce. Set a lettuce leaf on the wrapper to extend from the center over the top edge. Spoon about 2 tablespoons of filling onto the lettuce. Fold the lower half of the wrapper over the filling, then fold over the sides to enclose. Serve with the sauce. Eat out of hand, or with a knife and fork with the sauce poured over the *lumpia.*

Makes 12 to 14 *lumpia.*

# Hearts of Palm *Lumpia*
### *Lumpia Ubod*

F ollow the recipe for Sweet Potato *Lumpia* (page 118), substituting 1 cup carrot cut into ⅛-inch-wide by 2-inch-long strips for the green beans. Decrease the cabbage to 2½ cups, and omit the celery. Use one 16-ounce can hearts of palm cut into matchsticks in place of the sweet potato. Do not cook the hearts of palm; just stir them into the meat and vegetable mixture at the end of the cooking time. Proceed with the rest of the recipe.

Makes 14 to 16 *lumpia.*

*Variations*

Here are some suggestions for vegetables to replace sweet potatoes or hearts of palm: bean sprouts, snow peas, lima beans, bamboo shoots, or thin strips of jicama.

# Sauces for *Lumpia*

**Pineapple *Lumpia* Sauce**

    3 tablespoons cornstarch
    6 tablespoons firmly packed brown sugar
    1 cup water
    ¾ cup pineapple juice
    3 tablespoons cider vinegar
    6 tablespoons soy sauce
    2 cloves garlic, finely minced or pressed
    Drippings from filling if available

In a medium saucepan, combine the cornstarch and sugar and mix well. Add the water, pineapple juice, vinegar, and soy sauce and stir to blend. Stir in the garlic. Bring the mixture to a boil, stirring continuously until the sauce thickens and becomes translucent. Stir in any juices from the filling.

**Plain *Lumpia* Sauce**

    3 tablespoons cornstarch
    6 tablespoons firmly packed brown sugar
    2 cups chicken broth
    6 tablespoons soy sauce
    2 cloves garlic, crushed
    Drippings from filling if available

In a medium saucepan, combine the cornstarch and sugar and mix well. Add the chicken broth and soy sauce and stir to blend. Stir in the garlic. Bring the mixture to a boil, stirring continuously until the sauce thickens and becomes translucent. Stir in any juices from the filling.

**Peanut *Lumpia* Sauce**

    ¼ cup finely ground peanuts, or peanut butter
    3 tablespoons fish sauce *(patis)*
    4½ tablespoons sugar
    ¼ teaspoon dried red pepper flakes
    1 clove garlic, pressed
    5 to 6 teaspoons fresh lime juice

Combine the peanuts, fish sauce, sugar, pepper, and garlic in a saucepan and simmer 2 minutes. Stir in the lime juice; add a tablespoon or more of water to thin if needed.

# Chicken in Tamarind Broth
*Sinigang Na Manok*

Every country seems to have its own chicken soup—one that everyone knows. This flavorful dish is the chicken soup of the Philippines. Its tangy broth is flavored with the fruity sourness of tamarind. If tamarind is unavailable, substitute a tablespoon each of fresh lemon and lime juice.

⅓ cup white rice, preferably short grained
10 cups water
2 tablespoons vegetable oil
1 medium yellow onion, chopped
2 medium cloves garlic, minced
One 2½- to 3-pound chicken, or four
   chicken thighs, 1 breast, and 1 back
2 tablespoons fish sauce *(patis)*
⅛ teaspoon freshly ground pepper
Salt
8 pieces tamarind,* outer peeling removed, or a large walnut-sized piece
   tamarind pulp
3 ounces thick rice vermicelli *(pancit
   luglug)* or thin rice vermicelli *(bihon)*
1 cup icicle radish or daikon radish,
   cut into strips ⅛-inch wide by 2
   inches long
2 medium tomatoes, cut into wedges
1 bunch (8 to 10 ounces) mustard greens,
   washed and stems removed
5 green onions, thinly sliced
6 ounces cooked small shrimp (optional)

Rinse the rice in a strainer under running water for 30 seconds. Let the rice stand in 10 cups water at least 1 hour or overnight.

In a large soup pot, heat the oil and saute the onion and garlic until the onion is translucent and soft. Leaving the skin intact, remove as much fat as possible from the chicken and cut into 2-inch pieces. Add the chicken to the onions and cook, turning once until lightly browned. Strain the 10 cups of rice water into the chicken pot; discard the rice. Add the fish sauce, pepper, a little salt, and the tamarind.* Simmer the soup for about 45 minutes or until the chicken is very tender.

Remove the tamarind pieces and any seeds and a little broth. Mash them together well to extract the juice; strain the liquid back into the broth. Remove the chicken from the broth and remove the meat from the bones; discard the bones. Degrease the broth, bring it to a boil, and add the vermicelli, stirring to be sure the noodles separate while cooking; simmer 6 minutes for thick vermicelli and 1 minute for thin. Add the radish and tomatoes and simmer 1 minute. Stir in the chicken meat. Cut the mustard greens into ribbons and add to the pot; simmer 1 minute more. Add salt to taste.

If you are using the shrimp, remove a little broth from the pot and stir with the shrimp to warm them. Ladle the soup into bowls and sprinkle with sliced green onion and a few shrimp.

Serves 5 or 6 as a main dish.

*If substituting lemon and lime juice, add it to the finished soup rather than at the beginning of the cooking time.

# Bean Threads Sauteed with Shrimp, Chicken, and Chinese Sausage

*Pancit Sotanghon Guisado*

Taste this and you'll see why Filipinos love *pancit*. Bean threads are braised along with the chicken, soaking up flavorful pan juices, then topped with crisp stir-fried garnishes. The combination of these cooking techniques results in a voluptuous mixture of flavors and textures. The same treatment is often given to rice vermicelli, in which case the dish is called *pancit bijon guisado*. Annatto seeds or bottled annatto *(achuete)* water impart a traditional orange color to the noodles, but can be omitted without affecting flavor.

2 tablespoons annatto seeds, or 1 tablespoon bottled annatto *(achuete)* water
(optional)
⅓ cup tree ears
7 ounces bean threads *(sotanghon)*
1 whole chicken breast and 2 chicken
thighs
About 3 tablespoons vegetable oil
2 cups chopped yellow onion
3 Chinese sausages *(lop cheong)*, sliced,
or ⅔ cup diced smoky ham
2 cups chicken broth
1 cup water
3 teaspoons fish sauce *(patis)* or ¾ teaspoon salt
1 tablespoon finely minced garlic
1½ cups small, shelled raw shrimp
1 cup matchstick-cut carrots
1 cup sliced leeks, cut ⅛ inch by 2 inches
long
⅓ cup finely sliced green onions
2 limes, cut into wedges

---

If you are using the annatto seeds, soak them in ⅓ cup water. Soak the tree ears and bean threads in water to cover in separate bowls. Cut the chicken breast into quarters.

Heat about 1 tablespoon of the vegetable oil in a large skillet with a cover. Saute 1 cup of the onion with the sausage until the onion begins to turn translucent. Add the chicken and cook, turning once, until the chicken pieces are lightly browned. Add the broth, water, and fish sauce. Cover and simmer until the chicken is tender, about 45 minutes. Remove the chicken pieces from the broth, tear off the meat and shred it, and discard the skin and bones. Pour any escaping chicken juices back into the broth. Skim to degrease the broth. Mash the annatto seeds in the water and strain the water into the chicken broth, pushing the seeds against the strainer to extract the maximum amount of color; discard the seeds. Or add the bottled annatto water.

Drain the tree ears, remove any tough parts, and cut into strips. Drain the bean threads, cut them into 4-inch lengths with scissors, and add them to the chicken broth.

Cook, stirring occasionally, over medium-high heat until all but about ⅓ cup of the liquid is absorbed. Stir in the chicken meat. Remove the pan from the heat.

Heat 1 tablespoon oil in a wok or large skillet. Add the garlic and stir-fry until golden. Remove the garlic with a slotted or mesh spoon and reserve it. Stir-fry the shrimp until they are almost completely pink but still slightly underdone; remove them from the pan. Add more oil if necessary and stir-fry the remaining onion and carrot until they are barely tender and still crisp. Add the leeks and tree ears and continue to stir-fry until the leeks are softened. Remove the pan from the heat and stir in 1 teaspoon of the garlic and the shrimp.

Bring the bean threads to a simmer and stir in two-thirds of the stir-fried mixture. Transfer the noodle mixture to a large platter. Top with the remaining stir-fried mixture, and sprinkle with sliced green onions and the remaining garlic. Garnish the platter with lime wedges to be used as seasoning by the diners.

Serves 4 as a main course or 6 to 8 as part of a meal.

# THE PASTAS OF MALAYSIA, SINGAPORE, AND INDONESIA

T he national cuisine of Singapore is variety," promises a tourist booklet. If anything, this is an understatement, for Singapore, the crown jewel of the Malaysian archipelago, is the repository of about ten regional styles of Chinese cooking (its population is 75 percent Chinese), northern and southern Indian food, a wide range of Malaysian and Indonesian specialties, as well as British and Continental European restaurants, from its years as a British crown colony.

While eating establishments in Malaysia and Indonesia are not quite as diverse as those in Singapore, similar influences are found in the major cities. Together the two tropical countries separate the Indian Ocean from the South China Sea, and stretch thousands of miles over land and water from Thailand in the north to New Guinea in the south. Both claim a portion of Borneo and other far-flung, undeveloped islands as part of their nation. Not surprisingly, these geographic expanses create a diversity and a certain lack of internal cohesiveness enforced by local language differences and disparate social customs. Yet the countries share vital similarities, especially in more densely populated and urban regions, allowing those of us interested in Asian pasta to consider them as a unit. They share similar national languages and ethnic

identities, and were similarly influenced by Indian and Chinese immigrants. Throughout this area, Indian spices mingle with local flavorings, Chinese and Indian cooking techniques work together with intricate and spectacular results.

One of the best noodle dishes reflecting these cultural admixtures is *ketoprak*. Its making starts with locally grown lemon grass, chili peppers, and garlic ground or pounded together along with Indian curry spices. The mixture is fried with onions, then combined with tamarind juice and coconut milk, at which point the sauce is quite similar to those found in southern India. The addition of peanuts and sugar creates a uniquely Indo-Malay taste. Tofu, a legacy from the Chinese, is added; fresh-cut local limes and Indonesian-style fried shallots garnish the finished dish, which is served with Chinese rice vermicelli. What an exciting range of tastes and textures—sweet, sour, and hot with spicy Indian elements mellowed by coconut milk and ground peanuts.

The roots of the cuisine of the peninsula and archipelago go back to times before Christ, when Indian and Arab traders vied for power in the Spice Islands (the Moluccas, southeast of Borneo). For thousands of years, they were the world's only source of nutmeg, cloves, and mace. The trading ships, loaded with precious spices, had to come north; they stopped to trade at various ports on their way through the Strait of Malacca. The use of such spices as cinnamon, nutmeg, anise, cloves, and coriander was thus introduced to native cookery. Cooking techniques, religious practices, and customs of the traders also gained a strong footing. Even the Malaysian word for noodles, *laksa,* evolved from the Persian language.

The Chinese got a much later start in leaving their culinary mark. The Chinese traders of 9th-century Indonesia rarely got off their junks. Later, though, they settled somewhat anonymously throughout the islands. The Dutch arrived in the 16th century to find a scattered population of Chinese working in every province of Java. Eventually, bean sprouts, soy sauce, tofu, and, of course, noodles became a part of everyday cooking as did the use of the wok *(kawali* or *wajan).*

The early Chinese settlers in Malaysia were of the wealthy merchant class that traded and settled along the Strait of Malacca. But it wasn't until the fall of the Ming Dynasty in 1644 that thousands of immigrants, fleeing war and famine, poured into Malaysia seeking work in the tin mines. The European colonizers encouraged the migration as the Chinese were excellent workers. Along with these working-class immigrants came the popularity of one of their favorite foods—the noodle. Still favorites today, such noodle dishes as Hokkien *mi* and Teochew *char kway teo,* preparations from two different Fujian (south-

ern Chinese peoples), can be eaten everywhere in Malaysia and Singapore.

Even before these massive immigrations, early Chinese settlers (called Peranakan), born in Indonesia and the Strait of Malacca, began to develop their own very special "Nonya" cuisine. The women, called Nonyas, incorporated much of the already present Indian-Arabic aspects of the native food and altered ingredients (and occasionally cooking styles) to please Chinese-educated palates. Some dishes are predominantly Chinese and some are more Indian-Arabic.

The popular Singaporean *char kway teo* is almost purely Chinese. Fresh rice noodles are stir-fried with barbecued pork and an assortment of seafood, bean sprouts, oyster sauce, and fresh red chili peppers. Sometimes a bit of fiery *sambal* is stirred in—a Nonya touch. In *laksa lemak,* the cultural emphasis is reversed. In a *batu lessong* (mortar and pestle), a *rempah* of flavoring ingredients, including lemon grass, hot chilis, and often galingale, is pounded to a paste which is properly fried and cooked with coconut milk. Seafood, Chinese-style fish balls, and noodles are mixed in and fresh bean sprouts garnish the dish. A little tofu is sometimes added. Rich, smooth coconut milk mellows the fiery curry, while noodles, soaking up the creamy sauce, are balanced by the textures of seafood and crunchy bean sprouts—piquant but subtle and very addicting.

A wide assortment of noodle dishes is always available in Indonesia. Almost any time of day or night a noodle seller can materialize from around a corner or be found cooking in a tiny food stall. In Djakarta, rather than sit in a restaurant, I would walk to a street near Pasar Baru market when the heat of the day was subsiding. A row of stands constructed from thin stick posts and cloth, with gently sagging roofs, would light up after dark. In the harsh light of kerosene lanterns, each vendor would set out his specialties. The *sate* man was constantly fanning his tin drum filled with hot coals as he rotated skewered meats to crisp perfection. Next to him were two grandmothers wrapping countless *lumpia* in delicate pasta sheets. And in the many other stalls were other specialties: fried bananas, pickled green mangoes, or fresh fruit. I, of course, always gravitated toward the traveling noodle vendor. Crouched in front of a little burner and surrounded by baskets and bottles, he cooked with lightning speed. One hand traveled from bottle to basket while the other hand deftly stirred, scraped, and tossed the wok's contents. Finally, an aromatic tangle of noodles was nested in a bowl for the waiting customer, who ate as the man readied his gypsy wok for the next serving. (Something about this spontaneous cooking and eating style makes the food taste even more delicious.)

In each country such scenes were played again and again. In Malaysia, *makan malam* (night food stalls) offered bowls of *kari laksa kerang,* a spicy curry soup of mixed origins, or *popiah,* a Malaysian-style *lumpia*. And in Singapore, though their numbers are fast diminishing, you can still go to stall areas like Rasa Singapura or Newton Circus to eat Nonya or Chinese or Indonesian noodles under festive strings of lights in the equatorial evenings. □

# THE VARIETIES OF MALAYSIAN, SINGAPOREAN, AND INDONESIAN PASTA

### 1. **LAKSA** or **LAKSA MEEHOON**

Thick rice vermicelli used in typical coconut milk curry sauces or soups. Most easily found in the United States in Filipino markets as *pancit luglug* or as *lai fen* in Chinese stores. Thin rice vermicelli may be substituted.

### 2. **BEEHOON** (Malaysia, Singapore) or **BIHUN** (Indonesia)

Thin or average-width rice vermicelli. One of the most versatile noodles, turning up in curry-flavored and other stir-fried dishes, braised dishes, and soups. Can substitute for thicker rice noodles in any recipe calling for *laksa*.

### KWAY TEOW

Fresh ⅜-inch-wide rice noodles especially popular in Teochew-style dishes such as *char kway teow*. Chewy smooth texture also delightful in soups.

### 3. **BA MEE** (Malaysia, Singapore) or **BAKMIE** (Indonesia)

Thin Chinese egg noodle.

### HOKKIEN MEE

Same as the wider flat Chinese egg noodle.

### 4. **SOHOON** or **TUNGHOON** (Malaysia, Singapore) or **SOTANGHOON** (Indonesia)

Bean threads.

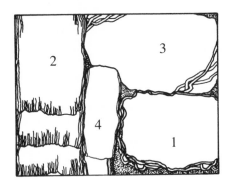

# *Teochew* Fried Fresh Wide Rice Noodles

*Char Kway Teow*

Variations abound for this typical Singaporean fresh-rice-noodle specialty, but I like this one with Chinese barbecued pork, shrimp, squid, scrambled egg, and just a touch of Serrano chili and oyster sauce.

¼ cup lard or vegetable oil
2 cloves garlic, minced
1 large yellow onion, slivered lengthwise
3 to 4 fresh chili peppers, seeded and minced
8 ounces Chinese barbecued pork (page 23), cut into strips ¾ inch by 2 inches and thinly sliced, or six pieces Chinese sausage, lightly steamed and thinly sliced
8 ounces raw, shelled shrimp
8 ounces small squid, cut into rings, or additional shrimp
2 cups fresh bean sprouts, straggly tails removed
2 pounds cut or uncut fresh rice noodles (page 15), or 14 ounces dried, flat rice noodles, cooked
About 4 tablespoons soy sauce
1 tablespoon oyster sauce
3 eggs, lightly beaten
Salt
Freshly ground pepper
4 green onions, thinly sliced

Heat half of the lard or oil and stir-fry the garlic, onion, and chili peppers until they are soft. Add the pork or sausage and stir-fry until lightly browned, about 1 minute. Add the shrimp and squid, and stir-fry several minutes more until the shrimp are opaque. Stir in the bean sprouts and toss well; remove the mixture to a platter.

Heat 1 tablespoon of the lard or oil to the smoking point. Add half the noodles and toss and stir until they are heated through, about 90 seconds. Add 2 tablespoons of the soy sauce and half the oyster sauce; mix them in and transfer the noodles to a platter. Cook the remaining noodles, adding 2 tablespoons soy sauce and the remaining oyster sauce. Return all the noodles to the pan.

Make a well in the center of the noodles and pour the eggs in. When they are about half set, toss them into the noodles and cook about 20 seconds more. Add the stir-fried meat and fish mixture and toss everything together well.

Taste and season with salt, pepper, and more soy sauce if needed. Garnish with sliced onion.

Serves 6 as the main part of a meal.

# Noodles with Indonesian Peanut Sauce

## *Ketoprak*

I discovered *ketoprak* at Melati, a Malay and Indonesian restaurant in London's Soho. The chef would not divulge his "secret" recipe (although other places served what seemed to be an identical dish), but the restaurant's hostess was most helpful with her description of how she cooked it at home. I went home and tried her recipe and came up with a dish tasting remarkably like the one I had eaten at the restaurant.

2 tablespoons tamarind pulp (not the
    concentrate), or 6 peeled tamarind pods
1 cup boiling water
1 pound fresh tofu
4 cloves garlic, minced to a pulp
1 fresh Serrano chili pepper
1 stalk fresh lemon grass, or the zest of
    one-half lemon
¼ teaspoon cayenne pepper
⅜ teaspoon ground cinnamon
½ teaspoon ground coriander
1 tablespoon sugar
⅝ teaspoon salt
1 medium-large yellow onion, minced to
    a pulp
⅔ cup vegetable oil
7 ounces rice vermicelli *(beehoon)*
One 8-ounce white potato, steamed
⅔ cup roasted unsalted peanuts
½ cup medium coconut milk (page 24)

3 limes
Crispy Shallots, purchased or homemade
    (page 136)

Mash the tamarind pulp in a bowl with the boiling water and let it soak about 30 minutes. Cut the tofu into ½-inch-thick slices. Arrange the slices on a double layer of terry toweling and cover them with another layer of toweling. Weight the tofu with a board or tray covered with heavy objects (I use books) and let it compress about 40 minutes. Cut the tofu into 1-inch by ½-inch pieces.

Combine the garlic and chili pepper in a food processor or mortar. Peel the tough outer stalks from the lemon grass and discard; slice the inner stalks and add them to the food processor or mortar. Pound or process the ingredients until they are almost a paste. Add the cayenne, cinnamon, coriander, sugar, and salt and mix or pound them into the paste until the mixture is almost smooth. Stir in the onions.

Heat ⅓ cup of the oil in a heavy skillet. Add the *rempah* from the processor or mortar and fry it briskly over high heat until any water evaporates. Turn down the heat to medium and continue to fry the *rempah*, stirring occasionally, until it gives off a fragrant "cooked" aroma and the oil separates out, 20 to 25 minutes.

While the *rempah* is cooking, soak the vermicelli in water to cover about 15 minutes until soft. Cook it in boiling water 2 minutes, drain, and rinse thoroughly with cold water.

Peel the potato and cut it into ½-inch cubes. Chop the peanuts in a food processor or by hand until they are finely ground but not a butter. Stir in 2 tablespoons of the oil. In a large pan, heat the coconut milk almost to the boiling point. Stir in the peanuts and the *rempah* and blend well. Cook over low heat until the sauce is thick, adding all but the final 1 tablespoon of the oil as you stir. Strain the tamarind into the sauce through a tea strainer, pressing down on the pulp to release the flavors.

Wipe the skillet and heat about 1 table-spoon of the oil. Fry the tofu pieces, turning once, until they are golden. Stir in the potato cubes until they are heated through. Transfer the tofu and potatoes to a plate. Stir the sauce into the noodles and heat over low heat just to warm the noodles through. Stir in the tofu and potatoes. Heap the noodles on a platter and garnish with lime wedges and Crispy Shallots.

Serves 4 to 5 as a meal or 6 to 8 as part of a meal.

# Malaysian Seafood and Noodles in Coconut Milk Sauce

*Laksa Lemak Melaka*

*Laksa lemak* Malacca-style is but one among hundreds of regional variations of this most popular noodle curry served throughout Malaysia and Singapore. *Penang laksa, nonya laksa, laksa Kelantan,* and *laksa Johore Bersantan* are variations of this noodle-in-a-spicy-coconut-gravy theme. All use thick (usually fresh) spaghetti-size rice vermicelli, seafood, and coconut milk sauce flavored with a *rempah,* or pounded and ground seasonings. According to Dorothy Ng in her book, *Complete Asian Meals,* "The best utensil for frying the *rempah* is an Indian clay pot, a *belanga,* rather than a *kwali* (wok). If a *kwali* is used then one must turn the heat to very low or some of the ingredients may be burnt." She also explains, "The *rempah* must be fried until it gives off a noticeably fragrant aroma and the oil separates or rises to the surface before adding any liquid or other ingredients to it."

1¼ pounds medium to large shrimp in the shell
About ½ cup vegetable oil
Water
1 or 2 Chinese fish cakes, or 16 to 20 fish balls (page 114), or 10 ounces lean white fish cut into ¾-inch chunks
¾ pound bean sprouts

1 pound dried thick rice vermicelli (spaghetti-size *pancit luglug,* in Filipino stores)*
¼ cup dried shrimp
One 1- by ¾- by ¼-inch piece dried shrimp paste *(blachan)*
5 candlenuts, or 5 macadamia nuts, or 5 Brazil nuts
3 stalks fresh lemon grass, tender part minced, or 6 tablespoons dried, chopped, and soaked lemon grass
Four ¼-inch slices fresh galingale, or 1½ teaspoons powdered galingale, or substitute
3 fresh, red Serrano chili peppers
8 dried Asian chili peppers, seeded
1 tablespoon grated fresh turmeric or 1½ teaspoons dried turmeric
3 cloves garlic, minced
2 cups very finely minced shallots or yellow onions
6 cups thin coconut milk (page 24)
1 cup thick coconut milk (page 24)
2½ teaspoons sugar
1 teaspoon salt or more
2 to 3 limes, cut into wedges
1 cucumber, peeled, seeded, and cut into strips ⅛-inch wide and 2 inches long
Mint sprigs
2 fresh chili peppers, finely shredded

Shell the shrimp, reserving the shells and setting aside the meat. Heat 1 tablespoon of the oil in a large skillet and fry the shells until they turn bright pink. Add 2 cups water, cover the pan, and simmer 15 minutes. Remove the shells. Cook the fish cakes, fish balls, or fish chunks in the same stock until firm. Remove the fish with a slotted spoon and set aside; simmer the stock until it is reduced to 1¼ cups. Set aside.

Blanch the bean sprouts in boiling water 1 minute. Drain and rinse them with cold water. Cook the noodles about 6 minutes in boiling water or until tender. Drain and rinse them with cold water. Refill the cooking pot with water and bring it to a boil while you are preparing the *rempah* (seasonings).

In a mortar or food processor, pound the dried shrimp, shrimp paste, candlenuts, lemon grass, galingale, fresh and dried chili peppers, turmeric, and garlic cloves to a paste. Heat about 5 tablespoons vegetable oil in the skillet, and add the shallots or onions and the contents of the mortar. Cook, stirring briskly over medium heat until the *rempah* gives off a "cooked" aroma and the oil separates from the solids. Add the shrimp and stir-fry until they are pink and firm. Remove them from the pan, leaving behind as much of the *rempah* as possible.

Add the reduced shrimp broth and the thin coconut milk and simmer 8 minutes. Add the shrimp, fish, thick coconut milk, and sugar, and simmer until heated through. Do not allow the sauce to boil. Stir in 1 teaspoon salt and the juice of half a lime. Taste and season with additional salt and lime juice if you like.

Using a strainer, dip the noodles, a portion at a time, into the boiling water just to warm them. Drain them well, divide them equally among individual soup bowls, and top with bean sprouts. Pour a serving of fish and sauce over the noodles and garnish it with cucumber and mint. Pass shredded chili peppers and lime wedges at the table.

Serves 6 to 8 as a main dish.

*You may substitute Chinese *lai fen* or thin rice vermicelli; cook as directed on page 15.

# Indonesian Shrimp and Noodle Soup

*Soto Udang*

The sparkling tang of tamarind and hot chili peppers flavors the sweet-sour-hot broth of this simple hearty dish.

One 14½-ounce can regular-strength
  chicken broth
Water
1½ tablespoons Indonesian soy sauce
  (*ketjap manis,* page 26)
2½ teaspoons palm or light brown sugar
1¼ pounds raw shrimp, in the shell
8 ounces bean sprouts (4 cups)
2 teaspoons peanut or vegetable oil
7 to 8 small fresh red Serrano chili
  peppers, thinly sliced
5 ounces rice vermicelli *(bihun)*
1½ cups finely minced yellow onions
2 large cloves garlic, crushed
3 ounces (½ cup) roasted unsalted
  peanuts, coarsely chopped
1 tablespoon tamarind concentrate mixed
  with 2½ tablespoons water, or 3 tablespoons tamarind water (page 33)
Salt
Freshly ground pepper

In a soup pot, combine the chicken broth, 3 cups water, soy sauce, and sugar, and bring to a boil, stirring to dissolve the sugar. Drop in the unshelled shrimp and simmer about 3 minutes, until they are pink and firm. Lift out the shrimp with a slotted spoon or Chinese wire mesh spoon and cool until they can be shelled. Remove the shrimp shells and tails and return them to the soup pot, setting aside the shrimp meat; cover the pot and simmer for 15 minutes. Strain the stock and discard the shells.

Blanch the bean sprouts in boiling water for 1½ minutes; drain, and rinse with cold water. Heat the peanut oil in a small skillet. Add the chili peppers and fry until they are crisp. Drain them on paper toweling. Mince half of the chili peppers very finely. Cook the noodles in boiling water about 3 minutes, or just until they are *al dente;* drain and rinse them with hot water. Mince the shrimp and mix them with the onions, garlic, and peanuts. Stir the tamarind concentrate into the soup, add the shrimp mixture and two-thirds of the minced chili peppers, and bring the soup to simmering. Simmer for 1 minute, then season to taste with salt and pepper.

Divide the noodles among 6 to 8 bowls, and top first with the bean sprouts, then with some of the shrimp mixture. Garnish with a little more of the fried chili peppers or serve the chilis as a condiment at the table.

Serves 6 to 8 as a main course.

# Beef and Sweet Potato Noodle Curry
# Garnished with Crispy Shallots

*Mee Rebus Java*

With beef and sweet potato as main ingredients (besides the noodles), this dish stands apart from the more typical seafood with coconut gravy noodle dishes, of which there are countless renderings throughout Southeast Asia.

1¼ pounds shrimp in the shell
About 7 tablespoons peanut or vegetable oil
One 14½-ounce can regular-strength chicken broth
Water
8 small dried Asian chili peppers, seeded
4 candlenuts, or 4 macadamia nuts, or 4 Brazil nuts
Three ¼-inch slices fresh galingale, or 1½ teaspoons ground galingale, or substitute
¼ teaspoon black peppercorns
1 tablespoon Chinese fermented black beans
1 cup minced shallots, or the white part of green onions, or red onions
6 ounces beef sirloin or top round cut into 2-inch by ½-inch by ⅛-inch slices
3 cups medium coconut milk (page 24)
1 teaspoon sugar
1 teaspoon salt
2 cups cubed sweet potato, steamed just until tender
1½ tablespoons rice flour or all-purpose flour mixed with 2 tablespoons water
3 cups bean sprouts
1 pound fresh, flat egg noodles (or the thinner egg noodles), or 12 ounces dried egg noodles *(bahmee)*
Garnishes: Crispy Shallots (recipe follows), fried *krupic* or Hawaiian-style potato chips, 3 hard-cooked eggs, quartered, 2 green onions, thinly sliced, lime wedges, sliced fresh chili peppers

Shell the shrimp, reserving the shells and setting aside the meat. Heat 2 tablespoons of the oil in a large frying pan and saute the shrimp shells until they are bright pink, about 1 minute. Remove from heat and add the chicken broth and ½ cup water; simmer 15 minutes. Strain the broth and discard the shrimp shells.

In a food processor or mortar, combine the chili peppers, nuts, galingale, peppercorns, and black beans, and grind them to a paste. Stir the paste into the shallots and pound slightly with the pestle, a meat mallet, or heavy jar. Heat 4 tablespoons of the oil in a large skillet or wok and fry the pounded ingredients until they are fragrant and the oil begins to separate. Add a little more oil and the beef, and stir-fry until the beef is browned. Then pour in the strained broth and coconut milk, and add the shrimp, sugar, salt, and sweet potato; simmer about 4 minutes. Add

# Fried Hokkien Meehoon Mee

the rice flour paste and boil the sauce, stirring, until it thickens; set aside.

Blanch the bean sprouts in boiling water 1½ minutes; rinse with cold water and drain well. Cook the noodles until *al dente* (page 14). Drain and rinse with warm water; drain well.

Divide the noodles among 4 to 6 bowls. Top first with the bean sprouts, then with a portion of the sauce. Garnish with the Crispy Shallots and any of the suggested garnishes.

Serves 4 to 6 as a main dish.

**Crispy Shallots**

Peel and slice 5 or 6 medium shallots very thinly, crosswise. Heat about ¼ cup peanut or vegetable oil in a medium skillet. Add the shallots and fry, shaking the pan almost constantly, until they are evenly golden. Quickly drain the hot oil through a fine strainer and spread the shallots on paper toweling to drain. If they are not yet crisp, bake them at 225° until crisp.

In Djakarta, Singapore, the market stalls of Kuala Lumpur—no matter where you eat it, this two-noodle (egg noodles and rice vermicelli) stir-fry, garnished with braised pork, shrimp, and squid, will make you wish for the recipe to take back home. Nonya cooks use smoking-hot lard to stir-fry the noodles and give them their characteristic smoky flavor.

Water
About 5 tablespoons soy sauce
1 teaspoon sugar
1-pound-piece pork shoulder
1 pound medium or small shrimp, in the shell
4 medium dressed squid, cut into rings
⅔ cup lard
1 large yellow onion, cut lengthwise into thin strips
6 cloves garlic, minced
1 pound 6 ounces fresh Chinese egg noodles* or 1 pound dried, cooked for stir-fry (page 14)
6 cups bean sprouts, straggly tails removed
5 ounces dried rice vermicelli, soaked 15 minutes and drained
3 eggs, lightly beaten
4 teaspoons cornstarch mixed with 2 tablespoons water

Salt

Freshly ground pepper

Chinese chives cut into 3-inch lengths, or sliced green onions

Lime quarters

Slivered fresh Serrano or jalapeño chili peppers

---

One hour or up to a day ahead, combine 6 cups water, 3 tablespoons soy sauce, and the sugar in a large saucepan. Bring to a simmer and add the pork. Cover and simmer until the meat is tender, about 50 minutes. Transfer the meat to a plate. Place about a third of the shrimp in a Chinese wire mesh spoon or strainer and dip them into the simmering stock until they turn pink; transfer to a plate and continue with the remaining shrimp. Cook the squid the same way. Peel the shrimp, set aside the meat, and add the peels to the stock; simmer 10 minutes, then strain the stock. Boil the strained stock, uncovered, until it is reduced to 2 cups. Cut the pork into thin strips, about 3/16 inch by 2 inches, and reserve.

Just before serving, heat about 3 tablespoons lard in a wok or very large skillet. Add the onion and stir-fry until it begins to turn translucent. Add the garlic and stir-fry until it is soft but not browned. Add about 1/4 cup more lard, and, when it begins to smoke, add the egg noodles and stir-fry rapidly as you toss the noodles; stir-fry 1 1/2 minutes until the noodles heat through. Add the bean sprouts and stir-fry about 30 seconds more. Transfer the noodles to a large platter to hold.

Heat another 1/4 cup lard to smoking. Add the vermicelli and fry, tossing continuously, 1 minute. Add the eggs and let them set as they cook, then toss them with the noodles. Add 1 cup of the shrimp-pork stock, cover the pan, and cook 1 1/2 minutes. Add the squid, shrimp, and pork and toss well. Add the bean sprout/noodle mixture and the rest of the stock and toss it in well. Add the cornstarch paste and toss until the sauce thickens.

Season to taste with salt, pepper, and soy sauce. Heap onto a platter and garnish the dish with Chinese chives. Serve with lime wedges and slivered chili peppers at the table.

Serves 6 to 8 as a main dish.

*Flat, 3/16-inch-wide egg noodles are preferred here, if you can find them, for a nice texture contrast. Otherwise use the thin, 1/16-inch-size egg noodles.

# THE PASTAS OF CHINA

ood food and good eating have always been central to Chinese culture. Even before the Chinese wrote, ancient pottery depicted food preparation and feasting. An early text, the *Shih Ching (Book of Songs),* from about 600 B.C., describes the elaborate food preparations of certain harvest festivals. Written one hundred years later, the *Analects of Confucius* examines in close detail the essential elements of great food: proper cutting, seasoning, cooking, and the balancing of flavors.

Food is a central theme in Chinese poetry, philosophy, and scholarly writings. Chroniclers and memoir writers offer lengthy dissertations on food and its relation to every aspect of life. While these writings show an appreciation for rustic simplicity in food and the importance of unadulterated, fresh ingredients, they are understandably more concerned with exotic and elaborate foods eaten by the wealthy or reserved for formal occasions and rituals. This is particularly true of the earliest recipes recorded, which, unfortunately, omit precise details of cooking procedures and measurements. As in the literature of other cultures, everyday foods such as pastas, though consumed in large quantities, were taken for granted and generally ignored in scholarly works.

Still, China's love affair with the commonplace noodle is well illustrated by many literary descriptions and personal memoirs. One legend tells us that during the Ch'ing Dynasty (1644 to 1911), the Son of Heaven, ensconced in his Forbidden City with thousands of kitchen servants at his command, occasionally sent a runner out to the night market for a bowl of Old Man Wang's spicy beef noodles.

The high degree of culinary consciousness achieved by the affluent filtered down to all Chinese foods, the humble noodle being no exception. Imagination and economy combined to create marvelous new interpretations of this staple, as shown by a 5th century recipe which suggests flavoring noodle dough with the water used for soaking dates.

Throughout history, as in modern times, the middle and even lower classes took full advantage of their well-developed culinary heritage during times of abundance. In the teeming cities of ancient China, everyone, from the lowliest beggar to the highest official, knew where to find the best foods, often without concern for elegant surroundings, as the following description from E. N. and Marja L. Anderson, in *Food in Chinese Culture,* reveals.

> It was a perfectly ordinary working class neighborhood wonton and noodle place, a small bare room with a few tables and

chairs, not a fancy restaurant; yet people from all walks of life flocked to it. It was famous throughout the Western territories and everyone yearned to eat there.

The noodle and its precursor, the dumpling, were first popular in the north, where cold winters and short growing seasons made millet and wheat, rather than rice, the staple grains. The specific origins of noodles, however, are unclear. The first Chinese word for noodle is *ping,* but this tells us little of precise origins because it is a generic word and refers to food made of blended flour and water, including breads and cakes. Whatever the precise source of noodles, large-scale commercial production was already well under way in Han China, about 100 A.D., following the introduction of wheat-milling technology imported from the Middle East. Third-century writer Shiu Hsi tells us that noodles "were an invention of the common people [of China], though some of their cooking methods come from foreign lands." He vividly describes a cook's skillful hands kneading noodle dough into a variety of shapes and the many ways noodles were cooked.

So impressed was Chinese anthropologist and food scholar, K. C. Chang, with the wide popularity of the noodle, that he was inspired to call its introduction "an entirely new chapter in Chinese culinary history." This is no small claim. Because grains have always been central to the Chinese diet, and no meal is considered complete without grain food, the introduction of so distinct a style of grain preparation was fundamental and profound.

Once ensconced, the noodle endured as a part of daily life. Even before the evolution of true restaurants, open-air food stalls in the marketplace supplied cooked foods to be taken home. The first examples were no doubt very similar to the food stalls found throughout Asian countries today. This style of fast-food merchandising benefited both the vendor, who could not afford real estate or rent, and a wide range of stoveless customers—from mobile merchants to students. They were open at almost all hours of the day and night. Accounts of urban life in the Sung Dynasty (960 to 1279) document the availability of foods at the night market as running straight through the "third watch" (3:00 to 5:00 A.M.) and starting up again at the "fifth watch" (7:00 to 9:00 A.M.).

By the time Marco Polo reached China in 1275, the country was enjoying a period of great prosperity. All foods, including noodles, became heir to the riches of the time. The adventurer's journals describe Hangchow as a port city visited by many ships bringing spices from the Indies and carrying away silks. Arab merchants eagerly traded with the Chinese; shops overflowed with precious goods. Restaurants, taverns, and tea houses flourished, serving every delicacy known in the empire; while in the marketplaces, street vendors continued to hawk their more simple, but delicious, foods.

Fierce competition for a discriminating clientele kept up the quality and originality of all foods—even the most inexpensive noodle dishes. Certain stall keepers (like Wei "the Big Knife," who kept shop at Cat Bridge and was known for his cooked pork) became famous for one special dish. Stimulated by a growing international trade, inventive cooks incorporated foreign ingredients. Stir-frying, which had been introduced in the 8th century, added another dimension to noodle preparation.

One of the most ancient forms of noodle preparation, hand-swung noodles, survives to this day. These slightly chewy yet soft noodles are incomparable and have been popular since at least the 2nd century A.D., when even the emperor enjoyed them. A more refined Beijing version was served to noblemen of the 16th century Ming Dynasty. Buwei Yang Chao, in her book *How to Cook and Eat in Chinese,* extolls their virtues by opening her discussion of noodles with, "There are noodles and there are noodles." Though noodle swinging is fast becoming a lost art, one occasionally runs across hand-swung noodles in the United States. Customers love to watch the cook pull, twist, and stretch the dough into two fat strands, then four thinner strands, then eight thinner strands, and so on until the divisions upon divisions become a fistful of silken noodles. So captivating is the experience that a noodle-making master from Wildwood, New Jersey, was invited to demonstrate his art on a popular television program. Friends of mine (noodle lovers as well) have found the art being practiced in Leeds, England, London, Toledo, Ohio, and Los Angeles. Be on the lookout in Chinatowns wherever you go. A demand may promote a hand-swung noodle renaissance.

It is no simple task to compress the vast possibilities for Chinese noodle dishes into one chapter. To best represent the scope of Chinese noodle cookery, I have included examples of each traditional method of noodle preparation and selected recipes that illustrate a range of ways noodles can be used—from deep-fried puffed noodles to cold noodle salads. I have organized noodles into their classic styles of preparation: soup noodles, stir-fried noodles (both hot and cold), noodles with braised toppings, and noodles that are themselves braised. To cover as much ground as possible, certain recipes are designed as basic methods with suggestions for creating many variations. Not included are *dim sum* (there are already so many good books on this vast subject) and savory wonton (every Chinese cookbook has a recipe). □

# THE VARIETIES OF CHINESE PASTA

"There are so many dialects and so many ways to pronounce [and transliterate] the Chinese terms for the various noodles," Madame Wong, coauthor of *Madame Wong's Long Life Chinese Cookbook*, told me in our interview. "For clarity, it's best to discuss them all in English and then give some Chinese pronunciations." I have taken her advice and listed the Chinese noodles by category, in English. The generic word for noodle in Chinese is *mian,* in Mandarin, and *mein,* in Cantonese. For brevity, the current Mandarin spelling has been used here in most cases. However, many packages are labeled in Cantonese or for other reasons may vary. The chart on page 34 will give all the names you will probably encounter for each noodle.

## BEAN THREAD NOODLES

Mung-bean-starch noodles, known by many names in English such as cellophane noodles, shining noodles, silver noodles, and glass noodles. Known officially as *fen si* (powdered silk) or sometimes called *sai fun* (long rice). Semi-translucent when dried, they become almost clear when soaked, then cooked.*

## RICE NOODLES

*Dried rice vermicelli.* Thin rice noodles that puff up when deep fried, called *mi fen.* For soups or stir-fried dishes, they are first soaked, then simmered. Thicker spaghetti-like rice vermicelli are called *lai fen.**

*Fresh rice noodles.* Fresh rice noodle sheets used in Chinese *dim sum* and many Southeast Asian dishes are known as *sha he fen*. They come in sheets which are folded, bagged in plastic, and usually sold in the produce section of Asian markets. Rice sheets also come cut into noodles approximately ¾-inch wide for soups and stir-fried dishes. Sometimes dried flat rice noodles are also labeled *sha he fen.**

*For cooking information see the General Instructions for Cooking Noodles section.

## SEAWEED STARCH NOODLES

Quite similar to bean threads, but thinner and more gelatinous, seaweed starch noodles *(yang fen)* are especially delightful in salads. Do not be put off by the source of starch used for these delicate transparent noodles. Prepare as you would bean threads.

## SOY BEAN SPAGHETTI

The name on many packages of pressed tofu cut into long noodle-like strips. Not a true noodle, but can be used as noodles. Their meaty texture and blandness are a good foil for spicy sauces and dressings. They are quite perishable and must be kept refrigerated.

## WHEAT NOODLES, DRIED

1. *Dried eggless noodles.* Used in northern-style dishes and known as *gan mian* (dried noodle) or *kuan gan mian* (broad dried noodle). Thin dried noodles containing a little egg are also available in Chinese markets. These should not be confused with true egg noodles which are usually available fresh. The best brand I have found for these wheat-with-egg noodles is Marco Polo Noodles made by the Quon Yick Company of Los Angeles.

*Precooked and dried wheat noodles.* Deep-frying and drying give body and a sturdy quality to *yi mian,* which must be recooked for use in soups and stir-fried dishes. The noodles are packaged in large round bundles or cakes.

*Shrimp- or crab-flavored noodles.* Fine wheat-flour noodles flavored with roe of shrimp or crab. Usually packaged in eight or nine nestlike bunches of noodles. Delicious simply stir-fried with ginger and garlic, and finished with chicken stock and soy sauce. Or they can be used as any dried Chinese noodles would be in soups or lightly pan fried.

*Very thin wheat vermicelli.* Known as *mi sua* in Fujian dialect. Most frequently found in the United States in Filipino markets as *misua* or *miswa.*

## WHEAT NOODLES, FRESH

2. *Fresh wheat noodles, nonegg.* Fresh uncooked wheat noodles *(sun mian)* are often labeled "chow mein noodles." They come in large boxes and may be found in the produce or noodle sections of most Chinese markets. Some brands contain a little egg but not enough to be called "egg noo- dles." Often found in supermar- kets packaged in airtight plastic packages. I have found these generally inferior to those purchased in a Chinese market.

3,4. *Fresh egg noodles.* There are two styles of the fresh, deli- cate, very eggy noodles called *dan mian:* the very thin string shape, the thinnest of which is the Cantonese-style; and the broader, very thinly rolled

³⁄₁₆-inch-wide noodle *(kuan dan mian)*—wonderful for cold tossed dishes. The shoe- string-style *dan mian* often come in bunches swirled into a nest. Fresh egg noodles should not be confused with the wheat noodles containing a little egg described above.

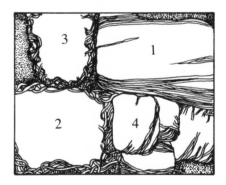

# Dumpling Knots in Winter
# Pork and Cabbage Stew

The dumpling knot, a predecessor to noodles, may well be the earliest surviving form of pasta. Quickly cooked, nourishing, and filling, such flour-paste foods have survived the ages. Before rice was widely distributed in the north, wheat and sorghum were the mainstays, and dumplings were a convenient and delicious way to cook wheat flour. Even to the present day in northern China, *geda,* a sort of wheat-dumpling stew, is commonly eaten. Long before the refined noodle came to be, grain pastes were made from roasted, coarsely ground grains and mixed with tea or water to make a primitive dumpling. No matter how rudimentary the dumpling knot, whether stewed or boiled, its chewy quality has gained it a following.

6 dried Chinese mushrooms
1⅓ cups all-purpose flour
Salt
1 large egg
¾ cup plus 2 tablespoons water
2 pork chops, about 6 ounces each, partially frozen
2 tablespoons vegetable oil
2 tablespoons soy sauce
⅓ medium Nappa cabbage, cut crosswise into 1-inch-wide strips
4 cups chicken broth
2 cups water
4 green onions, chopped

White rice vinegar
Hot chili oil

Soak the mushrooms in water to cover until they soften. In a large bowl, combine the flour and ⅜ teaspoon salt. Beat the egg and water together and blend it smoothly into the flour. Set aside.

Cut the meat from the pork chop bones and slice it into thin strips. Heat the oil in a wok or large skillet and swirl to coat the pan. Add the pork chop bones and fry them until they are nicely browned; transfer them to a plate and set aside. Add the pork meat and soy sauce to the pan and stir-fry until nicely browned, about 1 minute. Add the cabbage and stir-fry, scooping and turning until it wilts, about 5 minutes. Add the broth, water, and bones. Cover the pan and simmer 30 minutes.

Cut away the tough mushroom stems and slice the caps into strips. Add the mushrooms and green onions to the stew, and cook 5 minutes more. Discard the pork bones.

You are now ready to cook the dumpling knots, which can be cooked in the stew. However, since novice cooks often leave trails of dough (you'll see why), it is often best to cook the dumplings in water and transfer them to the stew. The dumplings may also

# Good Ole *Lo Mein*

be cooked a day in advance and reheated in the stew.

There are two ways to make the dumplings: 1) Using 2 wet teaspoons, slide about 1 teaspoon dough into 2½ quarts rapidly boiling salted water. Repeat with about 10 more dumplings, distributing the dumplings evenly in the pot. Or, 2) Tilt the bowl of dough slightly over the pot of boiling water. As the dough begins to flow over the edge, shave the rim of the bowl with a knife, in rapid succession, cutting the dough into thin strips that fall into the boiling water. Stir gently with chopsticks to loosen any dumplings that may stick to the pan. With either method, let the dumplings boil about 3 minutes until they are firm and are floating. Remove them from the pan with a slotted or wire mesh spoon and drain them briefly on paper toweling. Transfer them to a plate.

When you are ready to serve the dish, heat the dumplings in the stew. Serve the vinegar and chili oil as table condiments.

Serves 6.

Toss-fried noodles *(lo mein)* are probably one of the most well-known Chinese noodle specialties. Unfortunately, in the United States they have been associated with canned fried noodles and other misinterpretations of the genre. In the hands of a good chef (or even a home cook with good ingredients), *lo mein* dishes can rise to the sublime. So varied are the possibilities, hundreds of different dishes could be created from the master recipe below. Following it are but a few suggestions for variations. Once you get the knack of cooking the dish, you'll probably want to create your own *lo mein* specialty.

# Shrimp, Pork, and Two Red Pepper *Lo Mein*

12 ounces fresh thin Chinese egg noodles
or tonnarelli or spaghettini, or 8 ounces
dried noodles

1 teaspoon Oriental sesame oil

1 egg white

2½ tablespoons Chinese rice wine, or dry
sherry

2 teaspoons light soy sauce

½ teaspoon salt

5 teaspoons cornstarch

10 ounces pork butt, cut into strips ⅛-inch
wide and 2 inches long

6 ounces very small shelled, deveined
shrimp, or medium shrimp cut in half
crosswise

6 to 8 large dried Chinese mushrooms

½ cup chicken broth

3½ tablespoons soy sauce

½ teaspoon sugar

⅛ teaspoon salt

½ cup peanut or vegetable oil

3½ teaspoons minced ginger

1 tablespoon minced garlic

1 fresh red Serrano chili pepper, seeded
and minced almost to a pulp, or ¼ teaspoon *sambal oeleck*

1 red bell pepper, cut lengthwise into thin
strips

1 cup finely diced jicama

8 or 10 bok choy leaves, cut crosswise
into ½-inch ribbons

2½ teaspoons cornstarch, dissolved in
2 tablespoons chicken broth

Additional soy sauce

Cook the noodles for stir-fry (page 14); mix them with the sesame oil in a bowl and set aside. Mix together the egg white, 4½ teaspoons of the wine, light soy sauce, salt, and cornstarch, and divide the mixture between two medium bowls. Add the pork to one bowl and the shrimp to the other. Mix the pork and shrimp with the marinade to coat well. Marinate about 1 hour at room temperature or up to a day in the refrigerator. Soak the mushrooms in hot water to cover, weighting them with a small bowl or cup. When they are soft, squeeze the water from the mushrooms, cut away the tough stems, and dice the caps finely. Combine the broth, remaining 3 teaspoons wine, soy sauce, sugar, and salt in a small bowl.

When you are ready to cook, heat 3 tablespoons of the peanut oil in a wok, almost to the smoking point. Add the ginger, garlic, and chili pepper, and stir briskly about 15 seconds. (If you are using *sambal,* put it into the oil during the last 5 seconds of cooking.) Add 2 more tablespoons of the peanut oil and, when it is heated, add the pork and stir-fry briskly until it is about half cooked. Add the bell pepper and cook about 15 seconds until it begins to soften. Stir in the mushrooms, jicama, and white part of the bok choy, and stir-fry 10 seconds more. Add the shrimp and cook just until they begin to turn pink. Stir in the green part of the bok choy. Remove the mixture to a platter just before the shrimp are thoroughly cooked.

Wipe out the wok and heat the remaining peanut oil in it; swirl the oil to glaze the pan. Toss in the noodles and cook them over high heat, lifting and tossing them constantly until some of them begin to crisp. For crisper noodles, let them rest in contact with the hot wok several seconds at a time, then toss again. When the noodles are cooked to your liking, stir in the broth mixture. Rapidly mix in the stir-fried meats and vegetables. Stir the cornstarch and broth mixture and mix it into the noodles. Toss the noodles until the sauce is thick. Remove from the heat and season to taste with soy sauce. Transfer at once to a serving platter and serve immediately.

Serves 3 or 4 as the main part of a meal, or 6 to 7 as part of a multi-dish meal.

# Lo Mein Variations

### *Lo mein* with meat

• Use 12 ounces beef steak, or chicken breast meat, or pork cut into 2-inch-long thin strips in place of the pork and shrimp combination in the preceding recipe. Marinate in one bowl.

### Combination meat and seafood *lo mein*

• Substitute 2 to 3 Chinese sausages *(lop cheong),* thinly sliced, for the pork and use 10 ounces raw shelled shrimp. Marinate the shrimp only.
• Substitute 6 ounces beef, cut into thin strips, for the pork and 8 ounces bay scallops for the shrimp.
• Substitute 10 ounces chicken for the pork; retain the shrimp.
• Retain the pork and substitute 6 to 8 ounces squid cut into rings for the shrimp.

### Seafood *lo mein*

• Substitute 10 ounces squid rings or scallops for the pork.

### Vegetable substitutions

• For the jicama, substitute ¾ cup fresh, sliced water chestnuts, or ¾ cup sliced green onion, or ¾ cup slivered bamboo shoots, or 1½ cups bean sprouts.
• For the bell peppers, substitute 1½ cups broccoli florets, or 1 cup snow peas, or 2 carrots chopped into fine matchsticks, or 1 large yellow onion, cut finely.
• For the bok choy, substitute Nappa cabbage, or 2 cups finely cut white cabbage, or 1 bunch Chinese broccoli, or 8 leaves mustard greens, or 1½ to 2 cups bean sprouts.

# Roast Pork or Barbecued Duck *Lo Mein*

Here is another classic, this time with roasted meat or poultry. Try barbecued or roasted chicken, duck from a Chinatown market or deli, or use chicken or pork cooked any way.

10 ounces fresh, thin Chinese egg noodles or tonnarelli or spaghettini, or 7 ounces dried noodles
1 teaspoon Oriental sesame oil
2 tablespoons light soy sauce
2 tablespoons oyster sauce
½ teaspoon sugar
¼ teaspoon salt
¼ cup peanut or vegetable oil
2 teaspoons minced ginger
1½ teaspoons minced garlic
½ pound barbecued, roasted, or otherwise cooked pork meat, or barbecued or roasted chicken or duck meat, or cooked beef, shredded
2 green onions, sliced
2 cups coarsely shredded Nappa cabbage
2 cups bean sprouts

Cook the noodles for stir-fry (page 14); mix them with the sesame oil in a bowl and set aside. Combine the soy sauce, oyster sauce, sugar, and salt in a bowl and set aside.

Heat 2 tablespoons peanut oil in a wok and swirl it to coat the pan. Add the ginger and garlic, and stir-fry about 20 seconds. Add the meat and stir-fry until it is almost heated through, about 20 seconds. Add the onions and cabbage, and stir-fry 5 seconds. Add the bean sprouts and stir-fry 10 seconds more. Pour in the soy sauce mixture and stir to blend well. Transfer the meat and vegetables to a platter.

Wipe out the wok and heat the remaining oil. Swirl the oil to coat the pan. Add the noodles and cook them over high heat until some of them begin to crisp. For crisper noodles, let them remain in contact with the hot wok several seconds at a time, then toss again. When the noodles are cooked to your liking, add the pork and vegetable mixture and stir together well just until heated through. Heap onto a serving platter or individual plates and serve immediately.

Serves 2 as a main dish or 5 to 6 as part of a multi-dish meal.

*Variations*
• Substitute two thinly sliced Chinese sausages and 6 to 8 ounces small cooked shrimp for the cooked meat.
• Substitute 6 to 8 ounces cooked chicken and ⅔ cup smoky ham cut into matchsticks for the cooked meat.

# Chinese Rice Noodles, Singapore Style

Curry paste and rice noodles are both Singaporean ingredients in this modern Chinese dish. I particularly enjoy the mixture of meat with seafood, and the extra richness of egg scrambled into the noodle mixture.

3 eggs
1 tablespoon and ½ teaspoon Chinese rice wine, or dry sherry
1 teaspoon light soy sauce
1 tablespoon cornstarch
Pinch of salt
8 ounces tiny shelled, raw shrimp, or medium shrimp cut in half
8 ounces rice vermicelli
1½ tablespoons curry paste, or 1 tablespoon curry powder
2 tablespoons soy sauce
¼ teaspoon sugar
1 cup chicken stock
About ⅓ cup peanut or vegetable oil
1 or 2 small dried Asian chili peppers, seeded and crumbled very finely
2 teaspoons minced garlic
1 tablespoon minced ginger
4 to 6 ounces barbecued pork, shredded*
3 tablespoons Chinese-style ham, cut into pieces ⅛-inch wide and 2 inches long
4 green onions, quartered lengthwise and cut into 1½-inch lengths
1 cup frozen tender tiny peas, thawed
1 teaspoon Oriental sesame oil

In a medium bowl, mix together one egg white (reserve the yolk), wine, light soy sauce, cornstarch, and salt. Mix in the shrimp, coating each one well. Allow to marinate for an hour.

Soak the rice vermicelli in water to cover about 15 minutes, until soft. Drain well and spread on paper toweling. In a small bowl, combine the curry, soy sauce, and sugar, then blend in the stock smoothly.

Heat 1½ tablespoons of the peanut oil in a wok or Dutch oven. Stir in the chili peppers and cook about 10 seconds. Add the garlic and ginger, and stir-fry 15 seconds more. Remove the garlic mixture from the pan and reserve it. Add 1 tablespoon more peanut oil, allow it to heat, then stir-fry the pork and ham until the pork begins to brown slightly. Stir in the onions and cook 10 seconds longer; transfer the mixture to a bowl. Add a little more peanut oil and quickly stir-fry the shrimp until they are about 75 percent cooked. Transfer them to the meat bowl.

Heat about 3 tablespoons peanut oil and swirl it to coat the pan. Add the vermicelli and toss in the oil until the noodles are coated. Add the peas and toss about 20 seconds more. Make a well in the center of the noodles and pour in the egg yolk and two whole eggs. Allow the eggs to cook undisturbed until almost set, then scramble them quickly into the noodles. Add the curry sauce and shrimp, meats, and garlic mixture. Cover and simmer 2 to 3 minutes until all the liquid is absorbed. Toss to combine the ingredients, then heap the noodles onto a platter and serve immediately.

Makes 4 servings as a meal.

*Plain cooked pork may be substituted.

# Szechwan Red-Cooked Beef over Noodles

⅓ cup peanut or vegetable oil
2½ tablespoons minced ginger
1½ tablespoons minced garlic
2 cups chopped yellow onions
7 green onions, thinly sliced
1 teaspoon Szechwan peppercorns,
   well crushed
1 star anise
5 to 6 teaspoons hot pepper paste
   (see page 30)
2 pounds bottom round or other lean
   stewing beef, cut into ½-inch cubes
1½ teaspoons sugar
3 tablespoons soy sauce
1 cup beef broth
2½ cups water
4½ tablespoons cornstarch mixed with
   6 tablespoons water

1½ pounds fresh Chinese egg noodles
   or fettucelle or tonnarelli, or 1 pound
   dried thin egg noodles

---

Heat the oil in a wok or Dutch oven and add the ginger, garlic, and onions. Stir-fry briskly about 1 minute. Add about two-thirds of the green onions, and stir-fry 10 seconds more. Add the peppercorns and star anise, and stir-fry 10 seconds more. Add the hot pepper paste and stir-fry another 10 seconds. Add the meat and stir-fry about 1 minute, until every piece of meat is partially seared. Sprinkle the sugar and the soy sauce over the mixture and continue to stir-fry 2 minutes more.

Add the broth and water to the mixture and stir well. Bring the liquid to a boil, cover, reduce the heat to very low, and simmer until the meat is fork tender, about 1½ to 2 hours. The dish may be served right away with the noodles, or refrigerated and re-heated. Just before serving, blend in the cornstarch mixture and boil, stirring to thicken the sauce.

Cook the noodles as for sauced noodles (page 14). Serve the noodles in large individual bowls with the meat and sauce poured over them. Garnish each serving with sliced green onion.

Makes 6 servings as a main course.

# Cold Tofu "Noodle" with
# Spicy Sesame Sauce

The meaty, slightly chewy texture of the "noodles" (actually pressed tofu strips in this recipe) are a perfect match for the outspoken flavors in the sauce; the bland tofu seems to absorb and mellow their sharpness. If you can't get tofu noodles, please don't overlook this sauce—it is outstanding on egg or wheat noodles too.

> 8 ounces fresh pressed tofu noodle strips, or 10 ounces fresh Chinese wheat or egg noodles or fresh spaghettini (page 15), or 7 ounces dried noodles
> Spicy Sesame Sauce (following)
> ½ teaspoon Szechwan peppercorns, freshly ground (optional)
> 1 tablespoon roasted sesame seeds

If you are using the tofu strips, bring 3 quarts water to a boil. Place the tofu strips in a colander and pour the boiling water over them, gently turning them with tongs once or twice to expose all the strips to the water. Rinse the strips under warm water until the water runs clear. Allow the strips to drain, then chill them in a large bowl. If you are using the wheat noodles or spaghettini, cook them for cold noodles as directed on page 15.

Prepare the Spicy Sesame Sauce and cool it to room temperature. Pour the sauce over the chilled tofu strips or noodles and mix together well. Heap the noodles on a platter and garnish with ground peppercorns and sesame seeds.

Serves 4 as part of a meal.

### Spicy Sesame Sauce

> 1½ tablespoons vegetable oil
> 3 green onions, white parts only, minced
> 3 cloves garlic, minced
> ½-inch-long piece fresh ginger, minced
> 2 small, dried Asian chili peppers, snipped with scissors
> 3½ teaspoons Chinese red vinegar, or 3 teaspoons rice vinegar
> 3½ tablespoons soy sauce (or more to taste)
> 1 tablespoon sugar
> 1 tablespoon Chinese sesame paste, or tahini
> ⅓ to ½ cup chicken stock or broth
> 1 teaspoon Oriental sesame oil

In a small skillet or saucepan, heat the vegetable oil and saute the onions, garlic, ginger, and chili peppers until the garlic is soft but not brown. Turn off the heat and add the vinegar, soy sauce, sugar, sesame paste, and ⅓ cup chicken stock. Turn on the heat and simmer the sauce, stirring, for 2 minutes. (Because the density of sesame pastes varies greatly, you may want to add more chicken stock to the sauce.) Stir in the sesame oil.

# Composed Salad with Spicy Sesame Dressing

Double recipe Spicy Sesame Sauce
(page 152)
10 ounces fresh or 8 ounces dried thin
Chinese egg noodles, cooked for cold
noodles (page 15), or 8 ounces tofu
noodles (page 152)
⅔ cup each fine carrot matchsticks, diced
cucumber, and diced jicama
1 large whole chicken breast, cooked,
skinned, boned, and shredded
1 red bell pepper, cut into strips
About 1 cup jicama cut into ⅜-inch by
2¼-inch strips
½ peeled and seeded cucumber, cut into
half circles
Szechwan peppercorns, ground (optional)
Roasted sesame seeds
Chinese chives, cut into 2-inch lengths,
or thinly sliced green onion for
garnishing

---

Prepare the sauce. Chill the noodles, then mix them with the carrots, diced cucumber, diced jicama, and chicken. Using your fingers or rubber spatulas, toss them gently with the dressing. Heap the salad on a platter and decorate the circumference of the platter with the bell pepper, jicama strips, and cucumber half circles. Sprinkle the top of the salad with the ground peppercorns, sesame seeds, and chives.

Serves 6 to 8 as part of a multi-dish meal.

# T'ung Ching Street Szechwan Sauced Noodles

These noodles were once sold from handcarts on Copper Well Street. The carts eventually evolved into a restaurant and these are the noodles that made it famous.

Noodle purists may feel that any garnish that came between a well-made noodle and this strangely addictive sauce would ruin the dish. But I love both plain sauced noodles and the following Tossed Noodle salad.

**Plain Tossed Noodles**

14 ounces fresh Chinese egg noodles or
spaghettini, or 10 ounces dried noodles

*Sauce*

1 teaspoon Szechwan peppercorns
1 tablespoon finely minced ginger
1 tablespoon finely minced garlic
6 tablespoons Chinese black soy sauce
3 tablespoons plus 2¼ teaspoons
Chinese black vinegar *(chenkong)*,
or red rice vinegar
4 teaspoons sugar
3 tablespoons Oriental sesame oil
1 teaspoon chili oil, or more to taste

Chinese chives, cut into 2-inch lengths,
or green onions, minced

---

Cook the noodles as directed for cold noodles (page 15) and chill them.

Crush the peppercorns finely in a mortar. In a bowl, combine the ginger, garlic, soy sauce, black vinegar, sugar, sesame oil, and chili oil. Stir to thoroughly dissolve the sugar. Stir in the peppercorns. Allow the sauce to sit at room temperature about an hour.

Toss the sauce with the noodles and serve. Garnish the noodles with a few slivers of Chinese chives or a sprinkling of minced green onions.

Serves 8 as an appetizer.

## Cold Spiced Noodle Salad with Chicken and Cucumber

> 12 ounces fresh Chinese egg noodles or spaghettini, or 10 ounces dried noodles
> 12 ounces skinned, boned chicken breast, cooked
> 1 cup jicama, cut into pieces ⅛-inch wide and 2 inches long
> 1¼ cups cucumbers, peeled, seeded, and cut into strips ⅛-inch wide and 2 inches long
> ¾ cup shredded carrots
> 1 cup tiny cooked shrimp, or ⅔ cup Black Forest ham cut into fine dice
> Sauce mixture (see Plain Tossed Noodles, page 153)
> Lettuce leaves

Cook the noodles as directed for cold noodles (page 15), cut into approximately 8-inch lengths, and chill them. Cut the chicken into fine slivers. In a large bowl, combine the chicken, jicama, cucumbers, carrots, and shrimp or ham. Add the noodles to the mixture in the bowl and toss with half of the sauce mixture, using two rubber spatulas. Line a platter with lettuce leaves and arrange the noodles on them. Add more dressing to taste.

Serves 6 as the main part of a meal or 8 as an appetizer.

# Two Sides Brown

Legend has it that Two Sides Brown, sometimes called Two Faces Yellow, was the ancestor of American *chow mein*. But, oh, how different is this pillow of crisply-fried-outside, tender-on-the-inside, noodle cake when compared with the canned, crisp noodles of yesterday's American Chinese restaurants. Real Two Sides Brown provides a good backdrop for any stir-fry or braised dish with plenty of sauce.

Even if you lack the skills of a Chinese restaurant chef, it is easy enough to form the noodles into a pancake in a pie plate or cake pan while they are slightly warm, chill the noodle cake, and then saute it.

½ pound ¹⁄₁₆-inch fresh Chinese egg noodles, spaghettini or tonnarelli
1 teaspoon Oriental sesame oil
½ teaspoon salt
About ⅓ cup peanut or vegetable oil

**Basic method.** Barely cook the noodles in boiling water—they will cook further when they are fried. Immediately rinse the noodles under cold water, drain them, and spread them out on a tea towel or layers of paper toweling; pat them completely dry. Put the noodles in a bowl, sprinkle them with sesame oil and salt, and toss gently with your fingers to coat every noodle.

Heat a very heavy 12-inch skillet and add half the peanut oil, swirling the pan to coat it with oil. Heat the oil until almost smoking. Beginning at the pan's outer edge and working toward the center, coil the noodles into the pan. Press the noodles into the pan with a pancake turner, cover, and cook until the underside is browned, about 3 to 5 minutes. Loosen the pancake with a spatula. Place a very large plate, pan lid, or light cutting board over the pan and invert the noodle cake. Invert again onto another plate, lid, or board. Add the remaining peanut oil to the pan and,

when it is hot, slide the noodle cake back into the pan, press the cake with a pancake turner, and cook, covered, until the other side is browned (about 5 to 8 minutes). Loosen the cake and slide it onto a platter.

**Formed-cake method.** Cook the noodles slightly less than those you would rinse immediately with cold water; they will continue to cook by their own internal heat. Drain the noodles well, rinse them with warm water, and drain well again, swirling them in a colander to rid them of water. Spread them briefly on toweling. Put the noodles in a bowl, sprinkle them with sesame oil and salt, and toss gently with your fingers to coat every noodle. Heap the noodles into a 9- or 10-inch pie plate or round cake pan. Cover and refrigerate the noodles. (The noodles can even be weighted slightly with a light weight as they refrigerate.) Heat a very heavy 12-inch skillet and add 2½ tablespoons peanut oil. Turn the noodles into the hot oil all at once (or slide them out of the pie pan into the oil if that works better for you) and fry the noodles as directed above.

Garnish the noodles, leaving the rim of the cake showing, with any of the following toppings or with one of your own. Leftovers, wrapped tightly in foil, may be reheated in a moderate oven.

Makes 4 servings.

# Shrimp in "Lobster Sauce" on Two Sides Brown

This is a delicious example of how to use your favorite stir-fried or sauced Chinese dishes as a noodle garnish. Here, the famous restaurant dish of "lobster sauce," that is, sauce *for* not *of* lobster, is combined with shrimp to make an excellent topping for Two Sides Brown. It would also be fine on stir-fried or even plain boiled noodles.

> 1¼ pounds medium shrimp, shelled and deveined
> 1 egg white
> 2½ tablespoons Chinese rice wine, or dry sherry
> 2¼ teaspoons cornstarch
> 5 teaspoons soy sauce
> ¼ teaspoon sugar
> Pinch of salt
> 1½ cups chicken broth
> 1¼ cups peanut or vegetable oil
> 3 large cloves garlic, sliced
> 8 ounces ground pork
> 1½ tablespoons fermented black beans, rinsed and chopped
> 1 tablespoon chopped ginger
> 3 green onions, cut into 1½-inch lengths
> 2 tablespoons cornstarch dissolved in ¼ cup cold chicken broth
> 2 eggs
> 1½ teaspoons Oriental sesame oil
> 2 recipes Two Sides Brown (page 154)

Cut the shrimp in half lengthwise and make three shallow diagonal slashes on the back of each shrimp half. Whisk together the egg white, ½ tablespoon wine, and the cornstarch. Add the shrimp and stir until each piece is completely coated. Marinate for at least 1 hour. Combine the soy sauce, sugar, salt, chicken broth, and the remaining 2 tablespoons wine in a bowl and set aside.

In a wok or deep skillet, heat all but 2 tablespoons of the peanut oil. Drop in the garlic pieces and fry them about 10 seconds. Remove the garlic with a slotted spoon and reserve it. Add about a fourth of the shrimp, one piece at a time, and fry a few seconds until they are pink and barely firm. Remove from the oil and drain on paper toweling. Repeat with the remaining shrimp.

Pour the oil from the wok or skillet into a can and wipe out the pan. Heat the remaining 2 tablespoons of the peanut oil and fry the reserved garlic again about 10 seconds. Remove the garlic and discard it. Add the pork to the pan and cook, stirring over high heat, breaking any lumps as you stir. When the pork is almost browned, stir in the black beans and ginger. When no pink pork remains, add the onions, stir in the chicken broth mixture, and mix together well. Stir the cornstarch-broth mixture into the sauce and cook, stirring until the sauce thickens and

*Asian Pasta*

becomes clear. Remove from the heat and add the two eggs without stirring them. Cover the pan until the egg whites are set and the yolks are still runny. You may need to turn the heat on for a few seconds if the whites do not firm up.

Sprinkle the sesame oil over the pork and soy sauce and add the shrimp to the pan. Allow the dish to stand just until the shrimp are warmed through. Stir to distribute the egg evenly. Pour the shrimp in its sauce over Two Sides Brown or any other cooked noodles.

Serves 6 as the main part of a meal or 8 as a side dish.

# Tangerine Braised Duck on Two Sides Brown

8 to 9 medium, dried Chinese mushrooms
One 4- to 4½-pound duckling, cut into
    1½-inch pieces
1 large yellow onion, cut lengthwise into
    thin strips
2 cloves garlic, sliced lengthwise
5 slices ginger, sliced ⅛-inch thick
Peel of 1 tangerine, cut into strips and
    dried (page 33)
Braising Liquid (following)
¾ cup slivered bamboo shoots

1 tablespoon cornstarch
1½ tablespoons cold water
1 teaspoon Oriental sesame oil
2 recipes Two Sides Brown (page 154)
Chinese chives, or minced green onions
    and coriander sprigs

---

Cover the mushrooms with 1¼ cups warm water and weight them with a small bowl or cup. When the mushrooms are softened, remove them from the water, squeezing them over the bowl to release any liquid; remove the tough stems and cut the caps into strips. Reserve the mushroom liquid for the Braising Liquid. Cut as much fat as possible from the duck. Heat a large wok or two skillets and brown the duckling pieces, turning them occasionally. Spoon off and discard all but 1 tablespoon duck fat and brown the onion. Transfer the duck and the onion to a large pot suitable for braising.

Pound the garlic and ginger slices with a cleaver or the flat side of a chef's knife. Add to the duck and onion the garlic, ginger, and tangerine peel. Make the Braising Liquid (recipe follows) and deglaze the duck pan(s) with it, scraping the crisp brown bits from the pan(s). Transfer the braising liquid to the casserole and add the braising spices. Cover the pan and simmer the duck about 1½ hours. Add the bamboo shoots and mushrooms, and cook about 30 minutes more, or until the duck is very tender.

Remove the duck and vegetables with a slotted spoon. Pour the liquid into a glass measuring cup. Remove the anise, cinnamon stick, and the tangerine peel and discard. If there is less than 1¼ cups liquid, add more chicken stock to make up the difference. Degrease the liquid and return it to the pot. Mix the cornstarch and water together and add it to the liquid in the pot. Cook, stirring slowly over moderate heat, until the mixture boils and thickens. Stir in the sesame oil.

Make two recipes Two Sides Brown. The duck may be served with the bone, or you may want to remove the meat from the bone. Return the duck and vegetables to the pan to heat them. Pour the duck and sauce over the Two Sides Brown and garnish with chives cut into 2-inch lengths or a sprinkling of minced green onions and coriander sprigs.

Serves 6 as the main part of the meal.

**Braising Liquid**

⅔ cup soaking liquid from the mushrooms
¾ cup or more chicken stock or broth
⅓ cup Chinese rice wine, or dry sherry
5 tablespoons soy sauce
¼ teaspoon sugar
⅓ cup *hoisin* sauce
1 star anise

½ cinnamon stick
2 tiny dried Asian chili peppers, split, or
¾ teaspoon crushed Asian pepper

Mix the first six ingredients together to deglaze the duck pan; then add the anise, cinnamon, and peppers to the casserole.

# "Soup Noodle," Cantonese Style

The "soup noodle" is the mainstay of Cantonese noodle houses throughout the world. It is not a soup, but noodles in a little broth served with a variety of toppings. I first ran into them not in the Orient, but in Toronto, Canada, where, exausted from a day of hardcore sightseeing, I found myself in one of those wonderful hole-in-the-wall-restaurant areas that typify Chinatowns everywhere. Posted unceremoniously, the curled-edged menu of one of the restaurants listed a full page of soup noodle. Through the window I could see a few solitary diners concentrating single-mindedly on their servings of noodles. I went inside to join them. The food was so simple and delicious that I now look for soup noodle eating places wherever I am. I have found them in Seattle, New York, and San Francisco; in Los Angeles' Monterey Park and in London's Soho; and, yes, in Tokyo. Since space does not permit the inclusion of recipes for all the best-known soup noodles, I am providing instead a basic broth recipe and a few suggestions for creating your own variations.

# Quick Basic Broth for Soup Noodles

5 cups water
One 14½-ounce can regular-strength chicken broth
1 or 2 pork chop bones (optional)
About 1 pound of chicken bones, or backs, necks, and wings
1 teaspoon salt
6 peppercorns
1 tablespoon light soy sauce
1 slice ginger, crushed

Combine all the ingredients in a 3-quart pot. Bring the broth to a boil and cook, skimming any foam that rises to the surface after 15 minutes. Cover the pan and simmer the

stock at least 1 hour, or cook overnight in a crockpot. Strain and discard all but the broth.

Makes about 6½ cups of broth.

**Emergency Broth**

Say you've just rushed in, taken some frozen fresh Chinese noodles from the freezer, and you need broth within the next half hour. Here is a way to get almost-from-scratch-tasting broth, using canned broth. The canned taste will have been alleviated by the fresh ingredients.

Simmer one or two 14½-ounce cans regular-strength chicken broth mixed with ⅔ cup water for each can, a slice of onion, and any cooked chicken or pork bones you have* for about 20 minutes. Strain the broth.

*Try to keep a few leftover bones or a chicken back in the freezer for these occasions.

# Classic Barbecued Pork
# Soup Noodles and Variations

6 cups Quick Basic Broth (page 159)
2½ teaspoons Chinese rice wine, or dry
    sherry
Salt or light soy sauce
½ teaspoon Oriental sesame oil
1 pound broccoli, or variation (following)
1 pound Chinese Barbecued Pork (page
    23), or variation (following)
12 ounces fresh Chinese noodles (either
    flat or string shaped)
1 green onion, minced

Combine the broth and wine in a large pot and simmer a few minutes to blend the flavors. Remove from the heat and blend in salt or soy sauce to taste and the sesame oil.

Cut the broccoli florets from their stems. Peel the top half of the stems and cut into matchsticks. Discard tough portion of broccoli stems. Blanch or steam all the broccoli until it is bright green and crisp-tender. Cut the pork into 2-inch by ½-inch slices. Cook the noodles as for noodles to be used hot (page 14).

Divide the noodles among individual serving bowls. Heat the pork slices in the broth and ladle the pork and broth over the noodles. Top each serving with broccoli and a sprinkling of green onions.

Serves 4 as a main course or 6 as part of a multi-dish meal.

*Meat variations*

Try substituting poultry, such as roast or barbecued chicken or duck, for the pork. The usual way to serve it is to slice the breast and thigh meat, then cut the bonier parts into 1½-inch pieces. Put a little of both the meat and bony parts on each serving.

One pound plain roasted or simply simmered pork or beef, cut into ¾-inch by 2-inch thin slices, or Barbecued Meat Balls (page 74), makes a good soup noodle topping.

*Seafood variations*

Substitute 1 pound cooked shrimp, cooked scallops, or squid rings, 1 recipe fish balls (page 114) or shrimp balls (page 76), or fish cake purchased in an Asian market for the pork.

*Vegetable variations*

Replace the broccoli with cooked Chinese broccoli and leaves, Chinese chives, plain or braised bamboo shoots, blanched bean sprouts, blanched bok choy or Nappa cabbage cut crosswise into ribbons, blanched spinach or mustard greens cut crosswise into ribbons, tiny tender peas, blanched snow peas, jicama cut into matchsticks or fresh sliced water chestnuts.

# Fish-Fillet Soup Noodles
## with Dipping Sauce

Sometimes soup noodles are served with a dip or condiment on the side so diners can flavor their dish as they will.

> 1¼ pounds skinless fish fillets: whitefish, cod, haddock, halibut, scrod, sea bass, or rock cod, red snapper, or other rockfish
> 2 teaspoons Chinese rice wine, or dry sherry
> 1 tablespoon light soy sauce
> 1 tablespoon minced ginger
> ⅜ teaspoon salt
> Dash white pepper
> 1 tablespoon cornstarch
> 12 ounces fresh Chinese egg noodles, or 9 ounces dried egg noodles
> 4½ cups Quick Basic Broth (page 159)
> ⅔ cup water
> Dipping Sauce (following)

Wipe the fillets with damp paper towels and cut the fish into 1-inch by 2-inch pieces. Combine the wine, soy sauce, ginger, salt, pepper, and cornstarch and blend together well. Mix in the fish pieces, being sure to coat every piece with the mixture. Allow to marinate at least 30 minutes.

Cook the noodles as for noodles to be used hot (page 14). When the fish is marinated, combine the broth and water in a large pot and bring it to a boil. Drop half the fish pieces in, a piece at a time; cook the fillets 2 minutes, or until firm and opaque, then remove them with a slotted spoon or Chinese wire mesh ladle. Cook the other half of the fish, then return the first half of the fish to the pot.

Divide the noodles among individual serving bowls and pour the broth and some fish over the noodles. Serve with individual bowls of the Dipping Sauce.

Serves 4 as a main course or 6 as a first course.

### Dipping Sauce

> ¼ cup peanut oil
> ¼ cup minced green onions
> 1½ tablespoons minced fresh chili peppers, or 2 teaspoons Chinese chili paste
> ½ teaspoon sugar
> 2 tablespoons brown bean paste
> 2 teaspoons Oriental sesame oil
> 2 tablespoons chicken broth

Stir all the ingredients until the bean paste and oil are well mixed.

# Egg Noodles in Rich *Hoisin* Gravy

2 tablespoons *hoisin* sauce
2 tablespoons soy sauce
2 teaspoons Oriental sesame oil
3 cups chicken stock or broth
2 tablespoons peanut or vegetable oil
2 large cloves garlic, minced
1 tablespoon minced ginger
1 pound pork butt or boneless loin, coarsely minced (not ground)
1 tablespoon Chinese rice wine, or dry sherry
3 tablespoons cornstarch mixed with 6 tablespoons water or meat stock
Chili oil
1 pound fresh Chinese egg noodles, or 12 ounces dried
1½ cups bean sprouts, blanched
2 Oriental or pickling cucumbers, peeled, seeded, and cut into strips ⅛-inch wide and 2 inches long

In a bowl, whisk together the *hoisin* sauce, soy sauce, ½ teaspoon of the sesame oil, and the chicken stock. Heat the peanut oil in a wok and stir-fry the garlic and ginger about 45 seconds, until the garlic softens. Add the pork and stir-fry until it is nicely browned, about 2 minutes. Add the rice wine and stir-fry 30 seconds more. Add the *hoisin* mixture and blend it in well. Add the cornstarch mixture and stir until the sauce thickens. Season to taste with chili oil and keep warm.

Cook the noodles in boiling salted water about 1 minute, or until *al dente*. Drain well and spread on paper toweling a minute to absorb excess moisture. Toss the noodles together with 1½ teaspoons sesame oil. Divide the noodles among six bowls, pour on the meat and sauce, and garnish with bean sprouts and cucumber.

Serves 4 as a main course or 6 as part of a multi-dish meal.

# Gingered Lamb on Crisp Bean Thread Noodles

There are a good many ways to top these effervescent puffs of deep-fried bean thread. This especially pungent topping seems to best complement the wonderfully textured but bland fried noodle—a good marriage.

1 boneless shoulder or leg lamb chop, weighing 1 pound with the fat, partially frozen
6 wafer-thin ginger slices, peeled and cut into toothpick-size pieces
About 5 tablespoons peanut or vegetable oil
3 tablespoons minced ginger

½ cup minced yellow onion
2 small cloves garlic, minced
1½ cups regular strength beef broth
2 ounces bean threads (fen si)
8 fresh water chestnuts, sliced, or ⅔ cup
   finely diced jicama
½ red bell pepper
½ green bell pepper
1 teaspoon sugar
4 teaspoons soy sauce
1 tablespoon Chinese black vinegar, or
   rice vinegar
4 teaspoons cornstarch mixed with
   3 tablespoons water

---

Remove the fat from the lamb chop and mince it; you will need about ⅓ cup minced fat. Slice the lamb meat as thinly as possible, then cut each slice into ¼-inch-thick strips. Line up the meat strips and cut several at a time into tiny minced pieces. Put the ginger sticks into a small bowl of ice water and refrigerate.

In a skillet, combine 2 tablespoons of the oil and the lamb fat, and heat slowly about 5 minutes, until the fat is melted. Turn up the heat, add the minced ginger and onion, and stir-fry until the onion begins to look translucent. Add the garlic and stir-fry about 1 minute more. Add the minced lamb and stir-fry until it is nicely browned. Add the broth,

cover the pan, and simmer 6 minutes. Remove from the heat.

In a wok, pour oil to a depth of about 4½ inches. Heat the oil until a bean thread puffs and floats immediately upon contact with the oil. Add the noodles in four batches, pushing them down into the oil several seconds and turning them once when they rise to the surface of the oil. Drain each batch on paper toweling. Keep the noodles warm in a barely warm oven, or reheat them briefly in a 350° oven just before serving.

Just before serving, heat 2 tablespoons oil in the wok. Stir-fry the water chestnuts about 1 minute and remove from the pan with a slotted spoon. Next stir-fry the peppers until the color is bright and they barely begin to soften; remove from the pan.

Combine the sugar, soy sauce, vinegar, and cornstarch in a small bowl and add it to the lamb mixture. Cook, stirring, until the sauce thickens and is clear.

Drain the ginger sticks and stir them and the water chestnuts into the lamb and sauce. Transfer the bean threads to a large serving platter. Pour the lamb and sauce into the center of the bean threads, leaving a puffy white rim of bean threads around the edge. Garnish the sauce with the red and green peppers and serve immediately.

Serves 6 as part of a multi-dish meal.

# THE PASTAS OF KOREA

"We Koreans are spoiled," Heisun Chung told me. "When it comes to Chinese-style noodles, we like them hand-tossed, and in summertime we like our *naeng myun* [cold buckwheat noodles] freshly made." In Los Angeles, more restaurants in Koreatown than in Chinatown offer hand-tossed noodles, and numerous others make their own fresh *naeng myun* daily. Several Korean-American noodle manufacturers satisfy quality-conscious noodle lovers by selling fresh-frozen noodles in many Korean supermarkets.

Seoul, the capital of South Korea, is an Oriental noodle lover's paradise. Koreans love to eat noodles at the city's many Chinese and Japanese restaurants as much as they enjoy their own traditional noodle specialties. Restaurants serve noodles as part of a full meal, and countless tiny snack shops list at least one Chinese or Japanese noodle dish on the menu.

The huge East Gate Market, some 10 blocks square, loaded with everything from exotic silks to camping gear, is also a good place for foot-weary shoppers to try out some of the simpler noodle specialties. Hundreds of stalls are crowded under tentlike roofs. At the long wooden counters, perched on tiny stools, customers can order a variety of *gougsou* (noodle) dishes. Even though *mak gougsou* means "not well made," it is nonetheless a popular favorite. The use of machine-made noodles and the rather unglamorous circumstances in which the noodles are served account for its unfortunate name. But the broth and noodles, topped with sliced fish cake, pickles, and, if one likes, dried red pepper flakes, can be addicting. Another favorite is *bibim* (mixed up) *gougsou*, garnished with marinated vegetables, strips of deep-fried tofu, and sometimes fish cake, tossed with a chili sauce. *Ramen* dishes or Japanese *udon* dishes are sold here too.

The market is not the only place to find noodles. Throughout the city, especially near factories and college campuses, are shops offering seasonal noodle favorites—hot dishes in winter and cold in summer. Western palates will find *khong goug,* chilled noodles in an icy bowl of soy milk, surprisingly refreshing. Japanese-style buckwheat noodles on their basket trays are another summer standby for hungry students who often consume several trayfuls. At the end of the meal, the server tallies the bill by counting the stacked empty trays.

In wintertime, *khal gougsou* ("knife noodles")—chewy and thick wheat noodles in a hearty broth—provide rib-sticking fare. Not all stores cut their noodles by hand these days, but the ones that do usually have a long line of customers. *Khal gougsou* restaurants often stay open late at night to accommodate groups of men who have been out for a social evening.

For more formal or complex noodle dishes, one must go to a restaurant. Two classic examples are variations of *naeng myun* (cold noodles), based on fine, chewy buckwheat and potato-starch noodles. *Mool naeng myun* (see page 175) is the name for freshly made noodles in a bowl of chilled broth beneath many layers of elegantly arranged garnishes. *Bibim naeng myun* consists of the same noodles in a fiercely hot chili sauce laced with plenty of garlic and roasted sesame seeds. Both dishes are served in huge porcelain bowls, about 10 inches in diameter, and, in Korea, are usually reserved for warm-weather months. In Los Angeles they are available year-round, perhaps because of the mild climate or less traditional atmosphere. A dish that is closer to Chinese but still unmistakably Korean is *chap chae,* a festive looking stir-fried mixture of *dang myun* (springy potato-starch noodles, which resemble very coarse cellophane noodles), slivered meat, and finely cut vegetables.

The availability of all these noodle styles reflects Korea's past as a bridge between mainland China and Japan. Over the past 400 years, Korea has passed along Chinese artforms and other aspects of Chinese civilization to Japan, but not before they had been influenced considerably by Korean culture. Writing and simple rustic pottery are two examples. Superficially, especially in Korean cities, one gets the impression of strong Chinese and Japanese influences. A closer look, though, shows how strongly Koreans have clung to their ancient ways and traditions, never allowing outside influences to overshadow a characteristic Koreanness.

As with many Korean foods, garlic, soy sauce, sesame seeds, and oil and red pepper boldly flavor many noodle dishes. Others are more delicately subtle. Beef, though not often used elsewhere in the Orient, is a frequent noodle accompaniment in Korea—a possible legacy from Mongolian ancestors. □

# THE VARIETIES OF KOREAN PASTA

Though *gougsou* is the Korean word for noodle, the Chinese term, *myun,* is frequently used even in reference to non-Chinese-style noodle dishes.

In addition to the Chinese and Japanese noodles enjoyed in Korea, these are the specifically Korean noodle types:

## 1. DANG MYUN

You can't miss these huge packages—over a foot long and 8 inches wide—on the market shelf. The light, greyish tan noodles are a close relative of cellophane noodles, with the same resilient texture and transparency when cooked. They are made from potato and sweet potato starch and must be soaked in boiling water for 10 minutes before they are used in stir-fries, soups, or other dishes.

## 2. GOUGSOU

The Korean generic term for noodle and the word used for long thin wheat-flour noodles. They are used in soups and in *bibim gougsou,* garnished with *kimchee* (spicy Korean pickled cabbage) and spicy chili-garlic sauce.

## 3. NAENG MYUN

Literally means "cold noodle," and that is usually the way these buckwheat and potato-starch noodles are served. Some commercial brands use cornstarch in place of potato starch. *Naeng myun* are paler and chewier than Japanese buckwheat noodles *(soba).* The dried *naeng myun* require only about 1 minute of boiling; fresh-frozen *naeng myun* cook in seconds, just long enough for them to thaw. Package directions on the frozen varieties are usually quite reliable.

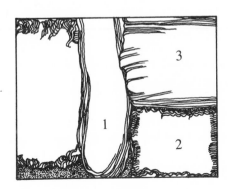

# Korean Vermicelli and Chicken
# and Sesame Seed Stir-Fry

4 or 5 dried Chinese or Japanese mushrooms
1½ pounds skinless, boneless chicken
   meat, partially frozen
6 green onions
About ⅓ cup soy sauce
8 ounces Korean vermicelli *(dang myun),*
   or coarse bean threads
2 medium carrots
⅓ pound green beans
⅓ cup vegetable oil
1 cup fresh bean sprouts
⅓ cup ground roasted sesame seeds
4 cloves garlic, minced
¼ teaspoon sugar
Freshly ground black pepper
Pinch of cayenne pepper

---

Soak the mushrooms in warm water to
cover until they soften, about 20 minutes. Cut
the chicken meat with the grain into ½-inch-
wide strips; then cut each strip into ⅛-inch-
thick slices. Mince the white part of one
green onion and combine it with 1 tablespoon
of the soy sauce and the chicken; mix well
and allow to marinate 20 minutes. Slice the
white and green parts of the rest of the onions
thinly and set aside. In a large pot, soak the
vermicelli in water to cover until it is soft,
about 20 minutes. Drain the mushrooms,
squeezing them dry; discard the tough stems,
and cut the caps into thin strips. Bring the
vermicelli to a boil and simmer ½ minute;
drain and rinse with cold water. Spread the
vermicelli on paper toweling to dry slightly,
then cut into 8-inch lengths. Cut the carrots
diagonally into very thin slices. Slice the
beans diagonally at ½-inch intervals.

Heat 1 tablespoon of the oil in a wok or
large skillet. Add the sliced green onions and
mushrooms, and stir-fry ½ minute. Add the
bean sprouts and 1 tablespoon of the sesame
seeds, and stir-fry ½ minute more. Transfer
the mixture from the pan to a small plate and
reserve it. Add another tablespoon oil to the
pan and stir-fry the carrots and beans for 5
minutes. Add the garlic, sugar, 10 turns of the
pepper mill, cayenne, 3 tablespoons of the
soy sauce, and 1 tablespoon of the sesame
seeds. Cook the mixture about 3 minutes until
the vegetables are crisp-tender. Transfer them
to a plate.

Add 1 tablespoon oil to the pan, add the
chicken, and stir-fry until the chicken is
opaque throughout. Stir in 1 more tablespoon
soy sauce, then transfer the chicken to a bowl
with a slotted spoon, leaving any pan juices
behind. Add 2 tablespoons oil to the pan.
When the oil is hot, stir in the noodles, and
stir-fry until they are heated through. Stir
in the mushroom mixture. Heap the noodles
onto a platter, and place the chicken in the

center of the noodles and the vegetables around the chicken. Sprinkle 1 tablespoon of the soy sauce and 1 tablespoon of the sesame seeds over the top.

Toss the dish at the table and pass the soy sauce and remaining sesame seeds as table condiments.

Serves 4 or 5 as part of a meal.

# Beef Dumplings in Soup
### *Mandu Kugk*

**M***andu*, the plump beef Korean-style dumplings, are a cross between pot stickers and wonton. They appear in soups, as in the following recipe, and pan-fried with a garlicky dipping sauce (see Pan-Fried Beef Dumplings, page 171).

> Half recipe Beef Dumplings (page 170)
> 4 ounces ground beef
> 2 green onions, whites only, minced
> 2 cloves garlic, minced
> Soy sauce
> 2 teaspoons Oriental sesame oil
> ¼ teaspoon salt
> Broth from cooking Beef Dumplings (page 170)
> ⅛ teaspoon freshly ground pepper
> Tops from green onions, thinly sliced

Make the Beef Dumplings. Freeze half for later use or for Pan-Fried Beef Dumplings with Dipping Sauce (page 171). Cook the other half of the dumplings as directed in the dumpling recipe, reserving the cooking broth. In a soup pot, mix the ground beef, onions, garlic, 2 teaspoons soy sauce, sesame oil, salt, and pepper, and cook over medium-high heat, stirring to break up the meat, until the meat is nicely browned. Add 6 cups dumpling broth, adding a little water if necessary to make 6 cups. Simmer 15 minutes. Season to taste with soy sauce. Add the cooked dumplings and simmer until they are heated through. Garnish with sliced green onion tops.

Serves 5 to 6 as a main dish or 6 as a hearty first course.

## Traditional additions

Remove the warm dumplings from the broth, then add *1 cup bean sprouts* or *2 ounces soaked Korean vermicelli (dang myun,* page 167); or drizzle *one or two lightly beaten eggs* into the simmering broth, breaking up any clumps with a fork. Simmer them 2 minutes. Return the dumplings to the soup and garnish with green onion tops. Any combination of additions may be used.

# Korean Beef Dumplings
*Kogi Mandu*

Take advantage of the versatility of these tasty dumplings, or *mandu,* by forming half of the dumplings into a hat shape for the Dumplings in Beef Soup recipe, and the other half into a flat triangular or flat semicircular form for the Pan-Fried Dumplings with Dipping Sauce. The dumplings may be frozen on a plate and then wrapped in foil.

> About ½ pound Nappa cabbage (one-third medium head)
> ¾ teaspoon salt
> 8 ounces minced or ground beef chuck
> ⅓ cup chopped green onions, white part only
> 1 clove garlic, minced
> 1 tablespoon soy sauce
> 2 teaspoons toasted sesame seeds, crushed
> 2 teaspoons Oriental sesame oil
> ⅛ teaspoon freshly ground pepper
> 35 to 40 round or square wonton wrappers
> 5 cups beef broth*
> Water

Sprinkle the cabbage leaves with ½ teaspoon salt and let stand about 15 minutes until they wilt. Squeeze out any moisture, then rinse and dry the leaves thoroughly. Chop the cabbage and measure 1⅔ cups.

In a medium bowl, combine the cabbage, beef, onions, garlic, soy sauce, sesame seeds, sesame oil, pepper, and ¼ teaspoon salt, and mix thoroughly. To make each dumpling, place 1½ teaspoons filling in the center of a wrapper using two spoons. Fold the wonton wrapper over the filling in a semicircle for the round wrappers or a triangle for the square wrappers. Seal the edges by moistening them with a little water and pinching them. (To form hat-shaped *mandu* for soups, moisten the corners of the semicircular dumplings and bring them together, pinching them so that the dumpling forms a sort of fat tortellini.) Keep both wonton skins and dumplings moist under plastic or damp towels as you work.

In a large pot, bring 5 cups of broth and 2 cups of water to a rolling boil. Drop in five or six dumplings and simmer until the skins are tender and the filling feels firm. Remove the dumplings with a slotted spoon. Cook the remaining dumplings, five or six at a time. When you have finished cooking the dumplings, reserve the broth for the Beef Dumplings in Soup recipe.

Makes 35 to 40 dumplings.

*The broth from Korean Broth with Pressed Beef (page 174) is ideal for this recipe. If you make it, there will be enough broth for Chilled Buckwheat Noodles and Beef in Cold Broth (page 173) and Beef Dumplings in Soup (page 169), and enough meat for the Chilled Buckweat Noodles and Beef in Cold Broth (page 173) and Korean Gardens' Cold Mixed Noodles (page 175).

# Pan-Fried Beef Dumplings with Dipping Sauce

*Koon Mandu*

Although the hat-shaped *mandu* used in soups may also be fried, my Korean friend, Sue Coe, told me she has childhood memories of her mother making hat-shaped dumplings with round pasta wrappers for soups and flatter triangular dumplings, made with square wonton wrappers, for frying. This is not a strict rule, however.

> ½ recipe boiled Beef Dumplings (page 170)
> 4 tablespoons soy sauce
> 1 large clove garlic
> ½ teaspoon sugar
> 1¼ teaspoons vinegar
> 1/16 teaspoon ground chili peppers or chili powder
> 4 teaspoons minced green onion
> 1¼ teaspoons roasted sesame seeds
> 1¼ teaspoons Oriental sesame oil
> ¼ cup vegetable oil

Drain the dumplings and put aside. Pour the soy sauce into a small bowl. With a mallet or side of a cleaver, crush the garlic to a paste between two pieces of wax paper. Stir the garlic into the soy sauce and stir in the sugar, vinegar, chili peppers, onion, sesame seeds, and sesame oil.

Heat half the vegetable oil in a large heavy skillet and add enough dumplings to cover the bottom of the pan. Fry the dump-lings over medium-high heat, turning several times until they are golden brown. Remove the dumplings and place on absorbent toweling. Repeat with the remaining dumplings. Serve the dumplings with individual dishes of dipping sauce.

Serves 4 or 5 as an hors d'oeuvre.

# Stir-Fried Korean Vermicelli with Beef and Vegetables

*Chap Chae*

Dang myun, potato starch vermicelli, are stir-fried *chow mein*-style with beef strips, lots of garlic, and a sesame and soy-flavored sauce of typical Korean flavorings in this recipe for *chap chae*.

> About ⅓ cup tree ears
> 1¼ pound beef top round or sirloin, cut into strips ⅛-inch-wide by 2 inches long
> 1½ teaspoons sugar
> 5½ tablespoons soy sauce
> 3 green onions, minced
> 2½ teaspoons minced garlic
> 1 tablespoon roasted ground sesame seeds
> ¼ teaspoon freshly ground pepper
> 1 tablespoon Oriental sesame oil

8 ounces Korean vermicelli *(dang myun)*, or coarse bean threads
Vegetable oil
2 eggs, lightly beaten
1 cup yellow onion, cut lengthwise into slivers
1 large carrot, cut into strips ⅛-inch wide and 2 inches long
1½ cups bean sprouts
½ pound Nappa or white cabbage, coarsely shredded (about 2 cups)
1 Oriental cucumber, cut into strips ⅛-inch wide and 2 inches long
¼ teaspoon salt
Cayenne pepper and soy sauce to taste

Soak the tree ears in warm water to cover until they are soft, about 20 minutes. Place the beef in a medium bowl. In a small bowl, combine ¾ teaspoon of the sugar, 2 tablespoons of the soy sauce, the green onions, garlic, sesame seeds, pepper, and 1 teaspoon of the sesame oil. Pour the sauce over the beef, stir to coat, and let marinate 20 minutes. In a large saucepan, cover the noodles with warm water until they soften.

Film a medium (6- to 8-inch) skillet with oil. Pour in half the egg and swirl it over the bottom of the pan to form a crêpe-like omelette. When the omelette has set, loosen it with a spatula and turn it out onto a plate;

repeat with the remaining egg. When the omelettes have cooled, roll them, one on top of the other, into a cylinder, slice crosswise into thin strips, and reserve. Drain the tree ears. Cut away the tough parts and cut into fine strips. Bring the noodles in the saucepan to a boil and simmer 1 minute. Drain and rinse the noodles in cold water.

Heat about 1½ tablespoons vegetable oil in a wok or large skillet. Add the yellow onion and carrot, and stir-fry until they begin to soften. Add the bean sprouts and cabbage, and stir-fry until they wilt. Stir in the cucumber and cook about 15 seconds. Heap all the vegetables onto a plate.

Heat another tablespoon oil in the wok and add the meat and mushrooms; stir-fry until nicely browned. Stir in the noodles and the remaining 3½ tablespoons soy sauce, ¾ teaspoon sugar, 2 teaspoons sesame oil, and ¼ teaspoon salt. Cook about 1 minute, blending together well. Stir in the vegetables to warm them. Season to taste with cayenne and more soy sauce. Heap onto a plate and garnish with the omelette shreds.

Serves 4 as a meal or 6 as part of a meal.

# Chilled Buckwheat Noodles
# and Beef in Cold Broth
*Mool Naeng Myun*

Ask most Koreans about their favorite noodle and they'll tell you nostalgically about the Seoul noodle shops that serve chewy flavorful noodles in an icy broth. The noodles are swirled into a nest (some restaurants offer scissors at the table to cut them) and topped with pressed braised beef, mild radish *kimchee,* hard-cooked egg, and slices of winter pear. The dish is easy to make, but requires cooking in stages to produce all its diverse components. Everything can be done in advance to make it very convenient to assemble, and you can use the pressed beef and leftover broth from *Bibim Naeng Myun* (page 175) and Dumpling Soup (page 169).

½ recipe White Radish Water Pickle (following)

½ recipe Pressed Beef (page 174), or 1 pound cooked lean beef, thinly sliced

1 recipe Marinated Cucumber (following), or 2 fresh pickling cucumbers sliced lengthwise

2 pounds fresh-frozen Korean buckwheat noodles *(naeng myun),* or 1 pound dried *naeng myun*

Ice cold broth from Korean Broth and Pressed Beef (page 174), or about 6 cups ice cold homemade beef broth

1 Asian pear or other hard pear

2 hard-cooked eggs, shelled and halved lengthwise

2 fresh red or green chili peppers, thinly sliced, or dried crushed chili pepper to taste

Dry mustard

Rice vinegar

Soy sauce

Minced green onions

Prepare the Water Pickle and Korean Broth and Pressed Beef 1 day or more in advance. Prepare the Marinated Cucumber a few hours or up to a day in advance of serving. Cook the fresh noodles* in about 3 quarts of boiling water about 45 seconds, until they are chewy but tender. Rinse with cold water, drain well, and chill the noodles. Or if you are using dried noodles,* soak them in water to cover 20 minutes, then cook 1 minute in 3 quarts of rapidly boiling water; drain, rinse, and chill.

When you are ready to assemble the dish, divide the noodles among four large soup bowls. Swirl the noodles to make a low nest for the other ingredients. Pour broth into the bowl to a level half-way up the noodle nest (about 1 cup broth). Peel, core, and slice the pear lengthwise into thin slices. Arrange about a fourth of the cucumbers in a circle of overlapping slices on top of the noodles. Repeat using six to eight pieces of radish, 4 ounces beef, and a fourth of the pear slices per bowl. Top with half a hard-cooked egg decorated with a few pepper shreds or a sprinkling of crushed pepper.

Mix 4 teaspoons dry mustard with 4 teaspoons water to make a paste. Serve the noodles with the mustard, vinegar, soy sauce, and green onions as table condiments.

Makes 4 servings as a meal.

*To make an even "nest" of noodles when serving, you must tie them at one end before cooking or soaking them so they will stay in one direction. Otherwise make neat mounds of noodles from the noodles that have been cooked without being tied.

### Marinated Cucumber

    2 pickling cucumbers or 1 salad cucumber
    2 tablespoons rice vinegar
    1 tablespoon sugar
    1½ teaspoons salt

Slice the cucumbers lengthwise into slices ⅛-inch thick and 2½ inches long. Stir the remaining ingredients together in a glass or ceramic bowl. Stir in the cucumber. Cover lightly and let sit at room temperature 4 to 5 hours or overnight. Refrigerate until ready to use. Use within 2 or 3 days.

### White Radish Water Pickle

    1 pound daikon radish, sliced 1½ inches by ½ inch by ½ inch
    2 cloves garlic, pressed
    2 slices ginger

    1½ teaspoons cayenne pepper
    1 fresh hot chili pepper, sliced lengthwise
    1 tablespoon salt

In a large bowl, combine the daikon and garlic. Put the ginger through a garlic press to get about 1 teaspoon juice; mix with the daikon along with the cayenne, chili pepper, and salt. Put a plate topped by a weight (a large can will do) on top of the radish. Allow the pickle to stand at about 90° overnight or up to 24 hours. Cover and refrigerate until you are ready to use. Will keep up to a week.

# Korean Broth and Pressed Beef
### (Tang and Pyuhkook)

    One 2-pound rectangular piece of beef brisket
    2 pounds meaty beef bones
    1 beef shin bone (optional)
    3 quarts water
    2 teaspoons salt
    Two ¼-inch slices ginger, flattened with the side of a cleaver or knife
    2 green onions, cut into 1-inch lengths
    2 cloves garlic, sliced
    1 teaspoon peppercorns
    2½ tablespoons soy sauce

# Korean Gardens' Cold Mixed Noodles

*Bibim Naeng Myun*

In a large pot combine the brisket, bones, water, and salt. Bring to a boil and simmer, skimming frequently, for 30 minutes. Add the ginger, onions, garlic, peppercorns, and soy sauce, and simmer on very low heat until the brisket is quite tender, about 2½ to 3 hours. Transfer the brisket to a cutting board; strain the broth and chill it. Remove any fat that coagulates at the surface of the chilled broth before using it.

Trim the fat from the beef and transfer the beef to a plate. Cover it with foil or plastic wrap, place the cutting board or another plate on it, then weight it with 15 pounds of weight. Allow the meat to sit at room temperature, weighted, about 4 hours. Turn the beef on its side, cover as above, and weight with about 8 pounds. After 2 hours, turn the beef and weight the other side. If the beef is too narrow to stand on its side, cut it in half, crosswise, place the two pieces together on their sides, and weight them as one piece. Chill the weighted beef wrapped in plastic wrap. To use the beef in the recipes, slice it very thinly across the grain.

Makes about 12 cups of broth and 8 to 10 servings of meat for noodle dishes.

I had been looking for a recipe for one of my favorite traditional Korean noodle dishes, *bibim naeng myun.* By a quirk of good fortune my search ended when I discovered that the grandparents of my friend, Sue Coe, own Korean Gardens Restaurant. It offers some of L.A.'s most outstanding Korean barbecue, and a specially trained chef makes noodles fresh daily. The restaurant's owners, Mr. and Mrs. S. Y. Kim, introduced me to their Seoul-trained noodle chef. I was allowed to watch the making of the spicy sauce for *bibim naeng myun,* and even given a sauce sample to compare with my recipe tests at home. Here's my recipe—it duplicates the hot garlicky flavors of the Korean Gardens' sauce.

1 cup Red Pepper Paste (following)
¾ cup soy sauce
4½ tablespoons sugar
2½ tablespoons minced garlic
4½ tablespoons minced green onions
2 tablespoons roasted sesame seeds, ground or crushed
½ cup Oriental sesame oil
6 tablespoons broth from Pressed Beef (page 174), or canned broth
3 pounds fresh-frozen buckwheat noodles *(naeng myun),* or 1½ pounds dried, or 18 ounces bean threads
1 large Asian pear or other hard pear

24 thin slices (about ½ recipe) Pressed
   Beef (page 174), or other cooked beef
1 recipe Marinated Cucumber (page 174)
About ½ recipe White Radish Pickle
   (page 174) (optional)
3 hard-cooked eggs

---

In a blender or food processor or by hand, combine the Red Pepper Paste, soy sauce, sugar, garlic, onions, sesame seeds, oil, and broth. Mix or process until well blended and almost smooth. Cook the frozen noodles about 45 seconds in 3½ quarts of boiling water or until they are chewy but tender. Rinse with cold water, drain well, and chill the noodles. Or, if you are using dried noodles or bean threads, soak them in water to cover 20 minutes, then boil 1 minute; drain, rinse, and chill.

Divide the sauce among six large wide bowls. Mound a sixth of the noodles in each bowl in the center of the sauce with a border of red sauce showing. Peel, core, and slice the pear lengthwise. Arrange the cucumbers in a circle of overlapping slices on top of the noodles. Repeat with the radish, four beef slices per bowl, and pear slices. Top with half a hard-cooked egg.

The usual way to eat the dish is to mix everything into the sauce. However, though I love the dish, I find it too spicy that way. So I just mix a little sauce into the noodles as I eat them, regulating the spiciness.

Makes 6 main-dish servings.

**Red Pepper Paste**

In the Korean markets, you will find bags of hot peppers, either crushed or ground. For this recipe, use the crushed rather than the powdery ground pepper. If you don't have access to a Korean market, try to get the hot dried red peppers called *New Mexico* or *Guajillo* chilis. Not all dried chilis are hot enough for this dish.

If you are using the crushed peppers, combine ¾ cup plus 1 tablespoon each pepper and water to get a cup of paste. Let the mixture soak 30 minutes. If using the whole peppers, with rubber gloves on remove the stems and seeds from 12 peppers. Tear the peppers into small pieces and soak them in 1½ cups very warm water for 35 minutes. Combine the soaked peppers and ½ cup of the soaking water in a blender or food processor and process to get a thick, slightly textured paste. Add a little more water if necessary.

PASTA, EAST WITH WEST

# PASTA, EAST WITH WEST

**W**hile leafing through a pile of women's and family magazines, I began to realize that the merging of Eastern and Western cooking methods and ingredients has worked its way into many cooking repertoires. Though publications of a trendier sort may portray the movement as somewhat esoteric, using such descriptive words as *Chinoise* and *Franco-Japonaise,* the mergings are already at home in unassuming kitchens. (I have seen signs advertising "teriyaki burgers.") It is hard to remember when fresh ginger, snow peas, and tofu were not supermarket staples; now such items as rice vinegar, sesame oil, and *hoisin* sauce are rapidly finding their places beside ketchup and Crisco. Home cooks are likely to cook Italian-style vegetables in a wok, and many salad dressings now include soy sauce and sesame oil.

The history of pasta in Asia reveals all sorts of culinary mergings. Its introduction to the West opens still more doors—so many that it was most frustrating to make just a few recipe choices for this chapter, when the sky's the limit. Imagine how many Western ingredients can be wrapped in a wonton skin, or how many permutations are possible when basic Occidental preparations such as vinaigrettes, stocks, and sauces are made with Oriental ingredients.

I started out making long lists of ideas. My first thoughts were rather ambitious, based on restaurant dishes that have impressed me the most: smoked duck and wild mushroom-filled wontons, paper-thin *sashimi* tuna in a delicate vinaigrette, a salad garnished with goose cracklings . . . the lists grew long and quite complicated. Finally, I decided that most of the recipes should instead use ingredients that are available in many supermarkets and that can be prepared with simple techniques producing dependably elegant results. The Giant Sole-Filled Ravioli with Malay Shrimp-Butter Sauce is an example. The filling can be blended in a few minutes, and twelve large raviolis are quicker to fill than sixty or so smaller ones. The wrappers are ready-made eggroll skins. For the sauce, I selected garlic, ginger, coriander, turmeric, cinnamon, and shallots from the gamut of Southeast Asian spice combinations to flavor a quick-cooking French-style stock based on shrimp, tomatoes, and wine. I then reduced the sauce with cream and finished it with a little butter.

My recipes are only an introduction to the conceivable mergings. I'm sure as you cook with Asian pastas, you too will discover many new ways to enjoy them. □

# East-West Mushroom Salad
# in Egg-Roll-Wrapper Bowls

You may, of course, serve the salad without the edible bowls, on plates of an Oriental design, perhaps.

4 large dried *shiitake* (Japanese) mushrooms

Vegetable oil for deep frying

8 to 10 egg-roll skins, 6¾ inches square

One 3.5-ounce (100 g) package fresh *enoki* mushrooms, tough ends trimmed

4 ounces *shimeji* (oyster) mushrooms,* cut apart

1 cup sliced fresh brown or white button mushrooms

About 6 cups torn, mixed lettuces: red leaf, butter, and Romaine

Freshly ground pepper

Vinaigrette Japonaise (following)

Soak the *shiitake* mushrooms in water to cover until they are softened, about 20 minutes. Squeeze the water from the caps. Cut away the tough stems and cut the caps into thin strips. Pour oil into a wok or deep kettle to a depth of 3 inches. Heat the oil to 375°, or until a piece of egg-roll skin dropped into the oil browns in about 1 minute. Lay one egg-roll skin flat on the surface of the oil and press in the middle of the skin with a ladle (to form a bowl) until it is completely submerged. Fry the skin, without removing the ladle, until it is golden brown and crisp, about 90 seconds.

Slip a Chinese mesh scoop under the skin and ladle, and lift them carefully from the oil, pouring out the oil in the ladle as you lift. Remove the ladle from the "bowl" and invert it onto paper toweling to drain. Repeat with the remaining skins. (The recipe serves eight, but you may need the extra skins in case one breaks.)

Toss all the mushrooms, including the *shiitake* strips, with the lettuce. Add a little freshly ground pepper and toss with just enough vinaigrette to coat the salad. Too much dressing makes the crisp bowls soggy. Serve the salad in the bowls.

Serves 8.

*If you can't find oyster mushrooms, use more *enoki* and button mushrooms.

**Vinaigrette Japonaise**

⅓ cup rice vinegar

2 tablespoons fresh lemon juice

½ cup safflower oil

1½ teaspoons Oriental sesame oil

½ teaspoon grated lemon zest

3½ teaspoons soy sauce

1 teaspoon Dijon mustard

¼ teaspoon sugar

2 teaspoons minced ginger

Combine all the ingredients in a jar. Cover the jar and shake vigorously. Let stand at room temperature several hours or overnight before serving.

# Mini-*Gyoza* with a Variety
## of Sauces

These East-West mini-dumplings, based on larger Japanese *gyoza*, are so versatile and easy to make I created many ways to eat them. As a hot dish, they are at home in a velvety Ginger Cream reduction or *Hoisin* Lemon-Butter Sauce. For lovers of cold pasta salads, the Miso Vinaigrette and Asian Salsa give the dumplings a completely different personality. The dumplings freeze beautifully, making them handy for entertaining.

1½ boneless, skinless chicken breasts
   (8 ounces meat)
1 teaspoon minced ginger
1 tablespoon minced shallot
1 teaspoon minced garlic
⅓ cup finely minced Nappa cabbage
2 ounces cream cheese, softened
¾ teaspoon soy sauce
About 32 round wonton wrappers, or
   *shao mai* skins, or *gyoza* skins

In a food processor or by hand, mince the chicken very finely. Add the remaining ingredients except the wrappers and blend the mixture thoroughly. Chill the mixture at least 1 hour for easier handling.

To fill the dumplings, keep a stack of wonton wrappers on a plate covered with a damp cloth. Have a small bowl of water and a damp towel handy to wipe fingers. Place three wrappers on a work surface and cut them in half. (You will make six dumplings at a time.) Dip your fingers in water and moisten half of each piece. With two spoons, place about ½ teaspoon filling in the center of the wet half of each dough piece. Fold the dough over and press it closed on the straight edge of the wrapper; carefully press along the straight edge with the tines of a fork to seal. Pick up the dumpling and pinch the remaining opening shut, then press along the edges with the fork.

To freeze the dumplings, place them in a single layer on a plate covered with plastic wrap, and freeze them solid. Then store in plastic freezer bags.

To cook the dumplings, bring a large pot of water to a boil. Add about one-third recipe frozen or unfrozen dumplings to the rapidly boiling water. When the water returns to boiling, reduce the heat to simmering. Gently loosen any dumplings that stick to the bottom of the pan. Simmer the dumplings until the skins are completely translucent, about 5 minutes. Lift the dumplings from the pan with a slotted or wire mesh spoon and let them drain on a rack. Repeat with remaining dumplings. If cooked dumplings are not eaten right away, they may be stored in layers between plastic wrap and reheated by gently steaming them in an oiled steaming basket. Serve warm or cold, as appropriate, with any of the following sauces.

Makes about 64 dumplings, or about 12 first course servings of about 5 small dumplings each.

### Ginger Cream

Here is a creamy reduction sauce with a taste you don't expect. It is enough for half a recipe mini-dumplings.

6 wafer-thin slices ginger
4 tablespoons minced ginger
3 tablespoons rice vinegar
⅓ cup sake
1½ cups chicken stock
½ teaspoon sugar
1½ cups heavy cream
1 teaspoon light soy sauce
5 tablespoons unsalted butter
Lemon wedges

---

Cut the sliced ginger into very thin strips and refrigerate in a bowl of chilled water. In a 9- or 10-inch skillet, combine the minced ginger, vinegar, and sake. Bring to a boil and cook until the liquid has reduced to about 1½ tablespoons. Add the stock and sugar, and reduce the liquid to about ⅓ cup. Add the cream and soy sauce, and simmer until the sauce is reduced to about 1⅔ cups and is thick enough to coat the back of a spoon. Turn the heat to very low and whisk in the butter 1 tablespoon at a time. Remove from heat and season to taste with a little lemon juice. Strain the sauce through a fine strainer.

To serve, place a pool of sauce on a plate warmed in a low oven, top with warm dumplings, and drizzle a little sauce over the dumplings. Garnish each plate with a few strips of the chilled ginger and a lemon wedge.

Serves 6 as a first course, with half a recipe Mini-Gyoza.

*Shrimp or sesame noodles with ginger cream*
Instead of using dumplings, serve 12 ounces homemade or 8 ounces dried, commercially made shrimp-flavored noodles with Ginger Cream sauce and garnish. (See page 204 for noodle recipe.)

or

Substitute 12 ounces sesame noodles for the dumplings.(See page 203 for noodle recipe.)

### *Hoisin* Lemon-Butter Sauce

4 large dried *shiitake* mushrooms
1 cup unsalted butter
5 tablespoons peanut oil
1 tablespoon minced garlic
4 teaspoons minced ginger
1 tablespoon Chinese rice wine, or dry
   sherry
¼ cup *hoisin* sauce
¼ cup chicken broth
3 tablespoons fresh lemon juice, or more
   to taste

Cover the mushrooms with warm water and weight them with a small dish. Soak them until they are softened (about 20 minutes), squeeze out the water, and cut them into very fine strips. Melt the butter over low heat, remove it from the heat and allow the milk solids to settle, then skim the foam that has formed on the top of the melted butter. Pour off the clarified butter leaving the solids in the pan, or pour the cooled, skimmed melted butter through a fine tea strainer. Keep the butter melted but not hot.

Heat the oil in a medium skillet. Add the garlic and ginger, and cook over low heat until they are softened. Add the rice wine and simmer about 1 minute. Remove the pan from the heat. Combine the *hoisin* sauce and broth, and stir the liquid into the ginger and garlic. Stir in the lemon juice, then whisk in the melted butter. Stir in the mushrooms. Taste the sauce and add more lemon juice if you wish. Pour over the heated *gyoza* and toss to coat before serving.

Makes enough for one whole recipe mini-*gyoza,* or about 1¼ pounds fresh noodles.

*Ginger noodle variation*
Make the ginger-flavored noodles described on page 203. Serve the cooked noodles with the *Hoisin* Lemon-Butter Sauce. You may want to lightly pan-fry the noodles before adding the sauce.

### *Miso* Vinaigrette

¼ cup dry sherry
3 tablespoons sugar
¼ cup dark or red *miso*
1 tablespoon soy sauce
⅓ cup white wine vinegar
1 tablespoon minced ginger
1 cup plus 2 tablespoons safflower oil
1 cup minced red radishes

In a small saucepan, combine the sherry and sugar, and simmer until the sugar dissolves and the alcohol evaporates from the sherry, about 1½ minutes. Stir in the *miso* until well combined. Add the soy sauce, vinegar, and ginger. Pour the mixture into a bowl and whisk in the oil. Stir in the radishes.

To serve the sauce, boil the dumplings, drain them and mix them with a little oil to prevent them from sticking together. Allow to cool at room temperature or refrigerate. When the dumplings are cool, carefully toss with the dressing.

Makes about 2½ cups, or 6 servings.

## Hiyamugi with Smoked Whitefish and Almonds

### Asian Salsa

4 tablespoons distilled white vinegar
2 teaspoons water
2 tablespoons fish sauce *(nam pla or nuoc mam)*
1 tablespoon sugar
4 cloves garlic, pressed or pounded to a paste
⅓ cup and 2 tablespoons peanut oil
3 small Serrano chili peppers, finely minced
3 cups seeded chopped tomatoes
½ cup minced shallots or the whites of green onions
⅔ bunch fresh coriander, coarsely chopped (about 1 cup chopped)
½ small bunch mint, coarsely chopped (about ⅔ cup)
1 teaspoon Oriental sesame oil

---

In a large bowl, blend the vinegar, water, fish sauce, sugar, and garlic until the sugar dissolves. Beat in the oil, then stir in the chili peppers, tomatoes, shallots, coriander, mint, and sesame oil. To serve the salsa, boil the dumplings, drain them, and mix them with a little oil to prevent them from sticking together. Allow to cool at room temperature or refrigerate. When the dumplings are cool, carefully toss with the dressing.

Makes 6 servings.

True to their heritage, these *hiyamugi* noodles are served cold. (*Hiyamugi* means cold wheat.) The dressing and garnishes, however, are completely unconventional. If the noodles are difficult to find, use any fine wheat noodle.

⅓ cup slivered almonds
8 ounces *hiyamugi*
1 teaspoon safflower oil
8 ounces smoked whitefish, flaked
2 cups daikon radish, cut into strips ⅛-inch wide and 2 inches long
1½ tablespoons minced shallots
1 egg yolk, room temperature
1¼ teaspoons *wasabi* powder, or freshly grated or prepared horseradish to taste
2 tablespoons white wine vinegar
¼ teaspoon salt
½ cup safflower oil
½ cup sour cream, at room temperature
*Kiaware* daikon (hot sprouts), or watercress sprigs, or minced chives for garnish

In a large skillet, toast the almonds without oil just until they begin to color. Transfer to a plate to cool. Cook the noodles in a large pot of boiling water 3 minutes, or until they are *al dente*. Rinse with cold water, drain on paper toweling, and mix them in a bowl with 1 teaspoon safflower oil. Fold in the fish and the daikon. (To cut the daikon by hand, slice it diagonally into long ovals, then into thin strips.) Chill the noodle mixture.

In a blender or food processor, combine the shallots, egg yolk, *wasabi* powder, vinegar, and salt. With the machine running, add the oil a drop at a time until the mixture thickens. Blend in the sour cream. Fold the sour cream mixture into the noodles. When you are ready to serve, fold in the almonds and garnish with the sprouts, watercress, or chives.

Makes 6 to 8 appetizer servings.

# *Ramen* Salad with Ginger-Sesame Mayonnaise

Noodles, vegetables, and chicken sparkle with the tang of a creamy ginger-flavored dressing.

- 12 ounces fresh *ramen* or Chinese egg noodles or spaghettini, or 10 ounces *chuka soba*
- 1 teaspoon vegetable oil
- 2 large carrots, cut into strips ⅛-inch wide and 2 inches long
- 2 yellow summer squashes, cut into fine matchsticks
- ¼ teaspoon salt
- 2 large or 3 medium leeks cut into ¼-inch-thick circles
- 3 boneless skinless chicken breast halves
- ⅓ cup lemon juice
- 2 tablespoons seasoned rice vinegar
- Ginger-Sesame Mayonnaise (following)
- 2 teaspoons toasted sesame seeds

Cook the noodles until *al dente*. (See page 14.) Rinse them with cold water, pat dry with toweling, toss in a bowl with the vegetable oil. Chill the noodles. Fill a large saucepan with water, bring it to a boil, and cook the carrots about 1 minute, or just until they soften. Remove them with a slotted spoon and rinse with cold water; drain on paper toweling. Repeat with the squash. In the same saucepan, bring ¾ cup water and the salt to a boil and cook the leeks about 1 minute. Remove them with a slotted spoon, and drain them. Chill the vegetables. Add the chicken to the leek water, cover, and simmer until the breast halves are just opaque throughout. Cool slightly and cut into thin strips; chill the chicken.

Make the Ginger-Sesame Mayonnaise, using 2 teaspoons of the lemon juice. In a salad bowl, combine the noodles, vegetables, chicken, mayonnaise, remaining lemon juice, and the vinegar and fold together. Sprinkle the salad with toasted sesame seeds just before serving.

Serves 8 as part of a meal.

### Ginger-Sesame Mayonnaise

3 tablespoons finely minced ginger, or
    ginger pressed through a garlic press
1 clove garlic, minced
½ teaspoon salt
1 egg yolk plus 1 teaspoon egg white
2 teaspoons lemon juice reserved from
    *Ramen* Salad ingredients
2½ tablespoons Oriental sesame oil
⅔ cup safflower oil

Have all ingredients at room temperature.
In a blender or food processor, combine the
ginger, garlic, salt, egg, and lemon juice;
blend well. With the machine running, drip in
the sesame oil and a little of the safflower oil
a drop at a time until the mixture begins to
thicken. Then add the remaining oil in a slow
fine stream with the machine still running.
Continue to blend or process until the mayonnaise is thick. If the mayonnaise separates,
beat in 1 to 2 tablespoons boiling water.

# Pan-Fried Noodles with Curly Endive, Pork, Pecans, and Honey-Bourbon Sauce

12 ounces lean pork loin, cut into strips
    ¼ inch by ¼ inch by 1½ inches
7 tablespoons Bourbon whiskey
1 tablespoon soy sauce
1 teaspoon cornstarch
4 teaspoons minced ginger
1 cup pecan halves
1 pound fresh Chinese egg noodles, or
    spaghettini
About ⅔ cup vegetable oil
½ cup unsalted butter, at room
    temperature
⅔ cup chopped yellow onion
2 cups beef stock
2¾ teaspoons honey
2 teaspoons rice vinegar
2¼ teaspoons cornstarch mixed with
    2 tablespoons beef stock
5 cups curly endive leaves, torn into little
    wisps

Combine the pork, 2 tablespoons of the
whiskey, soy sauce, 1 teaspoon of the
cornstarch, and 1 teaspoon of the minced
ginger in a bowl. Mix well and allow to marinate at least 30 minutes. In a dry skillet, toast
the pecans over medium heat, shaking the pan
and turning the nuts occasionally until they
begin to color lightly throughout; cool on a
plate. Cook the noodles for pan-fried noodles
(page 14). Rinse them with cold water, drain

them well, and toss them in a bowl with 1½ teaspoons vegetable oil.

Heat 1½ tablespoons each butter and oil in the skillet. Saute the onion until translucent and cream colored but not brown; transfer the onion to a plate. Heat another 1½ tablespoons each oil and butter in the pan. With a slotted spoon, lift the pork from the marinade and place it in the pan, reserving the marinade.

Saute the pork, stirring frequently, until it is nicely browned. Remove the pork from the pan, pour in the remaining 5 tablespoons whiskey, and boil briskly to deglaze, stirring any browned bits from the bottom and sides of the pan, about 3 minutes. Add the stock, the remaining 3 teaspoons ginger, and the sauteed onion. Boil the mixture, uncovered, until the liquid is reduced to 1⅓ cups. Add the honey, vinegar, and marinade. Remove the pan from the heat until you are ready to serve.

About 10 minutes before serving time, heat 2 tablespoons oil in a wok and stir-fry the endive just until it is lightly coated with oil and begins to wilt; transfer to a plate. (You may want to cook the endive in two batches; crowding steams it rather than stir-frying it.) Heat 2½ more tablespoons oil in the pan and stir-fry half the noodles until some of them begin to crisp. Transfer them to a large serving platter and place in a warm oven. Stir-fry the remaining noodles. Mix all the noodles and

the endive together, heap on the platter, and keep warm while you finish the sauce.

Whisk the cornstarch mixture into the sauce, then boil it about 1 minute until it thickens slightly. Turn the heat to low and whisk in the remaining butter, a tablespoon at a time. Return the pork to the pan to warm. Stir in the pecans. Pour the pork and pecan topping over the noodles in the center of the platter, leaving about a 1½-inch border of the noodles showing. Serve at once.

Makes 6 servings.

# Scallop Mousse *Agnolotti* with Lemon Grass Cream

Dumpling wrappers filled with a light seafood mousse comprise these *agnolotti*, which are set off by a delicately flavored, creamy sauce.

> 7 ounces scallops
> 6 ounces fillet of sole
> 1 tablespoon minced chives or green onion
> ⅜ teaspoon salt
> ⅛ teaspoon ground white pepper
> Dash cayenne pepper
> 1 egg, lightly beaten
> 6 tablespoons heavy cream
> About 32 round wonton, *shao mai*, or *gyoza* wrappers
> Lemon Grass Cream (following)

Mince half the scallops to the size of peas. Combine the remaining scallops and the sole in a food processor and process to the consistency of hamburger. Add the chives, salt, and peppers, and gradually add the egg while processing the mixture to a paste. Gradually add the cream until it is well incorporated. Fold in the minced scallops. Chill the mixture until it is firm, about 2 hours.

To make the *agnolotti,* keep a stack of wrappers on a plate covered with a damp cloth. Have a small bowl of water and a damp towel handy on which to wipe your fingers.

Place three wrappers on a work surface. Place a ball of filling, about 2 teaspoons, in the center of half of each wrapper. Moisten the wrappers all around the filling, fold the wrappers over the fillings, and seal the edges by pressing close around the filling. Make a decorative border by pressing the dough edges with the tines of a fork. As the *agnolotti* are completed, place them on a plastic wrap-covered plate; place another piece of plastic wrap between the layers. The finished dumplings should be cooked within 2 hours or frozen solid on the plate, then transferred to a plastic freezer bag.

To cook the *agnolotti,* bring a large pot of water to a boil. Add one-third of the dumplings, frozen or unfrozen, to the rapidly boiling water. When the water returns to a boil, reduce the heat and gently loosen any dumplings that stick to the bottom of the pan. Simmer the dumplings until the skins are completely translucent, about 5 minutes. Lift the dumplings from the pan with a slotted or wire mesh spoon and let them drain on a rack. Repeat with the remaining dumplings. Dumplings may be cooked ahead and reheated by steaming them in an oiled steaming basket. Handle the dumplings gently.

## Lemon Grass Cream

2 large or 3 small stalks fresh lemon grass
2 tablespoons vegetable oil
3 small or 2 medium fresh Serrano chili
    peppers, seeded
2½ tablespoons minced shallots
3 tablespoons white wine vinegar
⅔ cup dry white wine
¼ cup bottled clam juice
1¼ cups chicken stock
1¾ cups heavy cream
½ cup unsalted butter at room temperature
Cayenne pepper
2 lemons cut into wedges
Fresh chives

Peel away any tough outer layers of the lemon grass stalks, slice the white inner part, and mince in a food processor. Or pound the thinly sliced lemon grass in a mortar or *suribachi*. You will need ½ cup minced lemon grass.

Heat the oil in a large skillet and saute the chili peppers and shallots until they are soft. Add the vinegar, wine, and lemon grass and boil the mixture until the liquid is reduced to about 2 tablespoons. Add the clam juice and chicken stock, and boil until the mixture is reduced to about 4 tablespoons. Add the cream and continue to boil until the sauce is reduced to about 1¼ cups and is thick enough to coat the back of a spoon. The sauce may be cooked ahead to this point, then reheated and finished just before serving. Whisk in the butter about 2 tablespoons at a time. Season the sauce to taste with cayenne and lemon juice. Strain the sauce through a fine strainer, pressing the lemon grass to extract as much flavor as possible.

To serve, place a pool of sauce on warmed plates, top with the *agnolotti,* and drizzle with a little more sauce. Garnish with lemon wedges and strips of chives or a sprinkling of sliced chives.

Serves 6 as a first course.

# Chicken, Shrimp, and Herbed Cream Cheese in Rice Paper Chemise

The buttered rice paper wrapped in several layers around the shrimp and chicken filling takes on a flaky filolike quality.

> 4 to 5 medium, boneless, skinless chicken breast halves (1½ pounds meat), cut into strips ¼-inch wide and 1 inch long
> ¼ teaspoon salt
> 12 ounces raw shelled shrimp
> 3 green onions, minced
> 4 ounces herb and garlic flavored cream cheese at room temperature (such as Alouette or Rondele)
> Twelve 13-inch-diameter rice papers (*banh trang*)
> ⅔ cup unsalted butter, melted
> 12 large or 24 medium fresh spinach leaves

In a large mixing bowl, toss the chicken strips with the salt. Chop the shrimp by hand or in a food processor to about the size of large peas. Mix the shrimp, onions, and cheese with the chicken until thoroughly combined.

Preheat the oven to 375°. Brush three rice papers lightly with water on both sides and allow them to rest in a single layer. (See page 75.) Brush one paper with melted butter and place one large or two medium spinach leaves about 2 inches from the circumference of the paper. Spoon one-twelfth of the chicken mixture onto the spinach leaf. Roll the 2-inch edge of the rice paper over the filling, fold in the sides of the rice paper like a burrito or blintz, and brush the unbuttered surfaces from the reverse side with butter. Roll the rice paper, buttering the unbuttered surface after every turn. Place the closed packet seam-side down on a well-buttered, rimmed 10-inch by 15-inch baking sheet. Brush another paper with water so there are always two papers resting while you are filling the third. Continue this procedure until all twelve papers are filled.

Cover the baking pan with foil and bake at 375° for 15 minutes. Turn up the oven to 425°, remove the foil, and bake the rolls until they are lightly golden, 10 to 15 minutes more.

Makes 6 servings.

# Crisp-on-Soft Noodles with Marinated Squid Steak

In a wonderful play of textures (and flavors), crunchy fried bean threads contrast with soft egg noodles and crisp squid—all dressed with a Southeast Asian inspired cream sauce.

    ¼ cup sake, or dry sherry
    3 Serrano chili peppers, minced
    1 tablespoon minced ginger
    2 cloves garlic, minced
    ¼ teaspoon salt
    1 pound partially thawed calamari steak,
        cut into 2-inch by ¼-inch strips, or
        squid cut into rings
    12 ounces fresh, broad or narrow Chinese
        egg noodles, or spaghettini
    Vegetable oil
    1½ ounces bean threads (coarse if
        possible)
    ½ cup unsalted butter
    2 medium zucchini cut into strips ⅛-inch
        wide and 2 inches long
    ⅔ cup chopped shallots
    ⅔ cup chicken broth
    2 large lemons
    2¼ cups heavy cream
    ¾ cups chopped fresh basil, plus 12 basil
        leaves cut crosswise into strips

In a medium bowl, combine the sake, chili peppers, ginger, garlic, salt, and calamari or squid. Allow to marinate at room temperature 30 minutes to an hour. Cook the noodles for stir-fry (page 14), toss them with 1½ teaspoons vegetable oil in a bowl, and set aside. Into a deep pot, pour oil to a depth of 2½ to 3 inches. Heat the oil until a bean thread puffs instantly when dropped into the oil. Break up the bean threads or cut them with scissors to lengths no longer than 10 inches. Deep-fry one-third of the bean threads, pushing them down into the oil several seconds so all cook thoroughly. Transfer the first batch of bean threads to paper toweling and, using the same procedure, cook the remaining two batches of bean threads. (Bean threads may be cooked ahead and reheated briefly in a 350° oven.)

In a very large skillet or wok, heat 1 tablespoon each oil and butter and rapidly stir-fry the zucchini until they are just beginning to soften; transfer to a plate. Heat another tablespoon each oil and butter and saute the shallots until they are soft and translucent; transfer to a plate. Add a little more oil and butter and briskly stir-fry half the squid just until it is opaque. Transfer it to the zucchini plate and stir-fry the remaining squid, transferring it to the plate. Turn off the heat and add the shallots and chicken broth to the pan. Grate the zest of 1 lemon into the pan. Over high heat, boil the broth mixture until only 3

# Giant Sole-Filled Ravioli with Malay Shrimp-Butter Sauce

tablespoons remain. Add the cream to the pan and boil until it is reduced to about 1⅔ cups and is thick enough to coat the back of a spoon. While you reduce the cream sauce, reheat the fried bean threads in a 350° oven. Stir the chopped basil into the sauce and simmer 1 minute. Stir in 2 tablespoons lemon juice. Remove ½ cup sauce from the pan and set aside.

Stir the squid and zucchini into the sauce in the pan. Combine the egg noodles with two-thirds of the fried noodles and combine them with the sauce. Heap the noodles on a large platter, or divide them among six individual serving plates. Sprinkle the remaining crisp noodles over the top. Drizzle the reserved sauce over the noodles and garnish with the basil strips. Serve at once with lemon wedges.

Serves 6 as a main course.

C hinese egg-roll wrappers enclose a shrimp-studded fish mousse to make these silky ravioli. Served in a French reduction sauce, flavored with Indian-inspired Malay spicings, they combine the best of Eastern and Western cuisines. These huge ravioli are easy to make, and they freeze well. Except for the final addition of butter, the sauce may be made ahead too.

2 tablespoons vegetable oil
14 ounces medium shrimp in the shell
1¼ pounds fillet of sole
1 tablespoon fresh lemon juice
1½ tablespoons minced green onion
1 egg, lightly beaten
⅝ teaspoon salt
⅛ teaspoon ground white pepper
1/16 teaspoon ground nutmeg
1/16 teaspoon cayenne pepper
6 tablespoons heavy cream
12 egg-roll wrappers
Malay Shrimp-Butter Sauce (following)
Lime wedges
Fresh coriander leaves

Heat the oil in a large skillet. Saute 6 ounces of the unshelled shrimp until pink and firm, and set aside for the sauce. Saute the remaining 8 ounces shrimp, shell them, and return the shells to the pan and reserve for the sauce. Slice the shelled shrimp crosswise into pieces about the size of navy beans.

In a food processor, process the sole until it is almost a paste. Add the lemon juice and minced onion, and gradually add the egg while processing the mixture. Add the salt, pepper, nutmeg, and cayenne, and gradually add the cream while processing the mixture to a smooth mousse consistency. Fold in the sliced shrimp and chill the filling at least 1 hour until it is firm. In the meantime, you can make the first part of the sauce (recipe follows).

To make the giant ravioli, keep the wrappers in a plastic bag. Have a small bowl of water and a damp towel handy to wipe your fingers. Place two wrappers on a work surface. Mount one-twelfth of the filling on one half of each egg-roll wrapper. Moisten the area around the filling, fold the other half of the wrapper over the filling and press down as close to the filling as possible. With a ravioli cutter, cut a band from the folded egg-roll wrapper in a semicircle, leaving a ½-inch border around the mound of filling. (If you don't have a ravioli cutter, cut the dough with a knife and make a border by pressing the dough edges with the tines of a fork.) Lay the finished ravioli on a plastic wrap-covered, rimmed 10-inch by 15-inch baking sheet. Fill the remaining ravioli, keeping those you are not working with covered with plastic wrap. The ravioli should be cooked within 2 hours, or frozen solid in a single layer before being transferred to a plastic freezer bag. The ravioli may be cooked immediately and reheated by steaming a few minutes in an oiled steaming basket. Handle the ravioli gently.

Cook frozen or unfrozen ravioli, four at a time, in a large pot of boiling water for 6 to 8 minutes, or until the dough is completely translucent. Keep the cooked ravioli hot in a warm oven on a platter with ¼-inch of water, covered with foil. Drain the ravioli just before serving. If the cooked ravioli threaten to stick together, rub them sparingly with oil.

Serve the ravioli on a pool of Malay Shrimp-Butter Sauce, garnished with coriander leaves and lime wedges.

Serves 6 as a main course.

## Malay Shrimp-Butter Sauce

Shrimp shells in the pan from Giant Sole-
  Filled Ravioli recipe (page 192)
6 ounces cooked shrimp from Giant Sole-
  Filled Ravioli recipe (page 192)
2 tablespoons vegetable oil
½ cup chopped yellow onion
2 medium-large tomatoes, seeded and
  chopped
8 peppercorns
5 sprigs parsley
½ cup plus ⅓ cup dry white wine
½ cup water
3 tablespoons finely minced shallots
1½ teaspoons minced garlic
2 teaspoons minced ginger
3 tablespoons white wine vinegar
¼ teaspoon cayenne pepper
1 tablespoon ground coriander seeds
1 teaspoon turmeric
⅛ teaspoon cinnamon
1½ cups heavy cream
½ cup unsalted butter at room temperature
Fresh lime juice

Remove the shrimp shells from the pan
and reserve them. Mince the cooked shrimp
in their shells. Heat the oil in the skillet and
saute the onions until they are soft and pale
golden but not browned. Add the tomatoes,
peppercorns, parsley, ½ cup wine, water, and
the shrimp and shells. Cover the pan and

simmer the stock 40 minutes. Pour the stock
through a fine strainer, pressing the solid
material to extract all the flavorings. The
stock may be made and refrigerated a day in
advance.

In a large skillet, combine the remaining
⅓ cup white wine, shallots, garlic, ginger,
and vinegar. Boil the mixture, uncovered,
until it is reduced to 2 tablespoons. Add the
shrimp stock and boil until the liquid in the
pan is reduced to about ⅔ cup. Add the
cayenne, coriander, turmeric, cinnamon, and
cream, and boil the mixture until it is reduced
to about 1½ cups and is thick enough to coat
the back of a spoon. The sauce may be made
ahead to this point.

Whisk in the butter about 2 tablespoons at
a time until the sauce is smooth. Strain the
sauce through a fine strainer, pressing on the
solids to release their flavorings. Add 2 tablespoons of lime juice or more to taste. Serve
with the Giant Ravioli.

# Maggie Hale's *Udon* and
# Seafood Salad

Maggie Hale, my advisor on Japanese noodles, created this dish for her daughter's annual birthday celebration. She used *sirimi* crab (see Special Ingredients section), which I thought was outstanding. "Not all imitation crab is created equal," Maggie advises. "There are only a few really good brands." You'll have to experiment to see which brands you prefer. Of course, real crabmeat may be used.

12 ounces dried *udon* noodles
¼ cup almond or peanut oil
1 bunch (about 4 ounces) green onions
½ cup plus 2 tablespoons peanut oil
2 medium cloves garlic, minced
2 cups thinly sliced domestic mushrooms
6 to 8 ounces crabmeat, or *sirimi* "crab"
3 cups (about 1 pound) tiny, shelled
    cooked shrimp
7½ tablespoons rice vinegar
4 teaspoons ginger juice (squeezed
    through a garlic press)
4⅛ teaspoons sugar
3 tablespoons plus 2½ teaspoons soy
    sauce
3 large eggs
1 tablespoon prepared *dashi,* or chicken
    broth
Pinch of salt
One 3½-ounce package *enoki* mushrooms
    (optional)

Four 7-inch-by-8-inch sheets *nori,* cut
    into strips 3½ inches by ¼ inch (op-
    tional)

---

Cook the *udon* following the directions on page 44. Rinse the noodles with cold water, drain on paper toweling, and mix with 2 teaspoons of the almond oil in a large bowl. Chop the whites of the green onions and slice the green parts, keeping them separate. Heat 2 tablespoons of the peanut oil in a large skillet, and saute the onion whites and garlic until the onions begin to soften—about 1 minute. Add the sliced mushrooms and saute them, stirring until they soften slightly; then add the mushroom mixture to the *udon*. Stir in the crabmeat and shrimp, and chill. In a medium bowl, combine the vinegar, the remaining almond and peanut oils, ginger juice, 4 teaspoons of the sugar, and 3½ tablespoons of the soy sauce. Whisk them together well and set aside.

In a medium bowl, beat the eggs with the *dashi,* the remaining ⅛ teaspoon sugar and 1 teaspoon soy sauce, and a pinch of salt. Heat a 7-inch nonstick skillet and brush with a little oil. Pour in about 3 tablespoons of the egg mixture, swirling it to coat the bottom of the pan. Reduce the heat to low, cover the pan, and cook the omelette until it is firm. Turn it out onto a plate. Repeat with the remaining egg. When the omelettes are cool, roll them one on top of the other into a cylinder and slice into ¼-inch strips.

Gently blend the egg strips into the noodle mixture and fold in the oil and vinegar mixture. Trim the woody parts from the *enoki* mushrooms and either fold them in or reserve them to garnish the top of the salad. Fold three-fourths of the *nori* strips into the salad just before serving, and garnish the top of the salad first with the *enoki,* then with the remaining *nori* strips.

Makes 8 to 10 appetizer servings.

# *Soba* with Caviar

H ere the Western tradition of eating caviar with tiny buckwheat *blini* is given an Eastern character with delicious buckwheat noodles instead of crêpes. My favorite caviar for this dish is fresh salmon eggs *(ikura).*

12 ounces *yamaimo soba,* or regular dried
  *soba*
3 tablespoons walnut or peanut oil
3 tablespoons lemon juice
2 tablespoons rice vinegar
1¼ teaspoons sugar
2 teaspoons light soy sauce
1½ cups sour cream
3 to 4 ounces salmon eggs or other caviar
*Kiaware* daikon sprouts (hot sprouts), or
  watercress sprigs

Cook the *soba* until it is *al dente* (page 44). Rinse with cold water and drain on paper toweling. Toss the *soba* in a bowl with the walnut oil. Whisk together the lemon juice, vinegar, sugar, and soy sauce. Stir until the sugar is dissolved. Blend in 1¼ cups of the sour cream until smooth. Fold the dressing into the noodles, then fold in two-thirds of the caviar. Chill the mixture at least 1 hour.

To serve, mound the *soba* on individual serving plates or on a large serving platter. Top with a dab of sour cream and with some caviar in the center. Garnish the dish around the edges with the daikon sprouts or watercress.

*Variations*
**With smoked salmon.** Follow the recipe for *Soba* with Caviar, substituting 8 ounces diced smoked salmon for the caviar. Season to taste with extra lemon juice and, if the salmon is not salty, a little salt.
**With shrimp noodles and smoked salmon.** Follow the recipe for *Soba* with Caviar, substituting commercially made or homemade shrimp noodles (page 204) for the *soba* and 8 ounces diced smoked salmon for the caviar.

# Sweet Walnut Wontons with Dessert Sauces

The filling for these wontons is adapted from a delicious European strudel recipe I have been fond of for years. Served with either the Fresh Mango Sauce or the Apricot Brandy Sauce (following), they make a perfect ending for an Orientalized meal.

2 cups broken walnut pieces, about 9 ounces
2 tablespoons fine dry bread crumbs
1 cup sugar
4½ teaspoons fresh lemon juice
2½ teaspoons grated lemon zest
½ teaspoon vanilla extract
Milk
About one 1-pound package square wonton wrappers
1 egg, lightly beaten
Vegetable oil for deep-frying
About ½ cup powdered sugar
Choice of dessert sauces (following)

Chop the walnuts very finely until they are almost a paste. In a processor or mixing bowl, mix the walnuts with the bread crumbs, then the sugar. Mix the lemon juice, zest, and vanilla together and distribute evenly into the nut mixture. Add just enough milk to make a dry paste.

Put the wrappers on a plate and cover with plastic or a slightly dampened cloth.

Have a bowl of water and another damp cloth handy to wipe your fingers. Lay four wrappers on a work surface. Place 1 teaspoon of the filling in the center of each wonton wrapper. Moisten two triangles of dough with egg on opposite sides of the filling. Fold the dough over the filling diagonally with the points almost meeting to form a triangle that is slightly askew. Bring the two bottom corners together below the filling. Place the right corner over the left corner and pinch to seal. Repeat with the remaining wrappers, placing the finished wontons on a plastic wrap-covered, rimmed baking sheet, then covering the wontons with more plastic wrap.

In a large deep pot, pour oil to a depth of 2 inches and heat it to 360°, or until a piece of wonton wrapper dropped into the oil browns nicely in about 30 seconds. Add five or six wontons and cook, turning occasionally, until golden brown; do not cook them too fast. Remove the cooked wontons with a slotted or wire mesh spoon and drain on paper toweling. Keep the fried wontons warm in a warm oven while cooking the remaining wontons. A few seconds before serving, sprinkle lightly with powdered sugar sifted through a strainer. Serve the wontons on one half of a dinner plate; on the other half, pour a pool of sauce. Diners dip the wontons into the sauce.

Makes 8 to 10 servings, about 40 wontons.

### Fresh Mango Sauce for Walnut Wontons

2 very ripe mangoes
½ cup fresh orange juice
4 to 5 tablespoons Grand Marnier liqueur,
    or Cointreau liqueur
Powdered sugar

Roll the mangoes between the palm of your hand and a cutting board to soften them. Peel the mangoes over a bowl and scrape all the meat from the skin and pit into the bowl. Puree the mango, juice, and Grand Marnier in a blender. Add powdered sugar to taste—Cointreau is not as sweet as Grand Marnier, so you may need a touch more sugar if using Cointreau.

### Apricot Brandy Sauce for Walnut Wontons

Make this sauce the morning of your party, or even the day before.

3¼ ounces dried apricots (about ½ cup)
6 tablespoons brandy or Cognac
½ cup water
1 cup plus 2 tablespoons whole milk
3 egg yolks
6 tablespoons sugar
⅓ cup heavy cream

In a small saucepan, combine the apricots, brandy or Cognac, and water. Bring to boiling, reduce the heat, and simmer 1 minute. Remove the pan from the heat, cover, and let stand 30 minutes. Puree the apricot mixture in a blender until it is very smooth; leave it in the blender.

In a small saucepan, heat the milk to simmering and remove it from the heat. In a medium saucepan, whisk the egg yolk and sugar together, then pour in the hot milk, still mixing. Cook over low heat, stirring slowly with a spoon, until the mixture thickens slightly and will coat the spoon, about 5 minutes. Cool almost to room temperature. Blend the milk mixture into the pureed apricots. Strain the sauce and stir in the cream. Cover the sauce and chill at least 8 hours.

MAKING ASIAN PASTA AT HOME

# Making Asian Pastas at Home

## Chinese Egg Noodle Dough

Most Chinese cooks do not make their own noodles, wonton wrappers, or egg-roll skins because the products are available at nearby markets. But not everyone is near a Chinese market, and with a food processor and perhaps a pasta machine within arm's reach, the potentially time-consuming tasks of mixing, kneading, rolling, stretching, and cutting the dough take only minutes. I have included alternative directions for those who do not own these machines. The same dough may be used to make square or round wonton and egg-roll wrappers.

**For small processors**
   1¾ cups plus 2 tablespoons all-purpose
      flour
   2 tablespoons gluten flour*
   ½ teaspoon salt
   1 large egg
   About 7 tablespoons water
   ⅛ teaspoon Oriental sesame oil or
      vegetable oil
   About ⅓ cup cornstarch

**For large processors**
   2¾ cups plus 1 tablespoon all-purpose
      flour
   3 tablespoons gluten flour*
   ¾ teaspoon salt
   2 large eggs
   About 9 tablespoons water
   ⅛ teaspoon Oriental sesame oil or
      vegetable oil
   About ½ cup cornstarch

In a food processor fitted with a metal blade, process the flours and salt to mix them well. Beat the eggs with 5 tablespoons (6 tablespoons for the larger recipe) water. Turn on the machine and gradually add the mixture, processing just until the dough begins to form a ball. You may need to drizzle in the remaining water, but stop processing just before the dough becomes a ball. Process another 10 seconds if you are going to use a pasta machine to roll out the dough. Process the dough another 35 seconds if you are going to roll it out by hand. Turn the dough, which should be barely sticky, onto a very lightly floured board, and knead it about 1 minute. It should be satiny and not stick to the palm of your hand when you hold it 15 seconds. Cover the dough with plastic or put it in a plastic bag and let it rest half an hour to an hour.

*To mix by hand*, blend the flours and salt in a large bowl. Make a well in the center and crack the egg into it. Add all but 2 tablespoons of the water and blend it first into the egg and then incorporate the flour. Add enough water to make a lose but not gooey dough. Pick up about ⅓ cup of the dough and rub it vigorously between your hands for about half a minute to develop the gluten and shorten the kneading time. Repeat with the remaining dough. Turn the dough onto a floured board and knead at least 10 minutes until the dough is satiny and does not stick to the palm of your hand when held for 15 seconds. Oil the dough, cover it with plastic or put it in a plastic bag, and let it rest half an hour to an hour.

The dough may also be made in a heavy-duty mixer and kneaded with a dough hook.

*To roll out the dough with a pasta machine*, roll the dough into a sausage shape 1½ inches in diameter and cut it into thirds for the small recipe or quarters for the large. Cover the resting dough with plastic while you roll out the first piece. Flatten the dough piece to a rectangle about ¼-inch thick and lightly coat both sides with cornstarch. Pass the dough through the thickest setting. Then fold the dough into thirds, flatten it slightly, dust it with cornstarch, and run it through the rollers again, feeding in the unfolded end first. Repeat this procedure three times. Turn the machine to the next thinnest setting, dust the dough, and roll it through unfolded. Repeat this procedure with each setting up to the fifth setting, or until the dough is ⅛-inch thick for hearty noodles or ¹⁄₁₆-inch thick for delicate noodles and wonton or egg-roll wrappers. Spread the rolled dough on a tea towel

to dry slightly and become firm. After you roll out the remaining dough pieces, the first piece should be ready to cut.

Run the cornstarch-dusted dough through the ⅛-inch or ¹⁄₁₆-inch cutting blades of the pasta machine, cut the noodles in half, and dust them with cornstarch. Allow them to dry about 10 minutes before cooking them, or refrigerating or freezing them for future use.

*To cut the wontons or egg-roll skins*, lay one piece of rolled dough on a wooden board, and with a sharp knife and ruler mark off 3-inch squares for wonton or 7-inch squares for egg rolls. If you wish to make round wonton wrappers, cut the dough with a 3-inch-round cookie cutter, biscuit cutter, or opened tin can (*e.g.*, a tuna can). Allow the cut pieces to dry about 10 minutes, then dust them with cornstarch and stack them.

*To roll out the dough by hand*, it is best to use a long thin rolling pin about 16 inches long. If you are using a standard rolling pin, cut the dough into smaller pieces. Flatten one of the dough pieces into a circle on a cornstarch-dusted board. Place the rolling pin in the center of the circle and roll the dough away from you, then roll the pin toward you in a sweeping motion. Turn the dough a quarter turn and roll again. Continue rolling and turning until the dough is almost ¹⁄₁₆ inch thick.

Put terry toweling along the edge of a table. Dust the dough sheet lightly with cornstarch. Hang the dough from the towel by putting about a third of it on the towel and allowing the remainder to hang over the table. Stretch the dough as thin as possible, holding the end on the towel down while pulling the other end. Allow the dough to dry while you roll out and stretch the remaining dough. Fold the first noodle sheet accordion-style into 3- to 4-inch folds. With a very sharp knife or Chinese cleaver, cut the noodles by pressing straight down into the folded dough. Fluff the noodles onto a cornstarch-dusted surface and allowed them to dry about 15 minutes before storing as described above. The noodles should be dry and silky but not brittle.

A small recipe makes ¾ pound of noodles, a large recipe about 1¼ pounds.

*2 cups (3 cups for larger recipe) bread flour may be substituted for all the flour.

# Flavored Chinese Noodles

These flavored noodles can add a delicious, novel touch to traditional dishes. The following recipes are for processors with a large work bowl. If yours is small, divide the recipe in half and mix half at a time. A selection of simple sauces for these pastas appears in the East-West section, where substitutions using these noodles are specified.

### Hot Chili Oil-Flavored Chinese Noodles

Follow the instructions for the basic Chinese egg noodle dough, mixing in 2 teaspoons cayenne pepper and 1 tablespoon Chinese hot chili oil. Reduce the water by about 1 tablespoon.

### Ginger-Flavored Chinese Egg Noodles

Crush several chunks of ginger through a garlic press to get a puree and juice. You will need 3 tablespoons crushed ginger. Follow the recipe for basic egg noodles, blending the ginger with the eggs and reducing the water by about 2 tablespoons.

### Roast Sesame-Flavored Egg Noodles

Mix 2½ tablespoons Chinese sesame paste with 1 tablespoon Oriental sesame oil. Blend it into the dough as you mix in the eggs. Reduce the water by about 1 tablespoon.

### Coriander and Chili-Flavored Chinese Noodles

Mince seven medium Serrano chilis to a fine pulp. Mince enough fresh coriander to obtain ⅓ cup. Blend the coriander and chilis into the basic pasta dough along with the eggs.

### Coriander-Flavored Chinese Noodles

Blend ½ cup minced fresh coriander into the basic noodle dough. Reduce the water by about 1 tablespoon.

### Shrimp-Flavored Chinese Noodles

In a mortar or small coffee grinder, grind ¼ cup dried shrimp to a powder. Heat ⅓ cup chicken broth and add the shrimp, two individual packets dry chicken broth mix (4.5 grams each), and 4 teaspoons sugar. While stirring, simmer the mixture 1 minute, then cool to room temperature. Follow the directions for Chinese egg noodles, mixing in the broth mixture along with the egg. Reduce the water to about 4 tablespoons.

　　Serve with Lemon Grass Cream sauce (page 189).

# Homemade *Soba* Noodles

The following is a traditional recipe converted for use with a food processor and a pasta machine. Though you can make these noodles by hand, it is not easy to cut them into the thin, ⅙-inch strands without a machine, and this recipe works beautifully.

**For small processors**
　　1¼ cups buckwheat flour
　　⅔ cup all-purpose flour
　　⅓ cup gluten flour
　　1¼ teaspoons salt
　　About ⅔ to ¾ cup water
　　Flour for rolling out the dough

**For large processors**
　　1¾ cups buckwheat flour
　　1 cup plus 1 teaspoon all-purpose flour
　　6½ tablespoons gluten flour
　　1½ teaspoon salt
　　About 1¼ cups water
　　Flour for rolling out dough

---

　　Combine the flours and salt in a food processor or bowl; process or mix to blend well. Sprinkle 7 tablespoons (⅔ cup for large recipe) water over the dough and process or blend until it looks like cornmeal. Pick up a portion of dough in your hands and see if it will form a cohesive mass. If not, sprinkle on a little more water, blend it in, and try again. Process the dough 1½ minutes, changing the position of the dough every half minute, or knead it 12 minutes by hand. The dough will not quite form a ball in the machine, so turn the dough out onto an unfloured work surface and knead it 2 minutes. Let the dough rest covered with plastic wrap, 1 to 3 hours.

# Homemade Japanese *Udon*

Cut the dough in half for the small recipe and into thirds for the large and keep the remaining pieces covered. Pat one piece into a rectangle about ¼-inch thick. Lightly flour the dough and roll it through the pasta machine at the thickest setting. Fold the dough in thirds and feed the unfolded end through the rollers again. Repeat the procedure twice more. Lightly flour the dough again and pass it through the next finest setting twice. Pass the dough through the third and fourth settings, flouring the dough if necessary.

Place a lightly floured plate under the thinnest cutting blades. Roll the dough through the blades, allowing the noodles to fall onto the plate. Lightly sprinkle more flour over the noodles and gently toss to coat them with flour. The noodles are very delicate so be careful not to break them. Roll and cut the remaining dough pieces, allowing each to dry on its own plate. Allow the noodles to dry about 20 minutes.

The noodles may also be rolled and cut by hand as described for *udon* (following).

Cook the *soba* in rapidly boiling water 45 seconds to 1 minute, or until they lose their floury taste. These *soba* may be used in any recipe calling for *soba* or *udon,* or may be wrapped well in foil and frozen.

The smaller recipe makes about 1 pound *soba;* the larger recipe makes 1½ pounds.

*U*don are characteristically thick and chewy. This sought-after texture requires a high-gluten flour and plenty of kneading. For the flour, I blend all-purpose with gluten flour purchased in a natural-foods shop. Bread flour may be substituted. Knead the dough in a food processor or with a dough hook, or follow Elizabeth Andoh's advice and wrap the dough in plastic and knead it with your feet— much easier than hand kneading. *Udon* dough should be very dense, so add as little water as possible.

**For small processors**
> 1¾ cups plus 2 tablespoons all-purpose flour
> 2 tablespoons gluten flour*
> 1½ teaspoons salt
> About ⅔ cup water
> Additional flour and cornstarch for dusting the noodles

**For large processors**
> 2¾ cups plus 1 tablespoon all-purpose flour
> 3 tablespoons gluten flour*
> 2 teaspoons salt
> About 1 cup water
> Additional flour and cornstarch for dusting the noodles

*To make* udon *in a processor.* Combine the flours and salt in a food processor and process to mix. Add ½ cup water to the small recipe, or almost ⅔ cup water to the large, and process only until the mixture resembles cornmeal. If the dough will form a cohesive mass when you press it together, process it until it forms a ball, then process another 50 seconds. If the dough will not form a ball, drizzle just enough water to form a cohesive mass, then process to knead. Remove the dough from the work bowl; it should be satiny and not stick to your hands. Knead it by hand about 2 minutes. Put the dough in a bowl, cover it with a damp tea towel, and let it rest 2 to 3 hours.

To roll out the dough with a pasta machine, cut the dough into thirds for the large recipe or in half for the small, keeping the pieces covered with the damp towel. Gently flatten one piece to about ¼-inch thick. Dust the dough lightly with flour and pass it through the rollers at the thickest setting. Lightly dust the dough again, fold the dough into thirds, and roll it through again, inserting the unfolded end of the dough into the rollers. Repeat this two more times. Then roll the dough through the next setting without folding it; repeat. Set the rollers to the third thickest setting and pass the dough through again.

Pass the dough through the ¼-inch-wide fettuccini blades. Spread the noodles on a cornstarch-dusted plate and fluff them with your fingers to coat the cut edges. Allow the noodles to dry about 20 minutes until they start to become firm but not dry. To cook, boil the noodles continuously for 10 minutes.

Uncooked *udon* may be refrigerated 1 day or frozen 2 months well wrapped in foil. Thaw the noodles before cooking them. Makes 1 pound (small recipe) or 1½ pounds (large recipe).

*To make* udon *by hand.* Mix the dough in a bowl using as little water as possible. Knead the dough with a dough hook 5 minutes, or about 12 minutes by hand. Cover the dough and let it rest as directed. To roll the dough, cut it into thirds, keeping two pieces under a damp towel. On a lightly floured board, flatten the dough gently to about ¼-inch thick. Roll it into a rectangle. Place the rolling pin in the center of the dough and roll the dough by pushing it away from you, then roll back toward you in a sweeping motion. Turn the dough after several rolls and adjust the dough to get a rectangular shape as you roll. When the dough is about ⅛-inch thick, dust it lightly with cornstarch, fold it accordion-style into 4-inch-wide folds with a cornstarch-dusted knife, and cut into ⅜-inch-wide noodles. Avoid drawing the blade in a sawing motion;

just press straight down. Scatter the noodles on a cornstarch-dusted board or plate and fluff them to coat the cut edges. Allow them to dry, and cook them or store them as directed above.

*2 cups, or 3 cups for larger recipe, bread flour may be substituted for flours.

# Fresh Rice Sheets and Noodles

This is an easy and handy recipe. Although I live within driving distance of Chinatown, it is easier to prepare my own fresh rice noodles than to make the trek. Freshly made rice noodles are far superior to dried or frozen noodles.

1¼ cups rice flour
6 tablespoons tapioca starch*
5 tablespoons wheat starch* (not wheat flour)
1¼ teaspoons salt
2⅔ cup water
2 tablespoons vegetable oil plus oil for the pans

Combine the rice flour, tapioca starch, wheat starch, salt, and water; stir until smooth. Strain the batter through a fine strainer and stir in the oil. Let the batter sit half an hour.

Have ready an oiled baking sheet. Lightly oil two 8-inch-by-8-inch or 9-inch-by-9-inch square cake pans. Place an 8-inch round cake rack in a wok and add water to just below the rack. Bring the water to boiling. Have a pot or kettle of boiling water ready to replenish the water in the wok.

Stir the batter very well and add 5 or 6 tablespoons to one pan, allowing the batter to cover the bottom of the pan. Set the pan on the cake rack, cover the wok, and steam over high heat for 5 minutes. Remove the wok top without allowing condensed water to drip on the rice sheet. Remove the baking pan and cool in a sink filled with ½ inch cold water. Meanwhile, fill and steam the other pan. Loosen the cooled rice sheet and roll it out onto the oiled baking sheet. Turn the rice sheet so both sides are lightly oiled, then transfer it to a platter. Repeat the cooking, cooling, and oiling with the remaining batter.

Cover the rice sheets with plastic wrap and refrigerate at least 2 hours before cutting into ⅜-inch-wide noodles or shapes called for in the recipes.

Makes about 3 pounds.

*Available in Oriental markets.

# Fresh Rice Papers

I offer two recipes here: one uses rice flour, the other is a very satisfactory substitute using cake flour and cornstarch in case rice flour is hard to find. You may want to add more water to your batter to get the papers as thin as possible without having them fall apart. Test one first.

### With rice flour

    1 cup rice flour
    ½ cup cake flour
    ½ cup cornstarch
    ½ teaspoon salt
    2½ cups water
    2 tablespoons vegetable oil plus additional oil for cooking

Blend the flours, cornstarch, salt, and water together as smoothly as possible. Strain the batter through a sieve and stir in the oil. Let the batter sit half an hour.

Have ready an oiled baking sheet. As you cook the papers, stir the batter frequently so the ingredients do not separate. Use a 6- to 8-inch skillet, preferably with a nonstick finish. Heat the pan over medium heat, then turn it down. It is best to cook them over medium-low heat. Keep them cooking as long as possible until they become quite firm. Rub a film of oil over the inside of the pan. Pour about 2 tablespoons batter into the pan and quickly swirl it around to coat the bottom of the pan. Cover the pan immediately (the papers should steam rather than fry) and cook the paper over medium-low heat at least 30 seconds or up to a minute until the paper bubbles and is dry looking but not crisp. Loosen the edges of the paper with a spatula and turn it onto the oiled baking sheet. When the paper has cooled slightly, turn it over to oil the other side. Cook the remaining papers, and, as they cool, stack them. The finished papers may be used at room temperature. If you wish, the papers may be made ahead and refrigerated. Before using them they will have to be brought to room temperature or gently reheated, one at a time, in a lightly oiled skillet to restore their flexibility. When filled, the hot filling will warm them adequately.

### Without rice flour

    1 cup cake flour
    1 cup cornstarch
    ½ teaspoon salt
    1¼ cups water
    2 egg whites
    2 tablespoons vegetable oil plus additional oil for cooking

Blend the flour, cornstarch, salt, water, and egg whites together until smooth. Strain the batter through a fine sieve and stir in the oil. Let the batter sit half an hour. Cook as described in the preceding recipe.

## *Lumpia* Wrappers

2 large eggs
1¼ cups water
⅔ cup cornstarch
⅜ teaspoon salt
1½ tablespoons vegetable oil plus additional oil for cooking

Combine all the ingredients in a blender or food processor and blend until smooth. Transfer the batter to a bowl.

Heat a small 6- to 7-inch skillet and brush it lightly with oil. When a drop of water sizzles on contact, the pan is ready. Stir the batter and pour or spoon about 3 tablespoons of it into the pan. Quickly tilt the pan to spread the batter over the bottom as though making a crêpe. Cook over medium heat until the wrapper is set and dry on top, about 1½ minutes. Slide the wrapper out onto paper toweling to cool. Repeat with the remaining batter.

Makes about 14 wrappers.

# BIBLIOGRAPHY

Alejandro, Reynaldo Gamboa. "The Migration of Chinese Noodles to the Philippines: A Look into the Development of Chinese Philippine Cuisine." *Food in Motion: The Migration of Foodstuffs and Cookery Techniques. The Proceedings of the Oxford Symposium, 1983*. London: Prospect Books, 1983.

Andaya, Barbara W., and Leonard Y. *A History of Malaysia*. New York: St. Martin's Press, 1982.

Brennan, Jennifer. *The Original Thai Cookbook*. New York: Coward-McCan Inc., 1981.

Buck, Pearl. *Pearl S. Buck's Oriental Cookbook*. New York: Simon and Schuster, 1972.

Chang, K. C., ed. *Food in Chinese Culture*. New Haven: Yale Univ. Press, 1977.

Chao, Buwei Yang. *How to Cook and Eat in Chinese*. New York: Random House, 1945.

Cotterell, Arthur, and David Morgan. *China's Civilization: A Survey of Its History, Arts, and Technology*. New York: Praeger Publishers, 1975.

Davidson, Alan. *Seafood of Southeast Asia*. Singapore: Federal Publications Pte Ltd., 1976.

Dayrit, Pat Limjuco. *Favorite Filipino Recipes*. Australia: Paul Hamlyn Pty Ltd (Tradewinds Co.), 1975.

Daza, Nora. *Let's Cook with Nora*. Manila: — 1969.

Donnison, F. S. V. *Burma*. New York: Praeger Books, 1970.

Feng, Doreen Yen Hung. *The Joy of Chinese Cooking*. London: Faber and Faber Ltd., 1952–1979.

Gernet, Jacques. *Daily Life in China on the Eve of the Mongol Invasion*. New York: The Macmillan Co., 1962.

Haing, Lie Sek. *Indonesian Cookery*. New York: Crown Publishers, Inc., 1963.

Herklots, G. A. C. *Vegetables in Southeast Asia*. New York: Hafner Press, 1972.

Khaing, Mi Mi. *Cook and Entertain the Burmese Way*. Ann Arbor: Karoma Publishers Inc., 1978.

Kennedy, Victor, ed. *Sorties into Thai Cultural History*. Bangkok: Office of the National Cultural Commission-Ministry of Education, 1982.

Latourette, Kenneth Scott. *The History of Japan*. New York: The Macmillan Company, 1957.

Leeming, Margaret, and Mutsuko Kohsaka. *Japanese Cookery*. London: Rider and Company Ltd., 1984.

Leeming, Margaret, and May Huang Man-hui. *Chinese Regional Cookery*. London: Rider and Company Ltd., 1983.

McCawley, James D. *The Eater's Guide to Chinese Characters*. Chicago: The University of Chicago Press, 1984.

Miller, Jill Nhu Huong. *Vietnamese Cookery*. Vermont: Charles Tuttle Company, 1968–83.

Morris, Harriet. *The Art of Korean Cooking*. Rutland Vermont: Charles Tuttle Company, 1959–76.

Nagasawa, Kimiko, and Camy Condon. *Eating Cheap in Japan*. Tokyo: Shufunotomo Co. Ltd., 1972–80.

Needham, Joseph (Francesca Bray, ed.). "Science and Civilization in China," *Agriculture,* Vol. 6 Part II. London: Univ. of Cambridge Press, 1984.

Ng, Dorothy. *Complete Asian Meals*. Singapore: Times International Books, 1979.

Ngo, Bach, and Gloria Zimmerman. *The Classic Cuisine of Vietnam*. Woodbury, New York: Barrons Educational Series Inc., 1979.

Passmore, Jacki. *All Asian Cookbook*. London: Hamlyn Publishing Group Ltd., 1979.

Perry, Charles, "Notes on Persian Pasta." *Petits Propos Culinaires* 10. March 1982.

Perry, Charles, "The Oldest Mediterranean Noodle: A Cautionary Tale." *Petits Propos Culinaires* 9. October 1981.

Pinsuvana, Malulee. *Cooking Thai Food in American Kitchens*. Bangkok: Thai Watana Panich Press Co. Ltd., 1976–81.

Purcell, Victor. *The Chinese in Malaya*. London: Oxford Univ. Press, 1967.

Purcell, Victor. *The Chinese in Southeast Asia*. London: Oxford Univ. Press, 1965–80.

Skinner, William G. *Chinese Society in Thailand: An Analytical History*. Ithica, New York: Cornell Univ. Press, 1957.

Sing, Phia. *Traditional Recipes of Laos*. London: Prospect Books, 1981.

Steinberg, Raphael. *The Cooking of Japan*. New York: Time-Life Books, 1969.

Taneja, Meera. *The Hamlyn Curry Cookbook*. London: The Hamlyn Publishing Group Ltd., 1982.

Tannahill, Reay. *Food in History*. New York: Stein and Day, 1973.

Tropp, Barbara. *The Modern Art of Chinese Cooking*. New York: William Morrow and Company, Inc., 1982.

Yamaguchi, H. S. K. *We Japanese*. Yokahama: Yamagata Press, 1934–50.

Yew, Betty. *Rasa Malaysia*. Singapore: Times Books International, 1982.

# INDEX

*Page numbers in boldface type
indicate recipes.*

# COOKBOOKS FOR GOOD COOKS
## FROM ARIS BOOKS AND ADDISON-WESLEY